DIAGNOSTIC CLASSROOM OBSERVATION

This book is dedicated to my husband who, when we were only in our twenties, suggested that I get my doctorate.

I thank him for years of supporting my professional goals, even that cold, dark winter when I left him for months of research in sunnier climates with no one but our dear Chocolate Lab, Malcolm, to keep him warm.

I thank him for being my "first eyes" on this manuscript, for gracing our home with his magnificent art, and for being half responsible for our two (now adult) children whose talent, intelligence, sense of humor, and deep ethical convictions make me proud every day of my very fortunate life.

Thank you, Joseph.

DIAGNOSTIC CLASSROOM OBSERVATION

MOVING BEYOND BEST PRACTICE

NICOLE SAGINOR

CORWIN PRESS
A SAGE Company
Thousand Oaks, CA 91320

Cover art by Joseph Saginor.

For information:

Corwin Press
A SAGE Company
2455 Teller Road
Thousand Oaks, California 91320
www.corwinpress.com

SAGE Ltd.
1 Oliver's Yard
55 City Road
London EC1Y 1SP
United Kingdom

SAGE Pvt. Ltd.
B 1/I 1 Mohan Cooperative Industrial Area
Mathura Road, New Delhi 110 044
India

SAGE Asia-Pacific Pte. Ltd.
33 Pekin Street #02-01
Far East Square
Singapore 048763

Printed in the United States of America

Library of Congress Cataloging-in-Publication Data

Saginor, Nicole.
Diagnostic classroom observation: moving beyond best practice/Nicole Saginor.
    p. cm.
Includes bibliographical references and index.
ISBN 978-1-4129-5513-3 (cloth)
ISBN 978-1-4129-5514-0 (pbk.)

  1. Observation (Educational method) 2. School principals. 3. Teacher-principal relationships. 4. School supervision. I. Title.

LB1731.6.S34 2008
371.2′03—dc22   2008004904

This book is printed on acid-free paper.

08   09   10   11   12   10   9   8   7   6   5   4   3   2   1

Acquisitions Editor:	Arnis Burvikovs
Editorial Assistants:	Irina Dragut and Ena Rosen
Production Editor:	Veronica Stapleton
Copy Editor:	Julie Gwin
Typesetter:	C&M Digitals (P) Ltd.
Proofreader:	Dennis W. Webb
Indexer:	Kay M. Dusheck
Cover Designer:	Scott Van Atta
Graphic Designer:	Lisa Riley

Table of Contents

Preface

Diagnostic classroom observation (DCO), originally developed as a tool for principals and other supervisors of instruction, is a complete system of supervision and evaluation grounded in the real life of today's classrooms. Its primary audience is the building-level principal, providing guidance in a graphic way for the entire supervisory process from preconference, to classroom observation, to postconference and follow-through, to the improvement of practice. While the principal will be the primary beneficiary of the approach, this book has several secondary audiences, including teachers, teacher leaders, and mentors, guiding them to self-assess, consult with peers, and work to improve instruction by presenting vivid examples of the many indicators of successful teaching. It can also help superintendents and school boards or any others in charge of hiring who have included a site visit and classroom observation in their hiring practices. An additional secondary audience includes designers and implementers of teacher preparation programs. DCO can help create accomplished teachers *before* they acquire habits that impede maximum student learning.

This book presents the criteria, indicators, and examples of evidence of DCO. It includes a rationale for each indicator and examples of evidence. In addition, I give examples of many of the indicators with vignettes of how they play out in actual classroom settings for Grades K through 12. The vignettes presented offer a variety of ways of looking at the indicators of the tool. Some of them are positive examples of what it looks like when things are going well. Some depict instances when a well-prepared teacher can "seduce" an observer with a well-run activity that misses the mark. Still others demonstrate how the lack of adequate performance on a particular indicator can seriously affect student learning. These examples come from real-life observations done in the course of my career as a teacher, principal, professional developer, researcher, and consultant, unless specifically noted. These observations include examples from kindergarten through Grade 10. Some of these are composites. (Note that the concepts and strategies explicated should be easily transferable to more advanced classrooms, provided that the teacher and the supervisor have the depth of knowledge in the subject area to be able to make those connections.) The remainder of the examples described are based on portions of videotapes from various series developed to study math, science, technology, and literacy instruction by the Annenberg Foundation/CPB Math and Science Collection (1995, 1996, 2000, and 2002) and WGBH-TV as well as the Southwest Educational Development Laboratory (2000). Finally, I look at the sum total of the three observation criteria (implementation, content, and classroom culture) to see the role that they each play in creating a complete picture of truly effective instruction, demonstrating what it looks like when any one of them is seriously absent.

The observation criteria of DCO adhere strictly to the four assumptions on which it was built: an investigative environment; the merging of content and process; the deepening of learning through dialogue and collaboration, and the necessity for a safe, respectful culture that honors the individual and the collective learning community; and the effective use of technology. Each of the criteria directs the observer to carefully examine teacher choices and actions, student engagement and learning, and the interaction between the teacher and students. The Math/Science Version was the first to be developed, field tested, and used. The Literacy and Composite Versions followed. The format for each of the versions is the same, each containing four sections that are described below. The differences between the Math/Science and Literacy Versions rest in the particular content pedagogy for the disciplines. The Math/Science Version assesses classrooms by the ability to use inquiry, exploration, and scientific investigation to teach fundamental, enduring concepts as outlined in national standards. The Literacy Version focuses on the building blocks of comprehensive literacy from building fluency, depth of comprehension, and analysis and criticism in both reading and writing. The Composite Version is appropriate for the principal who evaluates instruction in many content areas. It combines elements of the Math/Science Version that apply to any good instructional event with key indicators from the Literacy Version that support reading and writing across the curriculum.

DCO was developed to address teaching and learning in real classrooms with the hope of making the benefits of research come to life for our students. The four sections of DCO paint a vivid picture of high-quality classroom practice and extensive student engagement. They are:

- Planning and organization of the lesson

   This set of criteria is concerned with the quality of the planning, organization, and structure of the lesson, *not* a written lesson plan. The planning section is designed to be used prior to the observation. It presents a set of questions that can guide a preconference and direct the teacher's attention to what the observer will be watching for. It includes a set of examples for each question to guide the observer's listening as well, and it suggests areas to probe if not immediately present in the teacher's response. Each numbered indicator is preceded by the letters "PO." The full Planning and Organization sections can be found in Appendices A (the Math/Science Version) and B (the Literacy Version), and a detailed discussion about how to use this section in the process of the preconference appears in Chapter 7.

- Implementation of the lesson

   This focuses on the effectiveness of the instructional event. Observations of both teacher and student activity are noted, including the efforts to engage students and the actual quality of their engagement. It emphasizes the ability of students to investigate concepts, construct knowledge, and become aware metacognitively of their own learning. Numbered indicators in this section are preceded by the letters "IM." Chapter 2 discusses in detail the implementation of math and science classes, while Chapter 3 does the same for literacy instruction. Each implementation indicator with its examples of evidence appears one by one with explanations and examples. In addition, the full Implementation sections appear in Appendices C (the Math/Science Version) and D (the Literacy Version).

- Content of the lesson

  Here we note the content's accuracy, level of abstraction, and connections to other concepts. The section emphasizes how to recognize conceptual closure, correction of student misconceptions, and clear guidelines for judging the effectiveness of student assessment, both formative and summative, which emphasizes student learning. It also notes the ability of the teacher to flexibly deliver the depth of content in accordance with national, state, and local standards. Content indicators are designated with the letters "CO." As with the implementation criteria, the content indicators are analyzed one by one with discussion and examples in Chapters 2 and 3, and appear in their entirety in Appendices C and D.

- Classroom culture

  This section assesses the learning environment, including the climate, classroom routines, behavior and the way it is monitored and managed, the level of student engagement, the nature of the working relationships, and issues of equity. Classroom culture indicators are identified with the letters "CU." Because this section is almost identical in both versions, Chapter 4 is dedicated to the issues raised by the classroom culture section with examples given from math, science, and literacy classrooms. Appendices C and D contain the Classroom Culture along with the Implementation and Content sections.

Each section describes standards of behavior for both teacher and students. While this can make the observation process more complex, the payoff comes in a number of ways. First, it more accurately portrays what actually occurs in the classroom—just like the shared juggling metaphor in which the teacher puts the ball into play, but what unfolds depends on the students' next move. Second, it gives the observer many opportunities to engage the teacher in a productive postconference that will focus on student learning and allow the teacher to reflect on the classroom event with less defensiveness and with a more problem-solving approach. The postconferences will be discussed in detail in Chapter 7 along with guidelines and suggestions for making this critical component of the supervisory process a worthwhile investment of time.

THE STRUCTURE OF THE OBSERVATION TOOL

Rather than present a complex rubric using value-laden terms, DCO lays out some clear criteria for quality teaching, a few key indicators of those criteria, and an accompanying set of bullets, which create not only a vivid picture of the quality indicator itself, but a sense of what that indicator looks like in a live classroom. The quality indicators appear in the left-hand column of the tool. To the right of each indicator is a series of bullets titled "Examples of Evidence." These are observable actions or elements to support the degree of presence or absence of the indicator. This column is called *examples* of evidence as there is no way to exhaust every possible way in which an indicator might be present. The purpose of the second column is to help paint the picture of a classroom where the particular indicator flourishes. Users of the tool are encouraged to add their own examples as appropriate for their own settings. Integration of technology is part and parcel of the other four sections. Quality elements of technology use in the classroom are woven directly into the tool to model the concept that technology is not to be viewed as an "add-on."

Chapter 1 presents an overview of the instrument and identifies the assumptions on which it is built and the knowledge base that supports those assumptions. It demonstrates the ways in which DCO aligns with previous work on classroom observation and qualities that distinguish it from them, enumerating the key distinctions of this observation system. A further look at the comparisons between DCO and three other well-known, effective observation systems (Danielson, 1986; Horizon Research, 1997; Saphier, Haley-Speca, & Gower, 2008) appear in Appendix E, where the areas of alignment and divergence are outlined.

Chapter 2 introduces the Math/Science Version of DCO. Using vignettes of actual classroom performance to illustrate specific indicators and examples of evidence described in the tool, it allows the reader to gain a graphic sense of how these indicators play out in real life. They demonstrate how math and science concepts must be taught in an inquiry-based environment but how inquiry alone can yield an engaging and seductive lesson, which is ultimately void of real learning, or what I have called the "neat activity syndrome." All indicators in this version are identified with the letters "MS" prior to the indicator number. For example, the third implementation indicator in the Math/Science Version is designated MS-IM#3. Technology indicators appear in shaded boxes and are prefaced with the letter "T."

"A good idea—poorly implemented—is a bad idea" (Guskey, 2002, as cited in Ainsworth & Viegut, 2006). An additional feature is called, "When good ideas go bad." These demonstrate the depth of understanding needed to take full educational advantage of the best practice research. These examples help to break through the veneer of best practice and give specific remedies to deepen learning. While the majority of examples of classes described in Chapter 2 are from the elementary and middle levels, there are examples from high school as well. Chapters 2 through 6 end with several suggested methods for administrative or supervisory teams to process together the concepts in the chapter and practice using the parts of the tool. These include discussions, co-observations, and scoring exercises using score sheets provided for training purposes only. (The score sheets appear in Appendix F, and their use is carefully described in Chapter 7.)

Chapter 3 has two sections that embody both "learning to read" and "reading to learn." Section 1 presents the Literacy Version of DCO, providing real-life examples of the indicators and good ideas going bad. Section 2 contains the Composite Version of DCO. It provides three additional implementation indicators and one content indicator that, when added to the Math/Science Version, become an instrument for the observation and supervision of any content-area class. Although the examples in this section are all from the high school level, they demonstrate how literacy skills integrated across the curriculum enhance learning of any content area and create a metacognitive element to the learning for all students in all grades. Literacy indicators are identified with the letter "L" prior to the indicator number. Indicators that are part of the Composite Version are designated as such. Chapter 3 ends as Chapter 2 does, with suggested discussion questions and activities to practice using the Literacy and Composite Versions of the tool.

Chapter 4 is the classroom culture component of DCO. As both the Math/Science and Literacy Versions are essentially identical, they are presented together, with any differences between them noted as they arise. A unique feature of the classroom culture criteria is the focus on "equity of access." This refers to many elements of the classroom climate. It encompasses fair and equitable treatment of students as individuals and equal access to the full educational resources of the learning environment, including teacher attention, grouping for maximum benefit to all students, and access to technology.

Chapter 5 focuses on assessment from the standpoint of the classroom observer. It dissects the activities that sometimes pass for assessment and helps you determine whether a teacher is effectively (or even actually) assessing his or her students. Different methods of assessment are discussed, exploring assessments at differing depths or styles of understanding, and examples of useful and not so useful assessment practices are presented to give a clear picture of what good assessment looks like when it's an integral part of instruction. The discussion section at the end of Chapter 5 focuses readers' attention on the assessment practices they have observed and offers some material for discovering what has been taught through analyzing what has been assessed.

Chapter 6 is called "Putting It All Together." This chapter makes the case that despite the common wisdom that nobody is perfect, optimal instruction must address each of the three main criteria. The chapter gives a graphic example of what happens when each criteria in its turn is missing from the instructional mix. There is a discussion about how to use this system to literally diagnose instruction so that you can focus your supervisory efforts for maximum strategic effect and have a real impact on improving instructional practice in your school.

In Chapter 7, I describe the training and research protocols that have helped DCO become truly useful in various settings, and I provide guidance for introducing DCO into your school for the maximum beneficial extent. I give some serious cautions and provide examples of the range of uses that this system can have. I discuss the scoring sheets that appear in Appendix F with information about how and when to use them, with strong caveats about how and when *not* to do so. Here, I speak directly to my primary audience: the building principal. For DCO to have an impact on actually improving instruction, the principal must be knowledgeable and aware of how to best use the instrument. I offer a variety of ways in which the approach can be introduced into a school or school system with suggestions for how to process the information in the book, apply its strategies, and use it to build a professional learning community, either of groups of principals or any of the other professionals who will read and want to use this book. I provide specific tools and guidelines for the preconference, observation, and postconference, which are the sum total of the supervisory process, to make the strongest case I can for principals as instructional leaders, despite the many pressures that draw their attention away from that critical responsibility. I challenge them to fearlessly face the shortfalls in instruction and instructional supervision to really make a difference.

ACKNOWLEDGMENTS

This book is the culmination of eight years that have encompassed my work and experiences with various people and organizations. I thank each and every one of them for their contributions to my evolving thinking regarding the observation and improvement of teaching and learning, which has resulted in the development of Diagnostic Classroom Observation.

It began at the Vermont Institute for Science, Math, and Technology (VISMT) in 1997. Vermont was designated in the early 1990s as one of several State Systemic Initiatives by the National Science Foundation (NSF). VISMT was a nonprofit organization established to lead Vermont's efforts to support the NSF goal to dramatically transform math, science, and technology education. VISMT was at the forefront of creating statewide standards and assessments, and it had a seat at the policy table for many initiatives, working in partnership with the Vermont Department of Education, the state's universities and colleges, and professional leadership organizations. My first expression of thanks goes to Frank Watson who, as executive director of VISMT, hired me to be the assessment specialist and then, by virtue of my experiences as a principal and superintendent in the state, enabled me to create programs of training and support for school leaders that were not in the original structure of the organization. My second thank you is for Douglas Harris, who, as the next executive director of VISMT (which became Vermont Institutes after the 10 years of NSF funding ran out), encouraged me to continue to develop leadership partnerships and resources, first as the director of leadership initiatives and then as the associate executive director of Vermont Institutes. He supported me throughout the entire process, which spawned Diagnostic Classroom Observation.

In my role as director of leadership initiatives, I supervised a cadre of accomplished math, science, and technology teachers called Teacher Associates. These teachers left their school districts for one to two years to become leaders in our reform efforts. We trained them in the new standards-based philosophy and method, cultivated their leadership skills, and turned them into first-class professional developers. During my work with the Teacher Associates, I came into contact with our outside evaluators, Science and Math Program Improvement (SAMPI), from Western Michigan University in Kalamazoo, MI. They were observing math and science classrooms across the state to determine the level of use of the standards-based approaches in our classrooms. To collect the data for their report, they were using an observation tool based on the original instrument developed by Horizon Research, Inc. At our request, they trained me along with the Teacher Associates in the use of the tool so that we could provide professional development to principals, who, until this time, had no programs created specifically to assist them in their part of the school reform taking place. I give thanks to SAMPI and to Horizon Research, Inc., for allowing us to use their materials in our work. I owe much to the select group of Teacher Associates (Marnie Frantz, Barb Unger, Don Hendrick, Gary Lashure, Paul Smith, Bruce Parks, and Pam Quinn) who worked with me to create and deliver a two-day training session to more than 200 principals and supervisors of math and science in Vermont. Special thanks go to Jean McKenny, who accompanied me for several years in these trainings in Vermont and eventually helped me bring the work to administrators, teacher leaders, and researchers in other states.

Over the years, I continued to refine the tool and the training to more explicitly describe what was going right and what was going wrong in the many classrooms that we observed. When the Technology Division at VISMT began to design a classroom observation instrument to assess the integration of technology into instruction, we decided to merge the work, and the Vermont Classroom Observation Tool (VCOT) was born. With major funding from VITA-Learn, a technology organization in the state, and technical support and assistance from the Education Development Center (EDC) and the New England and Islands Resources for Technology in Education Consortium (NEIRTEC), we rewrote and piloted the new version of the tool to cover the full spectrum of our work: science, math, and technology. My thanks go to VITA-Learn, Bill Romond from the Department of Education, Phil Hyjek and Kathy Johnson from VISMT, Wende Allen and Maureen Yushak from EDC and NEIRTEC, and the technology experts from Vermont who assisted in the writing and piloting of this version of the tool. I would also like to thank Peter Drescher for his work in videotaping several classroom segments for my research.

As Vermont Institutes expanded to include literacy grants and programs, the VCOT, continually being rewritten and refined, eventually expanded to include a literacy version. Assisting in this effort were David Liben, codirector of the Vermont Strategic Reading Initiative, and Karen Kurzman, writing and assessment specialist at Vermont Institutes.

I want to thank and recognize Cathy Miles-Grant, formerly of the EDC in Newton, Massachusetts, and coauthor of *Lenses on Learning,* another classroom observation protocol aimed at school leaders to help them develop a better eye for good math instruction and to assist them in helping teachers process the observation in a more collaborative mode. Co-teaching a course with her to a group of principals from two states lay the groundwork for Diagnostic Classroom Observation and extended my thinking about how to work with school leadership teams. Success in helping teachers actually change their practice was now a priority. Using the new perspectives gained from *Lenses on Learning,* I redesigned the VCOT training and replaced the two-day session with a credit-bearing course that I ultimately decided to only offer to entire administrative teams. This training was an inclusive approach involving the use of all the data gained from the observation, including student discussions and written work, to explore strategies for instructional improvement.

The final chapter of this story came through Mathematica Policy Research, Inc., which adopted the use of the VCOT in two national studies, one on teacher preparation programs and one on teacher induction. I would like to thank Paul Decker and Amy Johnson for selecting VCOT for their studies and for setting the stage for the establishment of interrater reliability on the five-point scale. Training just under 30 perspective classroom observers, I traveled to many states co-observing and double scoring with each of those observers who had passed our reliability test. Thanks go to Amy and to Debi Rubel for creating with me the "Gold Standard Panel," which set the scores to match for the test. Thanks go also to Mike Puma, one of those observers, who connected my work to a study being conducted by the Northwest Regional Education Lab (NWREL) in Portland, Oregon, on the strategic use of reading and writing in the content areas, or the CRISS project. It is for this study that I created the Composite Version of the tool with input from Maureen Carr and her advanced team from NWREL.

I would like to thank all the teachers who allowed me into their classrooms, regardless of the hat I was wearing when I was there: supervisor, consultant, or researcher. I would particularly like to thank Herrika (Rickey) Poor, Linda Fuerst, Olga (Teddy) Valencia-Reichert, Joe Beasley, and Bridget Fariel, who volunteered to share their practice specifically for the purposes of this book. A final thank you goes to Page Keeley, president-elect of the National Science Teachers Association and author of several important books on deepening student learning in science, who encouraged me to write this book and to make contact with Corwin Press.

As a result of these last eight years, VCOT has been used in more than 15 states and has developed into a complete system designed to improve teaching practice by crafting a total approach to instructional leadership. Diagnostic Classroom Observation is that system. Thank you, all.

Corwin Press gratefully acknowledges the contributions of the following reviewers:

Regina Brinker
Science Teacher
Christensen Middle School
Livermore, CA

Robert Brower
Superintendent
North Montgomery CSC
Crawfordsville, IN

Kermit Buckner
Professor
East Carolina University
Greenville, NC

Molly Burger
Principal
Middleton Middle School
Middleton, ID

Nicolette Dennis
Principal
Highland High School
Albuquerque, NM

R. Jon Frey
Director of Speech and Debate Activities
Aberdeen Central High School
Aberdeen, SD

John C. Hughes
Principal
Middle School 201
Bronx, NY

Mary Johnstone
Principal
Rabbit Creek Elementary School
Anchorage, AK

Marilyn Tallerico
Professor of Educational Leadership
State University of
    New York–Binghamton
Binghamton, NY

About the Author

 **Nicole Saginor, EdD,** has spent her thirty-five-year career in public education as a teacher, curriculum coordinator, principal, and superintendent. She was the associate executive director at Vermont Institutes, a nonprofit professional development organization, where she worked for eight years to strengthen leadership in the state, providing opportunities for support, networking, and professional development to school leaders. She received her doctorate in educational leadership and policy studies at the University of Vermont and holds a master's degree in French literature from Boston University. Her work has been used in several national research studies as the instrument for gathering data on classroom performance. She is currently the superintendent of schools in Saint Johnsbury, Vermont, where she also oversees curriculum and professional development.

She lives in the Upper Valley where central Vermont meets central New Hampshire at the Connecticut River. Her husband is a psychologist, an artist, and adjunct faculty at Dartmouth Medical School. They have two children: an actress/writer living in Los Angeles and a volcanologist completing his doctorate at Rutgers University.

Chapter 1

Defining the "Technology of Good Instruction"

[As with dual jugglers] the teacher introduces the ball into motion, building in the students the needed skills to enter the activity and keep the ball in the air. As the students gain expertise, more balls may be thrown in, new moves and rhythms attempted, other items included—a pin, a plate, a knife—thus filling the space with a rich array of knowledge, planned and unplanned. Any of these expansions may be initiated by either partner. To be successful, there must be constant synergy. This relationship is reciprocal; if one falters, the balls drop. (Saginor, 1999, p. 188)

The metaphor of tandem jugglers depicts what I have called "the space between the teacher and the students" (Saginor, 1999). What would a classroom be like that embodies that space where the magic occurs, where something that the teacher does, says, or sets in motion creates new meaning in the students, which we commonly call learning? The teacher must put the ball in play and carefully monitor and manage the process, all while opening the door for the unexpected. Every relationship, every aspect of the classroom culture, every conversation whether between teacher and students or among students alone reflects the quality of the decisions made and the level of understanding of the teacher. Capturing this very complex tangle of elements (the plan, the content, and the environment) is the object of Diagnostic Classroom Observation (DCO). We have become accustomed to referring to teacher actions recommended by the growing body of research as "best practices." Without putting all the pieces together, best practice can quickly degenerate into random acts of teaching, creating a veneer that looks on its surface as if it should be working but that frustrates both teacher and students in their inability to produce enduring learning.

This chapter will introduce you to the concepts underlying DCO, connect those concepts to some of the research that influenced its development, outline the elements that distinguish it from other observation protocols, and demonstrate how, in its entirety, it offers hope for the achievement of more than best practice: "best learning." The name, as it implies, describes a set of protocols that allows a classroom observer to look more deeply than was possible before into the complex dynamics of a classroom lesson, to diagnose the strengths and weaknesses, and to work with teachers to own the results of their teaching and to finally improve student performance. Using DCO and its accompanying protocols will allow you to break through the veneer of best practice and get at the stubborn habits that keep teaching practice from being its best.

Teacher observation protocols have typically focused on the teacher—what he or she says, does, or fails to say or do (Danielson, 1986; Glickman, 1990; Saphier & Gower, 1997). Assessments focus on student achievement—what students remember or can perform. New research about student discourse (Ball & Friel, 1991) directs teachers to listen to student conversations so teachers can analyze students' thinking in the moments of development. There is now some work that asks observers to note the ways the teacher interacts with student (mathematical) thinking to guide it from emergent stages to full conceptual understanding (Grant et al., 2002). The new edition of *The Skillful Teacher* (Saphier, Haley-Speca, & Gower, 2008) speaks about "getting inside students' heads" or "cognitive empathy." Analyzing either teacher practice or student performance alone tells only part of the story. It is in the interplay between the teacher and student, planned lesson and resulting learning, that the effectiveness of a teaching event can be judged. A teacher can implement the most well-thought-out plan with the most engaging activities, and students can score well on performance tasks or written tests, but neither of these measures the nature and depth of learning. We see teachers lead a lively discussion or plan an innovative activity, and we see students with their glitzy presentations at the end of a unit or passing a test with respectable scores, but these can leave us wondering how much of what they produced was a direct result of exposure to the teaching. It is in analyzing the interaction between the teacher's teaching and the students' learning that we begin to see how effective that teaching really is.

There has been much quality research about teacher practice that has informed the field and the creation of DCO (Danielson, 1986; Horizon Research, 1997; Saphier et al., 2008). DCO is completely compatible with these protocols and systems, and indeed, it draws on much of the same research that informs them. "Cross-walks" between these three evaluation tools appear in Appendix E. The work in teacher supervision, which focuses on classroom techniques that intentionally engage students in a more constructivist learning environment, forms the basis of Assumption 1 of DCO. Many schools have adopted some of these observation protocols for their supervision and evaluation systems. These school districts, pleased in general with an improvement in teacher practice, have not necessarily seen a rise in their student performance scores. In the face of new national standards, something more specific to the content pedagogy of each subject (Shulman, 1987) is necessary.

DCO is not a "values-free" approach. It is based on several basic assumptions that underlie the elements of the instrument. These assumptions, supported by research and experience, when implemented together, produce the highest quality teaching and learning. While these assumptions are not groundbreaking in and of themselves, applied together in this protocol, they are the essential building blocks of our best vision of the teaching and learning events known as lessons. This book documents dozens of actual classroom observations throughout the country where, despite the practices so well described in the current body of research and literature and so familiar in discussions in the field, classrooms operate as if the research either doesn't exist or is completely irrelevant to real-world classrooms. Some teachers continue to practice their craft behind closed doors, only intermittently challenged by their building principals, who are overwhelmed with safety issues, legal and budget battles, pressures from parents and school boards, and worries about test results. Ironically, the pressure of test results will only be relieved if principals pay attention to the details of instruction that create the conditions under which the learning measured by those test results takes place.

The book also contains many examples of exemplary practice, also from directly observed classrooms. There is much expert teaching happening in our schools, and not only in the best endowed of them. There is a generation of school leaders steeped in the best practice of the research whose schools embody the specific practices that the research extols. I have worked with and observed many of those teachers and their leaders. The essence of DCO comes from a blend of the research and my experiences as a building- and state-level school leader, a researcher, and a consultant.

ASSUMPTIONS UNDERLYING DCO

Assumption 1: The Best Instruction Happens in an Active, Investigative Environment

Ever since *hands-on* became a familiar term in our educational lexicon, teachers and textbook companies have developed ways of putting materials into the hands of students. Unfortunately, "hands-on," while clearly better than watching the teacher from afar, is necessary but not sufficient to fully engage the learner in understanding new concepts (Ball, 1992). We are now looking more deeply into what the materials that the students have their hands on are, what they are being asked to do with those materials, and how much of their own intellect is being required in the carrying out of learning tasks. The words *inquiry* and *investigation* have been used to describe the best lessons. Educators quibble about whether these take too much time to teach concepts taught more efficiently by teacher explanations or demonstrations. At the root of this argument are several forces. With the range of standards and high-stakes assessments driving many decisions, time becomes more precious to teachers. Administrators are pressured to ensure that all standards are included in the curriculum. But if student learning (and therefore performance on assessments) is the central concern, I would argue that the inefficiency of spending the time teaching content that few students will learn well and even fewer will be able to apply later is a more egregious waste of time than the use of inquiry as a regular part of an instructional program. A well-designed investigation does not have to be overly time consuming, and not every activity needs to be an investigation, but students should have multiple opportunities to engage in the active figuring out of concepts. While some teachers may argue that children need to have some content knowledge before they can be expected to handle an investigation, it is precisely through carefully designed active investigation that the content is learned—that very content that is seemingly more efficient if fed to the students by the teacher at the outset.

The Research Supporting Assumption 1

Students come to the classroom with preconceptions about how the world works. If their initial understanding is not engaged, they may fail to grasp the new concepts and information that are taught, or they may learn them for purposes of a test but revert to their preconceptions outside the classroom. (National Research Council, 2000a, pp. 14–15)

Research beginning in the late 1980s is showcased in a video series called *A Private Universe* (Annenberg Foundation/CPB, 1987). The researchers were curious about why it was that students of Harvard and the Massachusetts Institute of Technology, when randomly asked some simple questions about general scientific knowledge at their graduation, gave, in large numbers, naïve and incorrect answers similar to those given by elementary students to the same questions. In this study about student misconceptions, they noted that teacher explanations, regardless of their clarity and accuracy, do not interfere with previously held ideas unless challenged directly by the student's own new experience and thinking.

Box 1.1

A Private Universe: Can Teacher Explanations Shake Loose Previously Held Misconceptions? (Annenberg Foundation/CPB, 1987)

Perplexed at the number of Massachusetts Institute of Technology graduates who were unable to light a bulb with a single battery and wire, researchers examine an honors high school physics class in which concepts of electricity were taught. A top student is chosen by the teacher to be the subject of the study. The video episode follows the teacher as he explains complete circuits, light bulbs, and various concepts about electrical currents. Hands-on activities with sockets, wires, and bulbs follow the explanations with a few challenges built in.

One month following the unit, the researcher presents the student with a bulb, battery, and wire and asks her to light the bulb. Completely stumped, the student is unable to move forward because the researcher has not provided her with a socket as she had in her physics lab. Probing by the researcher further reveals that not only does she not know how to light the bulb, she has no idea why. She cannot explain the role of the socket and cannot correctly diagram how the bulb could be lit if she did have one. As a matter of fact, the mistakes she makes reflect the *very same misconceptions* she had about light bulbs when she was given a pretest at the beginning of the experiment. In other words, her prior misconceptions had not been challenged by the learning activities presented to her in class, although one presumes she must have done well enough on unit tests to have been chosen by her teacher for the research project.

Heavily influenced by this research, DCO uses the word *grapple* to denote what teachers need to orchestrate and principals need to look for when determining the likelihood of new learning for students. The teacher in Box 1.1 has done all the thinking for the students. His well-intentioned explanations and follow-up activities had not given the class the opportunity to put together the concepts for themselves.

A "metacognitive" approach to instruction can help students learn to take control of their own learning by defining learning goals and monitoring their progress in achieving them (National Research Council, 2000b, p. 18).

The important piece frequently overlooked is metacognition, even by teachers who, with the best intentions, have integrated investigation into their math or science classroom. An unlit bulb, a single battery, and a wire presented with an open challenge from the teacher ("See how many different configurations you can use to successfully light the bulb") can engage the students in *grappling* with the materials, hypothesizing, and finally concluding what exactly does make a light bulb light. The metacognitive element is introduced as students are asked to articulate in a variety of ways (diagramming, writing, orally explaining, or discussing) what that concept is and how they came to understand it. This is a prime example of *actual learning* taking place in an active and investigative environment. Investigation, coupled with articulated conclusions and metacognition, leads us directly to Assumption 2.

Assumption 2: Content and Process Do Not Eclipse Each Other; Both Are Needed and Work Together for Sound Instruction (Beware the "Neat Activity Syndrome!")

To develop competence in an area of inquiry, students must (a) have a deep foundation of factual knowledge, (b) understand facts and ideas in the context of a conceptual framework, and (c) organize knowledge in ways that facilitate retrieval and application (National Research Council, 2000b, p. 16).

Tiring of the argument over whether to teach content and information or to teach students how to think and learn, I began the process of observing teachers as a part of my principal's responsibilities. Knowing enough to value hands-on activities as a necessary component of active learning, I found myself in very "seductive" classrooms where engaged students were busily building, manipulating, and creating big charts for presentations. It all looked very impressive, and I would walk away smiling. That is, until I reached my office and asked myself what exactly the students had learned. I began to get alarmed when, in postconferences, teachers were unable to articulate the targeted student learning themselves. They could tell me the topic: magnets, states of matter, adding two-digit numbers. But they were unable to tell me several critical things: what specifically the students had learned about magnets, how the activity actually taught any specific concept about magnets (other than magnets stick to metal, which is not always true), or how they were assessing student understanding. What I discovered was that the assessment of learning had stopped at the completion of the activity (which in itself was certainly a "neat" thing to do) and had never reached the reflective or metacognitive level of analyzing what they had done and what it meant. I called this the "neat activity syndrome" and began to see it everywhere.

Appreciation of the active component of learning is certainly a first step toward leaving behind the dry lectures and textbooks with factual questions at the end of the chapter, all of which passed for quality instruction years ago. But it is a faulty assumption that because students have followed directions and completed an activity, they have learned anything substantial that they will be able to draw on in the future. This is the foundation of the content criteria of DCO and why it is not sufficient to simply develop a set of implementation criteria. The Content section directs the observer to note the specific concepts contained in the learning tasks, the degree to which the teacher can articulate those, and the skill in which those concepts come alive and gain meaning in the course of the lesson's activities. One of the key indicators notes the level of abstraction required from a hands-on activity and the nesting of newly learned concepts in a theoretical framework. It also focuses on the assessments, which are designed to monitor and eventually to evaluate student understanding. It is this section of the instrument that distinguishes it from other observation protocols, which focus primarily on professional practice as craft.

The Research Supporting Assumption 2

A relevant example is cited in *How Students Learn: Mathematics in the Classroom* (National Research Council, 2004), involving a comparison between students from a top technical college and elementary students, both groups making mistakes involving the concept of momentum in a computerized task, even though the college students could clearly articulate the concepts and would have performed well on a written test. This example leaves you with two questions: Were the elementary students exposed only to the activity without having the underlying concepts connected to what they were experiencing, and were the college students exposed to explanations and proofs without having to experiment themselves with the concepts and finally own them by articulating them as conclusions?

Box 1.2

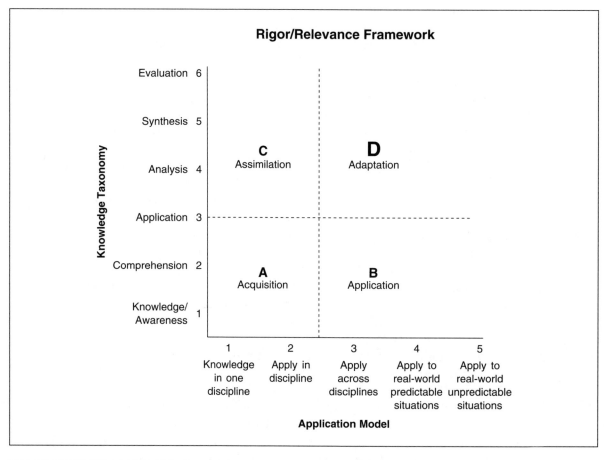

International Center for Leadership in Education, www.LeaderEd.com

The Rigor/Relevance Framework (Daggett, 1995) shown in Box 1.2 demonstrates the low level that many of our classes operate at in the name of "covering the content." When doing an in-depth analysis of American high school curricula compared with that of other countries (nine nations whose students were outperforming ours), it became clear that while our schools do well addressing the skills in Bloom's

Taxonomy, there is a huge gap between the level of application of those skills and two important measures:

1. the level of application required by the needs of the business world, and

2. the level of application being included in the curricula of European and Asian schools.

The U.S. curricula scored heavily in Quadrants A and C, yet when public expectations of the results of a publicly supported school system were graphed on the same matrix, the responses were almost exclusively found in Quadrants B and D (Daggett, 1995, pp. 52–53). These measures bode ill for the economic future of our students. This perspective on instruction is reinforced by the TIMSS studies. Called "a mile wide and an inch deep," our classes cover large amounts of material, giving the conceptual underpinnings of that content cursory attention. The literature on teacher knowledge (Ball, Lubienski, & Mewborn, 2001; Shulman, 1987) reinforces this notion. The implication is that one cause of this approach is superficial understanding on the part of some teachers. Another explanation is simply that our current teaching force was educated in a paradigm emphasizing teacher explanations, textbook chapters, and exercises focusing on definitions and procedures. Deep understanding and applications beyond the classroom uses were not part of the background of many of us who now find ourselves educating the generations of the twenty-first century.

If we continue to ignore the application skills and knowledge needed by our global economy, our businesses will easily find those who have them elsewhere. The importance of integrating the four quadrants of the Rigor/Relevance Framework into our instructional programs was powerfully expressed by Dr. Daggett who, addressing a group of school leaders in May 2000, noted that the idea of "going to work" is easily replaced by the new paradigm of "work coming to you." In our age of information technology, accessing workers overseas is as easy as hitting "send" on your e-mail. As long as our students lack the needed skills, outsourcing will by necessity continue to erode our students' opportunities. Examples of instruction that runs through the four quadrants are presented in Chapters 2, 3, and 4.

Assumption 3: Learning Is an Interactive Process Enriched by Dialogue and Social Interaction in a Safe, Respectful Environment

DCO values student discourse by including a dimension of student-to-student interactions in each of its criteria. In the Implementation section, it looks for the extent to which the lesson has been intentionally designed to use the benefits of learning through dialogue. The Content section focuses on the extent to which substantial learning is developing through student dialogue. In the Classroom Culture section, it asks observers to note the extent to which the students take it upon themselves to interact to maximize the learning of all. We also look for the sense of order and safety in the classroom: a culture in which expressing one's ideas is accepted, people challenge each other respectfully, and the debate of ideas freely takes place. We are social beings, and our learning, like most of our daily challenges, is enhanced by positive interpersonal relationships uninhibited by fear, anger, and distrust. Awareness of the diversity present in the classroom, whether it is gender, ethnic, socioeconomic, or related to learning styles, should be observable in teacher behavior. If it is observable in the students as well, there is a strong likelihood that the teacher has created those habits.

Cooperative learning took hold in our schools in the 1990s (D. W. Johnson, Johnson, & Holubec, 1994). Once again, the mere fact that students have been placed in groups to complete a task does not mean that any of the indicators for successful interaction are in place. We look for a purposeful environment, with tasks and group make-up designed to maximize the learning of each individual, and respectful listening and collaboration. We also look for teacher monitoring of group process, group tasks that are complex enough to warrant the "two heads are better than one" approach, lack of dominance of any particular students, and the encouragement of the more reticent ones. In short, we observe the structure, the content, and the style of the collaboration.

The Research Supporting Assumption 3

One of the first researchers to highlight the concept that social learning actually leads to cognitive development was Vygotsky (1978). He concluded that the level of potential problem-solving ability was enhanced both under adult guidance and in collaboration with more capable peers. Systems such as Cooperative Learning (D. W. Johnson et al., 1994) and Complex Instruction (Cohen & Lotan, 1997) demonstrate through their research that significant learning happens when students are asked to collaborate on a task, particularly one that causes them to "actively grapple" with concepts. Ball and Friel (1991) use the term *discourse* to describe the interpersonal process in which "knowledge is constructed and exchanged in classrooms" (p. 44).

But more than the constructivist power of dialogue in the classroom, its active inclusion as a pedagogical technique "disrupts the basic assumptions about how learning progresses and who gets to be a knower" (Tarule, 1996, p. 292). What has become an educational cliché, "The sage on the stage becomes the guide on the side," describes a new set of roles and relationships and places a degree of responsibility for learning onto the student.

What DCO makes clear, however, is that the teacher is *not* to abdicate ultimate responsibility for the learning in the classroom. It is still the teacher who must expose students to engaging material and help them make sense of it by attending carefully to their developing understanding.

> So what is the role of teaching if knowledge must be constructed by each individual . . . The first is to put the students into contact with phenomena related to the area to be studied . . . to engage them so they will continue to think and wonder about it. The second is to have the students try to explain the sense they are making and . . . to try to understand their sense. (Duckworth, 1987, p. 123)

Assumption 4: Technology Enhances Instruction

Technology has found its way into many of our nation's schools in the form of computer labs, banks of computers in classrooms, online capabilities, and a public who support maintaining a strong capacity for student access to information technology. What has moved more slowly than the provision of hardware and Internet capacity is the effective use of technology in the service of learning. Many schools approach technology as a separate entity, cloistering the computers in a library or lab with limited access and hiring technology experts in charge of all student use of the equipment. This approach leaves the average classroom teacher and his or her lessons as quite separate. Just as we learn to read for information, we can use technology as a tool for learning. But like any other innovation in education, training and support are necessary. DCO does not have a separate section dedicated to technology and its use in the instructional program. Instead, it is woven through each section of the instrument. This was a purposeful decision to model in the tool itself the philosophy that it was meant to embody. That is, technology is not an instructional add-on; it is instead to be naturally integrated into the daily program in a number of ways. Students are expected to be given the skills to use the technology and then are encouraged to use it in the further service of their learning. This can come in the form of using a spreadsheet when appropriate, accessing information ethically from the Internet, or using its presentation capabilities. Technology appears in the text in shaded boxes and paints the picture of a classroom in which technology is used as a matter of course, is accessible to all students, and is used by all to maximize the learning of whatever content is at hand. It leaves room for new technologies that are now readily available that were not known at the time the instrument was developed.

The Research Supporting Assumption 4

The International Center for Leadership in Education has done much research in educational practices in countries around the world. Our country has lagged particularly in its application of technology in our regular curricula. We have all noticed the proliferation of "international outsourcing" of jobs that require technological expertise. The National Standards for Technology Standards (International Society for Technology in Education [ISTE], 2000), and the Indicators of Quality Information Technology Systems in K–12 Schools (National Study of School Evaluation, 2002) support the need for technology to find its way into our national curricula with access available to all students. The National Educational Technology Plan (ISTE, 2000) contains seven action steps:

1. Strengthen leadership
2. Consider innovative budgeting
3. Improve teacher training
4. Support e-learning and virtual schools
5. Encourage broadband access
6. Move toward digital content
7. Integrate data systems

The elements of this plan addressed by DCO are Action Steps 1 and 3. Our training in the protocol targets both classroom and technology teachers and the administrators who supervise their instruction. Technology will not become part of our educational lives until the adults who are responsible for its use are as comfortable and adept as are the students they are teaching.

INTENDED USES

Supervision of Instruction

The primary use of DCO is supervision of instruction. The intended audience, as stated in the Preface, is the building principal or other direct supervisors of instruction. DCO informs classroom observers as they try to make meaning out of the very complex act of teaching and learning and helps them diagnose any problem areas while also giving them a clear picture of what good practice looks like. Because the most effective supervision happens in a school culture where there is joint responsibility for student learning, it is expected that as supervisors in a school or district become comfortable with the DCO system, they will share it with all teachers. Knowing what we do about the change process in schools (Evans, 1996; Fullan, 2001a, 2001b), new methods of classroom observation can feel threatening. Growth does not occur easily, and it occurs less easily in a climate that does not feel safe. Therefore, DCO is *not* recommended for use as an evaluative tool unless and until teachers have a deep understanding of the process and have experience working with the criteria and indicators in other contexts, such as study groups or peer coaching. DCO is an excellent anchor for faculty discussions about professional practice, supervision, collaborative lesson study, and peer mentoring.

Program Evaluation

A secondary use of the protocol is program evaluation. A school may be looking at K–12 student achievement results to attempt to identify factors contributing to low or flat student scores, or the faculty may be interested in analyzing the results of teaching with a particular text or program. By using DCO in a schoolwide audit or action research project, *without* results being used to target specific teachers, a principal can make the best recommendations for professional development spending. For example, it may be discovered that after many workshops in constructivist mathematics, teachers are skilled in leading the activities but weak in understanding the mathematical concepts contained in those activities. This might lead you to target future professional development at the building of math content knowledge, or you might find that teachers are prepared with content, but are not always in control of the behavior and establishing a positive culture in the classroom. These sorts of findings could suggest areas for a school to pursue in its annual goals or yearly action plan.

Large-Scale and Action Research

DCO has also been used in national research conducted by Mathematica Policy Research, Inc., and the Northwest Regional Educational Laboratory. These studies were researching a range of teacher performance issues, including competence linked to teacher preparation programs, new teacher induction programs, and use of the literacy strategies in the CRISS Project (Santa, Havens, & Valdes, 2004). Identifying patterns of strength or weakness in large numbers of teachers, these studies attempt to distinguish between different programs of training and support to establish the most effective. To use DCO (or any other measurement instrument, for that matter) for research, precision in training and interrater reliability are essential. A rigorous process of establishing interrater reliability was used for these studies using the score sheets that are described in Chapter 7 and appear in Appendix F. A description of these score sheets is cautiously provided. This book does not attempt to set standards for large-scale research.

DCO can have a role as part of action research in your setting. At the ends of Chapters 2 through 6, there are some ideas about how to incorporate DCO into your supervisory practice. Using the scoring sheets with the caveats provided, you can gauge professional growth or change in teaching practices as a result of any professional development training initiative.

Key Distinctions of DCO

DCO follows a number of well-researched observation and supervision protocols. Appendix E contains a "cross-walk" between DCO and three systems of classroom observation (Danielson, 1986; Horizon Research, Inc., 1997; Saphier et al., 2008) that demonstrates where they overlap and where they differ. There are some key distinctions between DCO and these systems that are worth noting:

The Process/Content Interaction

Equal emphasis is placed on *what* is taught and *how* it is taught, teachers' mastery of the content and the content-pedagogy, and students' ability to articulate and apply their learning.

Because learning is best served by transcending the argument over whether to stress facts or processes, each of those domains is given equal emphasis. Observers are directed to attend both to what concepts are being taught and how the teacher has arranged for the learning to unfold. Indicators of solid understanding of concepts and research-based pedagogy reside in the tool side by side. There is a strong emphasis on teacher content knowledge along with the ability to predict, diagnose, and untangle student misconceptions. Observers are directed to determine the extent to which the teacher can articulate the concepts contained in the activity, how the teacher has designed the lesson and assessments to capture the understanding of those concepts, and how flexible the teacher is in handling student misconceptions and unexpected occurrences. There is a similar focus on teacher skill in inquiry and constructivist teaching: the likelihood that the learning activities planned will lead to the understanding of the intended concepts, the balance between structured activities and open-ended ones, and the role of metacognition in helping students process the concepts at play in the lesson. The details describing how DCO paints the picture of quality instruction appear in Chapters 2 through 6.

Analysis of Assessments

How systematic and ongoing is the assessment; what sorts of assessments are being used? How does the teacher use information collected on student thinking for further instruction? How do assessments indicate to the teacher that the students have really "gotten it?"

Well-conceived and ongoing assessment is so critical to successful instruction that much attention is given to the specific assessment practices that contribute to success. Assessment as a whole-school or district activity has received much focus ever since the No Child Left Behind Act took effect. Classroom assessment as a concept has been written about and heralded as a major contributor to improvements in student performance (Ainsworth & Viegut, 2006; Black, Harrison, Lee, Marshall, & Wiliam, 2003; Reeves, 2006). What is missing are guidelines for classroom observers who may be unsure how to recognize those effective assessment approaches that actually do result in improved learning. Rather than leaving potential users with a vague directive to ensure that teachers are monitoring student progress, DCO's bullets give specific guidance about what, in the course of a normal classroom lesson, effective assessment looks like, both formative and summative. The assessment indicator is part of the discussion of the content section in Chapters 2 and 3 with examples given. In addition, Chapter 5 is devoted to delving into assessment as a classroom responsibility and gives explicit description about what constitutes valid and useful assessment.

Emphasis on Teacher Knowledge of Content and Underlying Concepts

How deep is the teacher's knowledge, and how flexibly can the teacher work with the concepts to untangle nascent or entrenched student misconceptions?

We often assume that each certified teacher is well-versed in his or her subject matter, but frequently, their knowledge is as the American curriculum itself has been described (TIMSS, 1995)—a mile wide and an inch deep. This can leave the teacher teaching rules and techniques, leaving the conceptual bases to the imagination of their students. A teacher whose content knowledge is limited to the procedural will be unable to work productively with students struggling over the concepts. His or her repertoire for remediation may consist solely of further drill and more examples or explanations similar to the ones that produced confusion in the first place. This strategy is not unlike a native speaker of a language who repeats to a confused tourist the same instructions that he didn't understand the first time, only spoken m...o...r...e...s...l...o...w...l...y and *loudly!* How can you tell if a teacher is flexible enough in his or her subject area to intentionally provide multiple pathways to learning? Indicators and examples of what depth of teacher knowledge looks like in classrooms appear in Chapters 2 and 3. Guidelines for diagnosing through postconference questioning and supervising teacher shortfalls appear in Chapter 7.

Emphasis on Teacher Skill in Inquiry and Constructivist Teaching

How adeptly do teachers translate concepts into activities designed to make those concepts clear?

With many of our new instructional programs chock full of ideas, it is common to see a classroom alive with student activity that appears engaging and purposeful. A teacher can run students very successfully through these activities with very little understanding of the concepts underlying them, and be incapable of posing the probing questions along the way that turn the activity into a true investigation or pushing the students to construct and articulate their new knowledge. The Implementation sections of the Math/Science and Literacy Versions in Chapters 2 and 3 give clues to look for that will help distinguish between the teachers who are facilitating the construction of knowledge in their students and those who are leading them in the neat activity syndrome.

Classroom Culture

How do the students behave in terms of classroom rules and social interactions? To what extent do students benefit from each other as learners? Do all students have equal access to all the educational resources of the classroom?

The ability of a teacher to set the tone of a classroom is essential. The culture that DCO looks for is one of a learning community in which purposeful activities are conducted by teacher and students in a respectful environment. Although intelligent and well-trained in pedagogy, teachers are ineffective unless they can manage the complexities of diverse students and create a safe place to learn. This, in itself, is not a distinction from other teacher evaluation methods. However, DCO pays particular attention to equity of access to the full educational resources in the classroom. This includes classroom discussion, group work, materials, technology, and the caring attention of the teacher. Well-meaning teachers can inadvertently isolate certain students or engage in patterns of exclusion that affect who benefits from the learning in the classroom. DCO raises the consciousness of both teacher and supervisor to see through habits of unintended bias, whether by gender, ethnicity, or ability. These enter our practice without our permission or knowledge and can derail the most expertly constructed lesson. An extended discussion with examples of ways in which teachers unknowingly allow some students to get left behind appear in Chapter 4 in the discussion of the classroom culture criteria.

A Strong Protocol for Professional Development of Principals, Supervisors, and Teacher Leaders/Mentors

How do we make sure that DCO is used as intended to support quality instruction?

Any observation protocol is as effective as the observer in whose hands it sits. In its early use, the use of the tool was restricted to those who had attended a certified training session of a minimum of two days. Certified training is now offered in a number of settings, including graduate-level courses and research training. The formats and processes of training are described in Chapter 7. However, this book is being written for those who will not have access to the certified training. Chapters 2 through 5 offer guidelines for discussion and group study that will help supervisors process the concepts in the book and use their current settings as action research labs for the improvement of instruction using DCO as the framework.

Guidelines for Preconferences and Postconferences

How do you use a preconference to help improve the lesson before it happens? How can you prepare yourself for an observation by indicating key areas to look for? How do you use the postconference to increase the likelihood that the teacher will use it to actually reflect on and improve instruction?

The hope of teacher observation is that the information gained during a session will be effective in helping a teacher reflect on his or her practice to actually improve it. DCO helps supervisors and teachers diagnose the "health" of the lesson by identifying the presence or absence of the key elements. While principals are not experts in all subjects, they may be required to supervise the teaching of them. The DCO guides for preconferences and postconferences help them pose the best "wonderings" to engage the teacher in the same construction of knowledge that DCO outlines for students. Engaging in a collaborative inquiry about teacher practice using the DCO criteria, indicators, and examples of evidence is less threatening to teachers and more likely to result in professional growth. The use of DCO in professional development and improvement in teaching practice is discussed in Chapter 7. Specific tools are provided for each part of the supervisory process: the preconference, the observation, and the postconference. These tools appear in their entirety in the appendices or are discussed in detail in Chapter 7 with examples of how to use these tools to maximize the benefit of instructional supervision.

FINAL THOUGHTS BEFORE PROCEEDING

Lessons can be learned from school systems that have consistently good results or have turned their results around. The TIMSS study (2004) points clearly to the most promising teaching practices that continue to produce superior results in countries like Singapore and Japan. The experience of the Lincolnshire Schools (DuFour & Eaker, 1998) teaches us the power of professional learning communities and the use of common assessments and analysis of student work to improve teaching practice and student achievement. While some educators lament the difficulties inherent in educating all students, the 90-90-90 Schools (Reeves, 2006) and the work of the Education Trust (2006) demonstrate that "the key variable is not poverty but teaching quality." In our honest attempts to find the silver bullets that make all teachers master teachers and ensure maximum learning for every student, we can bounce from good idea to good idea and end by having little to show for it. While there may be no silver bullets, we can choose to learn from success stories in our country and abroad, or we can choose to continue to dabble at the edges, engaging in the veneer of best practice but never really making the profound changes necessary for significant progress. DCO attempts to put together in one place what research tells us about the way students learn best. Its balanced approach to classroom observation addresses content and process, teacher practice, and student understanding. It challenges school leaders to demand a consistent level of professional practice from every teacher *and* from themselves. Until all adult professionals take responsibility for ensuring that their own skills and knowledge are commensurate with the level of achievement we now require from our students, we will continue to fall short of our goals.

Chapter 2

Ending the "Process Versus Content" Argument

In the mid-1980s, America was stunned by a study that compared student results in several developed countries. American education, the great economic equalizer of the post–World War II generation, was producing the least prepared math and science students in the group of nations who had participated in the test. We didn't just do poorly; we came in dead last. Goals 2000, one of the cornerstones of President George Bush's plan for educational improvement, boldly claimed that by the year 2000, we would be number one. The year 2000 has come and gone. The original tests have been repeated by the TIMSS (2004) studies. The good news is that we are no longer last. The bad news is that it may have more to do with the fact that additional countries have joined the testing program than that our gains have met the expectations of the hopeful Goals 2000 program. Countries like Japan and Korea who were ahead of us then still significantly outpace us.

The National Science Foundation has poured resources into innovative programs, creating statewide, rural, and inner-city systemic initiatives designed to radically change and dramatically improve math, science, and technology education. They have created partnerships between colleges, universities, and local school districts in attempts to bring the benefits of expertise and research to the average classroom. The Wallace/Readers Digest and Gates Foundations have funded leadership and other initiatives in virtually every state, and many other initiatives have gathered to address this critical, to say nothing of embarrassing, issue. Research and literature have proliferated, joining in with research on learning and the brain, setting clear paths for schools to follow. But change in schools comes at a slow pace. Willard Daggett in his May 2000 address to school leaders in Vermont noted the number of years it took to move the technology of the overhead projector from the bowling alley to the classroom (an assertion most probably repeated to many other audiences!). Ironically, at this writing, overheads are dinosaurs compared to LCD projectors and SMART Boards. Who knows what the next dinosaurs will be?

THE MATH/SCIENCE VERSION OF DIAGNOSTIC CLASSROOM OBSERVATION

Diagnostic Classroom Observation (DCO) was developed to address teaching and learning in real classrooms with the hope of making the benefits of the research come to life for our students. The high standards that it sets for instruction are evident in its criteria, indicators, and examples of evidence. In all the years since the National Council for Teachers of Mathematics (1989) first published its standards, setting forth a new paradigm of instruction, accompanied by the work of the American Association for the Advancement of Science (1989, 1993, 1998) and the National Science Education Standards (National Research Council, 1995), schools have been struggling to make science and math instruction more successful. The National Research Council (2000b) identifies five myths surrounding inquiry and its use as a teaching method in science. The myths, which grew out of a well-meaning desire for students to freely investigate scientific phenomena, include:

- All science subject matter should be taught through inquiry.
- True inquiry occurs only when students generate and pursue their own questions.
- Inquiry teaching occurs easily through use of hands-on or kit-based instructional materials.
- Student engagement in hands-on activities guarantees that inquiry . . . [is] occurring.
- Inquiry can be taught without attention to subject matter. (National Research Council, 2000b, p. 36)

The council warns that unfounded attitudes about inquiry "threaten to inhibit progress . . . by characterizing inquiry as too difficult . . . or by neglecting the essential features" (p. 35). These "essential features" include having students cite evidence, formulate ideas, communicate, and justify explanations that are connected to scientific knowledge.

The danger to math and science instruction in misunderstanding this basic premise of the new standards was twofold. First, there was the tendency of teachers who lacked a deep understanding of the concepts to adopt a purely activities approach to instruction with math manipulatives and scientific "inquiry" galore, leaving the program no cohesion and not establishing conceptual understanding. This left no foundation on which to build. Second, schools rushed to adopt the new standards-based programs and provided their teachers with insufficient training to get the mileage out of the programs. Their training might even have been limited to the publisher's presentation, which might in turn be limited to understanding the structure of the text and how the program was laid out. These teachers were left to their own devices. Many just taught step by step from the book, assuming that the careful development that had gone into the math series would be enough to ensure that as long as the students were completing the chapters and passing the skills tests, they would be getting what they needed to know.

It was to quell this argument about whether the teaching of content or the teaching of the inquiry process should guide instruction that DCO has developed its Implementation and Content criteria for both math and science. It is the firm belief, backed by all the current research and literature, that one must have specific skills and knowledge and that the best way to teach those is through active investigation that exemplifies (or at least approximates) the way mathematicians and scientists actually do their work. This investigation is sometimes guided and sometimes open ended, but it always results in the articulation of what was learned.

THE IMPLEMENTATION CRITERIA

This section focuses on how the teacher implements the planned instructional activities and how successfully the students are engaged in productive learning. It speaks to the preparation and execution of the lesson and directs the observer to look carefully at what both the teacher and students are doing at all times. Successfully implemented lesson plans do not always produce the learning that they seem to be designed for. Frequently, observers can be lulled into a false sense of security by a "neat activity." We have all walked into classrooms where there seems to be purposeful activity, students are busy handling manipulatives or making charts and journal entries, and there is a general sense that the lesson is being conducted as planned by the teacher. Yet we may walk away with questions as to what was actually being learned. This section directs the observer to analyze the level of probing, deep thinking, and constructing one's own knowledge that has been built into the plan.

Box 2.1

Indicator MS-IM#1	
Indicator	**Examples of Evidence**
MS-IM#1. Teacher demonstrates confidence as a facilitator of mathematical and scientific learning and growth	• Teacher speaks fluently and in depth about concepts • Teacher allows student questions and can expand on topic as necessary • Lesson is not overly scripted; teacher demonstrates ability to adapt the task as necessary to guide and deepen student learning • Teacher encourages students to actively grapple with concepts • Teacher presents himself or herself as a learner along with students, indicating what he or she doesn't know and voicing satisfaction about learned information

Indicator MS-IM#1 has to do with the comfort level of the teacher in teaching the math or science concepts that are at the core of the lesson. It goes deeper than the teacher's preparedness to run the activity. Math texts, science kits, and curriculum materials offer supports for teaching that are meant to standardize instruction, but the most scripted lesson with all the pieces provided cannot take the place of a knowledgeable teacher who has the confidence to lay out an activity for the students to grapple with, ultimately guiding them to understand important concepts. Here we look for a teacher who can discuss the concepts or present the day's tasks without hanging on to the book for dear life. How does the teacher cope with the unexpected and probing question from a student? We may be in the habit of saying that it's OK to not know everything and that it is better to acknowledge the limits of your knowledge than to fudge your way through an erroneous explanation, but it's not OK to not know *anything* about the topic and to not be able to speak with some level of depth about it. We are looking for a teacher who handles questions honestly with a lack of defensiveness. Frequently, the more controlled the lesson is, the fewer questions allowed, and more restricted the latitude given to the students, the less confident the teacher is to handle the content.

Box 2.2

Indicator MS-IM#2	
Indicator	**Examples of Evidence**
MS-IM#2. Periods of teacher-student interaction are probing and substantive	• Questions expose and draw on students' prior knowledge • Questions and dialogue emphasize higher order thinking (students compare, contrast, classify, use analogies and metaphors; Marzano, 1999) • Teacher probes with challenging activities in addition to questions • Students are encouraged to develop a metacognitive sense of their learning

MS-IM#2 looks at how deeply the teacher probes student thinking. The first step in substantive learning is accessing a student's prior knowledge. Building on preexisting research (Cobb, 1994, as cited in National Research Council, 2000a; Piaget, 1978; Vygotsky, 1978), new research determines that "new knowledge must be constructed from existing knowledge . . . teachers need to pay attention to the incomplete understandings, the false beliefs, and the naïve renditions of concepts that learners bring with them to a given subject" (National Research Council, 2000a, p. 10). Assessing prior knowledge is not only critical for exposing students' naïve and possibly incorrect assumptions to tackle them, it can often establish already known concepts that a teacher, always pressed for time, can pass through quickly to build on the next level. (Note that having students inform you that "we learned that last year" is *not* a sufficient assessment of students' prior knowledge!)

We often focus on teacher questions to indicate the extent to which students are being engaged in higher order thinking. Yet it is not just the questions per se that expose that element of teaching. While questioning techniques are critical, sometimes the most probing lesson is one in which the teacher does very little actual questioning. With groups engaged in investigations, we may not hear questions being asked at all. The third bullet directs the observer to look at the activity posed. How much independent thinking is required for the students to approach and complete the task? Is it overly directive, or does it allow for multiple approaches? There may be a single correct answer, but do the students discover it for themselves? A well-developed task is the highest form of a probing and substantive question.

Box 2.3

Good Implementation Ideas That Go Bad (MS-IM#2)

The idea: K-W-L ("What do you know? What do you want to know? What have we learned?" [Ogle, 1986])—engaging students by activating prior knowledge.

A good preassessment accomplishes a few goals:

- It allows a teacher to not have to teach what students already know.
- It exposes misconceptions that will have to be tackled for learning to progress.
- It gets students to share what they know and learn from each other.

HAS IT GONE BAD?

To what use does the teacher put that collective knowledge? Does it sit idly on a chart for the rest of the unit? Is there follow-up to the more promising ideas? Are any of the ideas actively engaged in the new activities? Are the learning activities set up to prove or disprove the theories expressed at the outset? Is there closure at the end of the lesson or unit that revisits those initial ideas to sort out the promising concepts from the misconceptions?

The idea: During group work, the teacher circulates to facilitate learning. Questions and discourse emphasize higher order thinking.

This is a way for teachers to work with students individually to:

- identify misconceptions as they are developing,
- work with students who need individual attention, and
- probe student thinking to push them from where they are to where they need to go.

HAS IT GONE BAD?

After the problem has been posed and the students begin to work on it, listen carefully to the interventions of the teacher. What is the level of questioning the teacher engages in with individual students and small groups? We know the good "tag lines" to listen for: "Could you tell me where you got that answer?" "Why do you think that?" The key is what the teacher *does* with the answers. Does the teacher listen politely and move on, or does he or she probe further? If the student is off-base, how adeptly does the teacher pose the next question so the student has something new to consider that will lead to the next level of understanding?

Box 2.4

Indicator MS-IM#3	
Indicator	**Examples of Evidence**
MS-IM#3. Teacher's instructional choices are effective in engaging students in active and thoughtful learning	• Students are engaged and excited about finding answers to questions posed by the activity • Objectives are clearly stated (sometimes in an inquiry; this comes out later in the lesson and might not be observed at first) • Activities are likely to lead to student learning in the stated objectives • Teacher does not dominate discussions • Tasks are challenging; teacher sets high expectations • Both teacher-directed instruction and constructivist methods are used as appropriate for task and diverse learning needs

MS-IM#3 has two parts: the level of engagement of the students both in the intensity and the extent of their involvement. How deeply are they engaged, and how many of them are actively engaged? Ideally, *all* students will exhibit excitement and purposeful activity. Engagement is an important first step, but the more pressing question is how likely that engagement is to lead the students to new learning. Is real thinking needed to complete the task? Are the students thinking hard, knowing that a high level of accountability will be applied? Has the teacher used a variety of teaching techniques to reach all students?

Box 2.5

Good Implementation Ideas That Go Bad (MS-IM#3 and MS-IM#4)

The idea: Students learn best when they have their hands on the materials and are actively engaged. Inherently more engaging to students, this approach also:

- challenges students' intellect,
- helps them construct their own knowledge, and
- rewards curiosity and perseverance.

HAS IT GONE BAD?

Is this a "cookbook" activity that looks hands-on but is essentially procedural in nature? Is it tied directly enough to the concepts being taught so that when completed, the students will understand something that they didn't before? Or is it a case of the "neat activity syndrome?"

Hands-on Example 1

A high school science lab is handed a sheet that describes step by step the experiment that they are to conduct with all details, including the amounts of materials and specific methods to be followed. Results produced are exactly as predicted by the teacher or the students have done something wrong. Students are asked to explain the results, but they are not required to ask any follow-up questions, to make any connections to previous lessons, or to choose a variable to alter, predict a result, and design a new investigation.

HAS IT GONE BAD?

Is the activity so rote that coming up with the right results is less a function of understanding than of correctly following the procedure? Is the activity so complicated that following the directions and carrying out the steps become the focus of instruction with the concepts getting lost in the shuffle?

Hands-on Example 2

A fourth-grade teacher wants to use a game with manipulatives to demonstrate the concept of fractions. Students are provided papers containing fraction bars divided into wholes, halves, quarters, thirds, and sixths. The problems begin with inaccurate use of scissors resulting in differing sizes of equivalent pieces. The activity involves multiple rounds of folding the pieces, leaving the students with so many folds in each piece that the visual of what a "half of a half" looks like is completely lost. Behavior issues begin to dominate, and by the time the bell rings, there has been no opportunity to complete the task, much less compare results or reflect on the concepts.

Example 2.6

MS-IM#1, MS-IM#2, and MS-IM#3

WHAT DOES A CONFIDENT TEACHER LOOK LIKE? WHAT DOES PROBING AND SUB-STANTIVE TEACHER-STUDENT INTERACTION LOOK LIKE? WHAT DOES SUBSTANTIVE STUDENT-TO-STUDENT INTERACTION LOOK LIKE?

A sixth-grade teacher is reviewing long division problems. The issue of when you can "cancel zeros" in reducing fractions comes up as a result of a division problem with a remainder being expressed in fraction form. The teacher lets go of the planned lesson on division when he becomes aware that the concept about canceling zeros is not understood by most of the class. He asks the students to work in groups to come up with a theory about when it is allowable to cancel zeros. Students work together and volunteer several theories, some of which are incorrect and some of which are partially right. The students work together seriously, sifting through their prior knowledge to think of ways in which to handle the challenge put to them. Their theories range from making sure the zeros are in the same column to canceling other matching numbers if they are in the same column. In each case, the teacher probes further with questions such as "Why do you think that?" "Is everybody comfortable with that?" and offers confounding factors that will lead students to discovering a flaw in their theory (i.e., presenting a fraction in which both zeros are in the tens column, but neither number is divisible by ten or a multiple of ten). By the end of the lesson, students come upon a method of proof that will tell them if the canceled zeros have yielded two equivalent fractions. By dividing the numerator by the denominator in each case, they will determine if the decimals indicate an exact match. If they do, then the cancelled zeros were allowable. The teacher then sends them home with a prompt to think back to when they first learned about the shortcut of canceling zeros: a lesson in prime factoring. He indicates that they will revisit that concept on the next day to finally agree about the rule. By allowing his students to grapple with a misconception, regardless of where that may take them mathematically, he has demonstrated his comfort in being able to handle the mathematics and to continue to probes the students' thinking, even in the face of some disappointing misconceptions (MS-IM#1). The students have demonstrated the ability to apply prior knowledge (MS-IM#2), and the engagement and excitement to persevere and be the developers of mathematical theory (MS-IM#3).

From Grant et al. (2002).

MS-IM#4 poses the familiar question of balance: When does a teacher engage in direct teaching, and when do the students get to discover the important concepts? While not every activity needs to be an inquiry, DCO does ask that the instructional program provide for consistent, as opposed to rare, chances for students to own their own thinking. There are a number of ways in which this can happen. Certainly one of the most powerful is to engage students as active participants in asking the questions, designing the investigation, and articulating what they have learned. Good inquiry, however, exists on a continuum, with the teacher at one pole posing the problem,

Box 2.7

Indicator MS-IM#4	
Indicator	**Examples of Evidence**
MS-IM#4. Students have opportunities to construct their own knowledge (Note: if this is not directly observed in the lesson, teacher can identify when and how in the unit this will occur.)	• Investigative tasks are essential elements of the lesson • Curiosity and perseverance are encouraged • Students apply existing knowledge and skills to new situations and integrate new and prior knowledge • Students make notes, drawings, or summaries in a journal or lab book that becomes part of their ongoing resources • Students have opportunities to do more than follow procedures; they ask their own questions, choose their own strategies, or design investigations • Students manipulate materials and equipment • Teachers and students discuss which technologies to use for various products and processes and why to use them

providing the means to solving the problem, and structuring the manner in which the answers are presented (guided inquiry), and at the other pole, providing open-ended tasks where students pose their own question, design their own investigation, and devise their own strategies for analyzing data and presenting conclusions.

Example 2.8

MS-IM#4

WHAT DOES "CONSTRUCTING ONE'S OWN KNOWLEDGE" LOOK LIKE?

A fourth-grade class is doing a geometry unit on circles. They are learning about circumference, diameter, and radii. The teacher wants them to discover that there is a fixed relationship between the circumference and the diameter of a circle (which we know of as pi) and that the circumference is approximately three times the diameter. They will arrive at 3.14 a bit later.

Instead of giving them the information or providing the formula, the teacher sends the students in pairs around the room measuring the circumference and diameter of everything round they can find in the room, noting each measurement on a chart. When they are all done (taking into account some errors in measurement), they have a chart of comparison between circumferences and diameters of all sorts of circles. They notice the "circumference divided by three relationship" from some of the easy examples, but as they use their calculators to test that relationship with all the circles on their charts, the fact that all the answers hover around three emerges. Ultimately, these students will have generated the concept of pi, which the teacher now has the opportunity to refine and have them use in future explorations of circles. These students are likely to always remember that the circumference of any circle is about three times the diameter, because they have discovered it themselves.

From Annenberg/CPB Math and Science Collection. 1995. Science images. (Videotape). Burlington, VT.

Box 2.9

Indicator MS-IM#5	
Indicator	**Examples of Evidence**
MS-IM#5. The pace of the lesson is appropriate for the developmental level of the students, and there is adequate time for wrap-up and closure of the lesson	• Students have time to engage in the tasks, and there is adequate time to practice new skills • Teacher "wait time" is sufficient to allow all students to have a chance to think of answers • Teacher adjusts time periods to accommodate students if necessary • Time is available for students to review, reflect on, and articulate what was learned, either through class discussions, journal writing, completion of data sheets, or presentations

If the lesson does not involve an inquiry, students can construct their own knowledge by having time to ponder in their math or science journals, integrate prior knowledge with new learning, apply new knowledge to a task of their choice, ask questions that will be answered by the teacher, read and investigate questions on their own, or describe their learning in nonlinguistic ways. These options allow even the most directive teacher to begin to turn over some of the responsibility for learning to the students.

Pacing can be gauged in several ways. It can be monitored minute by minute by noting how quickly the teacher speaks, moves from task to task, speaks before the children have a chance to think of an answer, or jumps to the first right answer that pops out of the crowd. We note this by looking at "wait time" and judging how many different students have a chance to respond to teacher questions before the quickest among them has grabbed the floor. But there is a more subtle aspect to pacing, which has to do with the overall lesson and its flexibility to allow students to work at their own speed. What are the strategies for students who work at different paces? Look for how many children are staying in from recess to complete work from the morning versus how many have follow-up tasks to move ahead more deeply. If too many don't complete their work while too many others languish with little important left to do, then the pace is working for virtually no one.

The lesson should have a beginning, middle, and end. The end may not be where the teacher planned it to be when the bell rings or the art teacher shows up. But does the teacher, seeing the end of the time period approaching, give time to stop and take stock of where students are in the process? It is this part of the lesson that is frequently missed. There is some research that suggests the literal evaporation of new learning without a period of reflection or closure to help it gel (Jernstedt, 2005). The research even reports that people learning a new task have a better chance of remembering what they've learned if they take a nap directly after, as opposed to continuing on with another activity. So (barring naptime in our upper grades), closure of some sort—journaling, gathering ones thoughts on a chart, noting questions that remain unanswered, and making plans for where to go next in the pursuit of the answers—is critical for student success.

Example 2.10

MS-IM#5

WHAT DOES GOOD PACING LOOK LIKE? HOW CAN PACING CONTRIBUTE TO STUDENT LEARNING?

A fourth-grade teacher is teaching a lesson on nonstandard measurement. Students gather together on the rug to review what they did yesterday. They recall that they have used numbers of paces to express distances in the classroom. Today, they will use paces to map out distances to give directions to others about how to reach various spots in the classroom. They have assigned partners for this task and a chart to record where they began and where they traveled. As the pairs work, the teacher joins one after another, asking them to show her where they are traveling and attempting to follow their directions. It becomes apparent to at least one group that the teacher is having difficulty arriving at the proper location because the size of her paces is different from the students'. After about ten minutes, the teacher calls them back to the rug for about three minutes. At this time, she asks them to share any problems they were having and tell the group how they solved those problems. Determining that they are all on the right track, she gives them ten minutes more to complete the task. Near the end of the period, the students are back on the rug with their charts and are asked to report anything that they noticed while doing the task. One group reports the finding about the problem with the difference in size of the teacher's paces. The students are left at the end with this thought, which will be important for the next day's task when students will find themselves walking into walls as they attempt to follow each other's directions from the classroom to the library. In this way, the activity leads them to understand the need for standard measurement.

The lesson has a beginning, middle, and end, each segment of which contributes in its own way to student understanding. Wait time, think time, time to engage in the task, *and* time to process learning up to that point are all present.

Box 2.11

Indicator MS-IM#6	
Indicator	**Examples of Evidence**
MS-IM#6. Periods of student-student interaction are productive and enhance individual understanding of the lesson	• Students have opportunities to collaborate in pairs or small groups • Student group work is structured to lead students to greater understanding; outcomes are clearly stated • Student discussions demonstrate thinking and learning about the concepts contained in the activities

Ever since "cooperative learning" (Johnson, Johnson, & Holubec, 1994) became popular, teachers have learned that they should have some group work as part of their instructional program. But merely having students assigned to groups or tables or teams does not guarantee productive interaction, which enhances individual understanding. The first step in MS-IM#6 asks whether students have multiple opportunities to work in groups, because we do know that dialogue can further individual learning and that there is a social component to learning. But knowing how to look at groups and how they are structured can help an observer identify when groups are working for all the students, or only some, or none.

A well-structured group task begins with well-structured groups. The size and make-up of the groups is key. Pairs tend to work best, but the teacher needs to monitor groups of any size carefully to ensure that every student in the group is equally involved. Strategies for tracking individual thinking need to be in place. Teachers frequently complain that they don't know how to assess individuals when a group grade is given. Math and science journal writing at the end of the activity gives each child a chance to process what the group accomplished and what approaches they took. As the teacher circulates, note the extent to which he or she engages each child through questioning and encourages each child to handle the materials, propose solutions, and take responsibility for group presentations.

This is also a time for the observer to note the level of student discourse. How probing and substantive is the conversation? Are the students really discussing the task and applying what they already know to find solutions? Are they building off each other's ideas? Are they taking the first good idea and going with it whether it seems to be working or not? See Example 2.12 for the "Discourse Rubric." This is useful for training students who have not had experience in real collaboration, particularly on the secondary level, to engage in content-laden discourse.

There is much to be said about the workings of groups. DCO has three indicators to assess the success of group process and learning. We will revisit group work in the content section and the classroom culture section as well.

Example 2.12

MS-IM#6

WHAT DOES STUDENT-TO-STUDENT INTERACTION THAT ENHANCES INDIVIDUAL UNDERSTANDING OF THE LESSON LOOK LIKE?

A seventh-grade class has been studying body systems, in particular the circulatory system and heredity. They have been given a mystery to solve: A patient presents himself to a doctor's office with certain symptoms, and the task is to ultimately find out what disease he has. The students have a clinical history that the doctor has taken from the patient and evidence collected by the doctor, which includes blood samples and models of the patient's red blood cells. They are to begin to hypothesize what might be wrong with him.

The students are arranged in same-sex pairs, and they begin to read the history together and to discuss the various issues. After they have had a chunk of time to do this, they now turn to their across-the-table-mates (another pair of students) and share their working hypotheses. The disease is sickle cell anemia, and the patient history leads them to posit that the disease is probably hereditary. The odd-shaped red blood cells have several groups wondering whether the misshapen red blood cells may not carry enough hemoglobin and therefore not enough oxygen, causing the shortness of breath. They do not yet know what the disease is, but they have, through examining evidence together and discussing it, noted two critical factors central to this disease.

From the Annenberg/CPB Math and Science Collection (1995).

HOW CAN YOU ENCOURAGE STUDENTS TO ENGAGE IN COLLABORATIVE, PROBLEM-SOLVING DISCOURSE WHEN THEY ARE NOT USED TO IT?

This Discourse Rubric trains students and rewards them for real conceptual discussions, good listening, and collaborative problem solving. Students earn points for collaborating to complete tasks, in addition to getting credit for correctly doing the work (used primarily in Grades 6 through 12).

4 points	3 points	2 points	1 point
Students independently discuss and collaboratively complete task	Students discuss and complete task with some prompting from teacher	Students need multiple prompts from teacher to get them to either discuss or complete task	Students in group not talking to each other but doing work by themselves

Example 2.13

MS-IM#6

WHAT DOES A HIGH SCHOOL LESSON LOOK LIKE WITH NO STUDENT-TO-STUDENT INTERACTION (OR WHEN THE TEACHER IS HAVING A CONVERSATION WITH HIMSELF OR HERSELF)?

A high school algebra teacher has assigned homework in which the students have to determine the slope of a number of lines on a graph. Students have papers on their desks in front of them. The teacher places a transparency with the exercises and answers filled in on the overhead projector. She goes through each of the examples, briefly explaining each response. She occasionally stops to ask if everyone understands or if there are any questions. There rarely are in this class, where teacher explanations are presented and accepted as "the only way." If a student does ask a question, it is answered quickly and with similar language to the original explanation. A follow-up question by the student is even rarer. If the teacher poses a question to the students, one or two students call out the right answer. Satisfied, she continues with the lesson. When the test is given at the end of the week, few students pass, and the teacher is annoyed that the students didn't study.

HOW CAN THIS LOOK DIFFERENT?

A high school algebra teacher assigns homework that contains examples that are essential to understanding slope. Students come in, are assigned partners to review the homework, and are instructed to come to consensus for each solution. The teacher circulates and applies the Discourse Rubric so that students earn points for sharing and discussing their work. After a sufficient period, the teacher asks the groups one by one to volunteer to give their answers to a question and explain their solution. Other pairs of students are given an opportunity to question or challenge the proposed solution, and the teacher checks to make sure that each pair has come up with a valid response. If there is general understanding, the teacher proceeds with the lesson. If there are significant misconceptions, the teacher is ready with some reteaching or differentiated activities.

Box 2.14

Good Implementation Ideas That Go Bad (MS-IM#5)

The idea: "Wait time" is sufficient to allow all students to think of answers.
Waiting before allowing students to answer a question:

- promotes the participation of all,
- discourages the dominance of a few students, and
- prevents the automatic discouragement of those who take a bit more time to process information.

HAS IT GONE BAD?

Has "wait time" become "dead time," where the slower students just sit while others wag their arms, put their fingers on their noses, or otherwise anxiously wait for the teacher to call on them? Or has the teacher given the students some thinking strategies, such as jotting their thoughts on paper or sharing them with a partner? These encourage everyone to take a stab at the answer in a low-risk way and allow all students to give themselves credit for their answers even if they weren't called on.

The idea: Students have opportunities to collaborate in pairs or small groups (MS-IM#6).
Grouping students for selected tasks:

- takes advantage of the natural tendency to learn through dialogue,
- allows students to learn some things at their own pace, and
- gives students the opportunity to learn by doing.

HAS IT GONE BAD?

Are group tasks unclear, causing students to lose focus? Does each student have a role? Does the task require that the students communicate to solve the problem or complete the task? Do students use the discussions to enhance their learning, or are they just "going through the motions?"

Box 2.15

Indicators T-IM#7 and T-IM#8	
Indicators	**Examples of Evidence**
T-IM#7. Teacher models technology integration	• Teacher uses the equipment in class and suggests technology tools to expand student learning • Teacher has backup plans in case of a problem with the technology
T-IM#8. Students use electronic resources efficiently and productively	• Students use planned strategies to contact resources and collect information • Within a lesson or unit, students use many available resources, including the Internet • Students process and evaluate the information collected • Students communicate appropriate school-related information through the use of electronic tools (e.g., newsletters, Web pages)

Even in the most well-endowed classroom, technology integration cannot happen unless the teacher is comfortable with the technology, can model its use, and helps the students devise strategies for using their technology skills in new ways. Now that many students have access to information technology in the classroom and in labs, teachers can still struggle with how to use the computers in substantial ways. Students need guidance in how to navigate the Internet with purpose, how to discriminate between fact and opinion, and how to evaluate the depth and reliability of the information. Although PowerPoint presentations are impressive and should be mastered, we must learn to harness the power of the technology tools to enhance learning, not merely showcase it. We will revisit technology integration in the content section to look at some meaningful ways to enhance learning with technology.

THE CONTENT CRITERIA

To avoid the neat activity syndrome, the content section of DCO focuses the observer on the actual concepts that are at the center of the lesson being observed. It is not necessary to be a scientist or mathematician to effectively supervise instruction or to use this tool. It is necessary, however, to know what kinds of questions to ask the teacher and the students, and to know how to listen to their answers. Knowing that questions of content must be addressed is a beginning. Becoming adept at speaking to teachers about their math and science may seem daunting to those among us who became school leaders with other than math or science degrees. I can, however, guarantee that you can become not only skilled at asking the right questions, but skilled at cutting through technical talk to determine if the lesson you are observing is being taught for the mastery of specific math and science concepts.

Box 2.16

Indicator MS-CO#1	
Indicator	**Examples of Evidence**
MS-CO#1. Academic standards are central to the instructional program	• Content is aligned with the appropriate national or state standards • The standard and content is clearly identified and understood by students OR • The standard and content will intentionally emerge from the activities

Math and science national standards have done much to guide curriculum and instruction over the last decade or so. Yet teachers can persist in teaching what they have always taught in the ways they were taught themselves even in the face of the most compelling evidence of how learning actually happens. The first step in an observation is to establish the source of the lesson. The teacher should be able to identify for the observer the standard being addressed, whether from the national, state, or local guidelines. Students should be aware of this as well, although it is not necessary to have the teacher stand up and announce the name and number of the relevant standard. What is most important is that the knowledge outlined in that standard will intentionally emerge from the teaching of the lesson.

An excellent resource for science teachers at all levels is the Science Curriculum Topic Study (Keeley, 2005). This book outlines the connections between topics studied and the bigger concepts inherent in them, knowledge that is essential for every teacher of science to have. Using the sources of national and state science standards from the American Association for the Advancement of Science (1989, 1993, 2001) as well as the *National Science Standards* and *Inquiry and the National Science Standards*, the Curriculum Topic Study guides teachers topic by topic from the big ideas and the conceptual development to the lessons that they will need to prepare for their students. These resources make it easy to delve more deeply into the concepts and grow beyond superficial approaches.

Box 2.17

Good Content Ideas That Go Bad (MS-CO#1)

The idea: Lessons should be aligned with state or national standards and should be posted or otherwise made known to students.

Aligning lessons with the standards:

- takes advantage of the best practice established by national standards research,
- focuses teachers on exactly what to assess as they prepare students for higher levels and for state tests, and
- helps students know where they are headed with the unit being studied.

HAS IT GONE BAD?

Are the standards applicable to each lesson either posted on the board or on student worksheets listed in code form (e.g., HSS:9:17) without the words associated with that code evident to students? Are the standards listed, but the connection of the activity or assignment to the standard not discussed or even mentioned? Are the assessments focused on the procedures without assessing the underlying conceptual understanding?

Example From Grade 8 Mathematics

Standard: Students demonstrate proportional reasoning.

Students are given multiple examples where they have to calculate a particular percentage of a given number (find 3.9% of 330), find the percentage that one number is of another (13 is what percentage of 330), and use proportions to figure percentages (13:330 = x:100). Students dutifully perform each operation as modeled by the teacher and are successful as long as the procedure is the same for each example. But as they move on in the chapter, the examples are mixed so that the student needs to decide which algorithm to perform. At this point, the students fall apart, and more than 60% of the class fails the chapter test.

Box 2.18

Indicator MS-CO#2	
Indicator	**Examples of Evidence**
MS-CO#2. Teacher shows an understanding of the concepts and content of the lesson	• Teacher can articulate clearly what concepts are intentionally contained in the activities • The activities and instructional strategies are crafted to lead to the understanding of those concepts • Teacher provides accurate information • Teacher asks questions that reflect substantive understanding of the topic • Teacher elicits more than just facts or introduces confounding factors to deepen thinking • Teacher encourages students to question, probe, explain answers, and extend knowledge

Having established that the lesson you are about to observe does correspond to age-appropriate national or state standards, you need to establish the teacher's ability to understand the content at a deep enough level to do more than run through the activity. Poorly planned math and science investigations can go far afield, and there are two misguided strategies that unsure teachers use to cope with the uncertainty inherent in letting students loose to explore:

• Overly control the activity so that the outcomes are predictable.
• Let an investigation go on and on with no closure, allowing student ideas to flourish but not helping students sort out which ideas hold the most promise for understanding the concepts at hand.

In either case, the teacher has controlled what he or she will be required to know. In the first case, the knowledge is predetermined and restricted ("cookbook" labs are an example of this). In the second, no demonstration of actual content knowledge is required since there will be no conceptual closure or articulation of any specific concepts. Sometimes these lessons can end in presentations by students that reflect what the students did, but not necessarily what they learned. (This is the neat activity syndrome.)

Box 2.19

Good Content Ideas That Go Bad (MS-CO#2)

WHAT HAPPENS WHEN THE MATH CONTAINED IN A LESSON IS NOT THOUGHT THROUGH?

A first-grade teacher who, by all other standards, is a talented and thoughtful teacher, attempts to teach her students to tell time. They have just completed the unit on counting money, which is frequently taught near the "time unit." They begin the lesson with a quick review of their understanding of counting money, and it is evident that the students are comfortable counting by fives, tens, and twenty-fives to a dollar. It is also clear that they know the values of pennies, nickels, and dimes and that they know that a quarter equals twenty-five cents.

As they get into the time unit, the students develop a misconception that "quarter after six" means "twenty-five minutes past six." The teacher is caught unaware by this misunderstanding and has no plan for counteracting it. She is left with telling them that they are incorrect, that twenty-five had to do with money, and now they are doing time. It is clear that the confusion is not allayed.

The issue that she has failed to take into account is that when teaching both money and time, you are dealing with fractions. The key concept about fractions at the most basic level is that they express a "part to whole" relationship. Therefore, a quarter equals one fourth and is only equal to twenty-five when the whole is one hundred. Beginning by understanding the whole you are dealing with is a critical first step. Moving to fractional expressions needs to wait until the value of the whole is firmly established in the children's minds. Money and time are not usually taught as fractions units. But understanding the underlying math contained in the lesson is important not just because the teacher might have to end up teaching more than he or she counted on. It is important to be able to foresee the possible misconceptions and to factor them into lesson plans.

Box 2.20

Indicator MS-CO#3	
Indicator	**Examples of Evidence**
MS-CO#3. Teacher collects and assesses evidence of student progress to enhance teaching and learning	• Assessment is systematic and ongoing so that teacher can track student progress and adjust instruction • Student misconceptions are identified so that they can adjust their thinking • Agreed-on standards are used to judge the quality of student products and performances • Assessments are varied (journals, performance tasks, presentations, tests) and target concepts *and* skills • Students self-assess by using rubrics or reviewing past work to see their progress • Assessments clearly indicate conceptual closure

Conceptual closure differs from lesson closure in that it has to do with student learning of a well-articulated concept. In the case of the "finding the circumference" example, conceptual closure will come when the students understand that there is a fixed relationship between the diameter and circumference of any circle, that it is known as pi, and that this relationship is useful in understanding and working with circles in a variety of ways. In the "canceling zeros" case, students will come to conceptual closure when they understand that the only time you can "cancel zeros" is when both the numerator and denominator are divisible by ten or the same multiple of ten. During a typical classroom observation, you will frequently see students working toward this level of understanding, but you rarely get to witness the final "aha!"

So how, then, do you know if they ever get there? A preconference with the teacher will tell you whether the teacher can not only articulate what the concept is, but what it will look like when the students have gotten it. Then it will be necessary to determine what sorts of evidence the teacher plans to look for or collect to monitor the student thinking along the way and to identify when each student has really arrived. While a test or quiz may be the most common piece of evidence collected, there are many other ways the teacher can assess progress and achievement. Other formats include journals, diagrams, constructed response questions in which students have to describe their understanding, student conferences, exit questions, or quick-response questions that students complete before they leave the room. *Uncovering Students' Ideas in Science: 25 Formative Assessment Probes* (Keeley, 2004) is an excellent source for both specific assessments and formats that teachers can draw on for their own classrooms.

Formative assessment (checking for understanding along the way in some systematic form) is a promising strategy in raising student achievement (Black, Harrison, Lee, Marshall, & Wiliam, 2003). Many teachers feel that they already do this. What many of them do, in fact, is what I've called "assessment by wandering around." They claim that they know where their students are and that they are constantly assessing them. However, if a teacher is circulating among working groups of students, we need to ask him or her two key questions:

- What understanding are you looking for?
- How are you keeping track of who is where along the continuum of understanding?

This is a central tenant of *Understanding by Design* and building a unit of study using "backwards design" (Wiggins & McTighe, 1998). Well before a teaching event occurs, a teacher must have a clear idea of the concepts that he or she is going to teach and what it will look like when those concepts have been understood. The "essential questions" that must be answered will guide both the assessments used and the instructional activities chosen that will lead students to that concept. There is nothing wrong with circulating to check informally on student progress to determine that students understand the task, are staying on track, and are not stuck in confusion. But circulating does not rise to the level of assessment unless there is a specific goal and a method of recording each child's status at that time.

Box 2.21

Good Content Ideas That Go Bad (MS-CO#3)

The idea: Teachers should be continually assessing students' understanding. Formative assessment:

- helps untangle misconceptions before they become fixed;
- informs instruction, allowing teachers to adjust according to student progress; and
- results in deeper learning and student accountability.

HAS IT GONE BAD?

Does the teacher assure you that, despite no recorded data, he or she knows exactly where the students are at all times? Does the teacher wander about, randomly interacting with students, and call this "formative assessment?" Does student work consist primarily of workbook pages with fill-in-the-blank or circle-the-response questions or fact-based quizzes? Do final projects get graded primarily according to their neatness, organization, and completeness? Do assessment rubrics fail to identify the understanding of specific concepts, relying on general statements such as "student represents concepts accurately?" Do the majority of formal assessments happen at the end of the unit?

Example 2.22

MS-CO#3

WHAT DOES AN ASSESSMENT LOOK LIKE THAT IS SYSTEMATIC, IS ONGOING, HELPS IDENTIFY AND UNTANGLE STUDENT MISCONCEPTIONS, AND HELPS THE TEACHER KNOW WHEN AND HOW TO ADAPT INSTRUCTION?

Activity: Students are investigating forces and motion by constructing rolling vehicles and sending them down a ramp. Their task is to choose a variable to investigate, formulate a hypothesis, and design and carry out an experiment that will test that hypothesis.

At this time, the teacher wants to assess student understanding of two elements of scientific inquiry:

- Develop a testable question (hypothesis)
- Write a plan related to the question and prediction that includes:
  - o a procedure that lists significant steps sequentially, and
  - o a description of which variable will be manipulated or changed and which variables will remain the same ("fair test").

Formative assessment: The teacher circulates around the room with a clipboard and visits each group, asking students what variable they are investigating and what their hypothesis is.

1. Teacher notes if:
   - an appropriate variable has been chosen,
   - the hypothesis proposed is a testable question, and
   - the design is in fact a fair test.

2. If those conditions are met, teacher moves on to the next group. If not, the teacher probes thinking, asks questions, or poses a problem that pushes students through their misunderstanding to a better plan. In either case, the teacher records results.

3. If, after stopping at a few groups, the teacher discovers that most groups are struggling with this task, the class is called back together, and together they review what a testable question is and how to design a fair test for that question.

Box 2.23

Indicator MS-CO#4	
Indicator	**Examples of Evidence**
MS-CO#4. Students are intellectually engaged with concepts contained in the activities of the lesson	<ul><li>Students are engaged in substantive discourse about the concepts with teacher and other students</li><li>Students do more than just guess; they check their hypotheses to discover important concepts that lead them to learn the concepts</li><li>Student responses reflect real thinking, not just "canned answers" or simple procedural steps</li><li>Students come to conceptual closure about what they have learned by the end of a unit</li></ul>

It sounds trite to say, "If there is no learning, what is the point of teaching?" In fact, typically much more teaching than learning takes place in schools. We know this from repeated tests of student performance whose results do not reflect the effort of the teacher. We have learned that student intellectual activity is a required ingredient for learning. In the Implementation section, we talk about the efforts of the teacher to engage the student in active and thoughtful learning. In MS-CO#4, we look for evidence that students are using their brains in the service of learning whatever content is in play in the lesson. We find that evidence in their conversations; in their responses, written and oral, to teacher questions or challenges; and in their final products. It is this indicator in the Content section where group work is critical. Things to monitor include the quality of the discourse within the groups and the ways the students are using each other's thoughts to help them adjust their own thinking. Are they wildly guessing, or are they bringing their knowledge to the table? Are they moving forward in their understanding? Are they getting it?

When you are observing a classroom, you may only see evidence of the students beginning to engage in an idea and may not be present for the moment of "conceptual closure." It is dangerous to assume that while you see students on their way to developing a skill or understanding, they will necessarily arrive at that understanding. Some strategies for assuring that the targeted learning has in fact occurred are:

- Ask to be invited back on the day that the students will present their conclusions.
- (If you happen to be a principal and are lucky to have found the time to visit the class once) Ask if a few students ranging in abilities could come down to your office to show you and *explain to you* their final work.
- See if the results will be part of a student display that you can come to see at your convenience.

Box 2.24

Indicator MS-CO#5	
Indicator	**Examples of Evidence**
MS-CO#5. Connections are made between concepts in this lesson and previous and future lessons in the unit, other subjects, or applications in the real world	• Teacher identifies the connections • Student activities and discussions lead to having them make connections • The connections made are more than just mentioning them; they are used to further understanding of the current concepts • Teacher provides examples and students discuss real-world applications • Students are provided with opportunities to actually apply new learning in the real world

We frequently hear an opening to a class lesson that begins something like this: "Now, yesterday we were discussing . . . " Or, "Is there someone who would like to remind us what we were doing yesterday?" The research on "prior knowledge" (National Research Council, 2000a) indicates that people learn best when new learning is related to what is already known. We also know from brain research that the more connections you make as you are learning something, the more likely it will be that you will remember it. So the connections that you see teachers helping students make are a critical component of their eventual success. Mentioning yesterday's lesson is better than not, but a mere mention does not rank high as a substantial connection. The more the connection is meaningful and integral to the next steps, the more valuable that connection is. If the connection comes not just from yesterday's lesson, but represents a real-world application, it becomes more useful still. The Rigor/Relevance Framework (Daggett, 1995) demonstrates the importance of applying new knowledge to other situations, both in and out of the classroom. It is this element of application and connection that keeps the classrooms of Japan, Singapore, and Chinese Taipei scoring above the United States at the fourth- and eighth-grade levels (TIMSS, 2004).

Box 2.25

Indicator MS-CO#6	
Indicator	**Examples of Evidence**
MS-CO#6. The lesson incorporates abstractions, theories, and models as appropriate	• Teacher explains and students discuss how concept fits in an existing theory or relates to other theories • Students create models and other nonlinguistic representations that depict the concepts • Models portray concepts accurately • Models help students make the connections to the abstract concepts

Manipulatives, science kits, and hands-on activities have found their way into our math and science classrooms, but as suggested by indicator MS-CO#2, manipulatives in the hands of a teacher who does not understand the concepts contained in them risk being reduced at best to a neat activity. What must happen for the concept to be learned is the "nesting" of that activity in the bigger math or science idea at play. Ball (1992) suggests that manipulatives are not the panacea that they were once thought to be. Because models and manipulatives may confuse as well as inform the building of mathematical and scientific understanding, Indicator MS-CO#6 looks for models (and accurate ones, at that) *and* the connection between the models and the appropriate concept or theory. These connections need to be explicit and must be articulated ultimately by the students in the form of presentations or assessments.

Box 2.26

Good Content Ideas That Go Bad (MS-CO#6)

The idea: Models help students understand concepts.
Using or constructing models can:

• help students visualize abstract concepts, making them more concrete or real to them,
• provide opportunities for students to manipulate materials during investigations, and
• serve as another way for students to construct their own knowledge.

(Continued)

(Continued)

HAS IT GONE BAD?

Do the models portray the concepts with enough accuracy to prevent misconceptions? Does making the model become the main activity, burying the concept in papier-mâché and paint? (Note this notorious but popular example: Students construct a papier-mâché volcano that erupts with a mixture of baking soda and vinegar. Neither of these elements represent in any real way what a volcano is or how it erupts.) Is using the model the end of the activity, or are students asked to relate it back to the abstractions or theories it represents?

Box 2.27

Good Content Ideas That Go Bad (MS-CO#6)

WHAT DOES SCIENCE LOOK LIKE WHEN MODELS ARE INACCURATE AND DISCONNECTED FROM THE CONCEPTS THEY PORTRAY?

A fourth-grade teacher is teaching a lesson about water filtration and how dirty water can become drinkable. He has several models to show the students:

- dirty water melted from road ice,
- plastic cups of water tinted blue with food coloring poured through various materials such as pebbles, sand, and sawdust, and
- a plastic soda bottle cut in such a way as to make a water filter with paper towels, sand, and gravel.

The classroom discussions range from how one could get the road ice to get cleaner, to referring to the plastic cups of blue water as examples of "aquifers." Students do some wild guessing about how to make water cleaner and make some observations about what is happening to the water in the plastic cups. They finish by constructing water filtration systems according to step-by-step instructions that the teacher presents, using foam cups, paper towels, and sand, adding some alum at the end. The role of alum is not explained.

There are several valuable science concepts at play here—perhaps too many. There is the concept of aquifers and how, through the water cycle, we end up with drinkable water. There is the idea that dirty water can be processed and made drinkable by human-devised systems. The models used each represent one, but not both, of those concepts, and some not so accurately (i.e., aquifers are systems found in the earth through which water flows, while a plastic cup does not allow flow-through and the blue water never gets clearer). The lesson goes back and forth between the various models, and the students are potentially left with unanswered questions. There is lack of closure or any connection between the models and how we ultimately obtain, either through natural or man-made systems, clean and drinkable water.

From Annenberg/CPB Math and Science Collection (1995).

Box 2.28

Indicators T-CO#7 and T-CO#8	
Indicators	**Examples of Evidence**
T-CO#7. Students use electronic resources to support the learning of the content of the lesson	• Students collect resources and conduct collaborative research (e.g., World Wide Web, CD-ROM) in a focused, productive way for specific educational purposes • Students are taught skills needed for critical analysis of information obtained through the use of electronic resources • Students demonstrate the ability to distinguish fact from opinion or bias, and they consider the reliability and validity of their sources
T-CO#8. Students understand appropriate use of technology tools	• Students and teachers select technology tools appropriate to the learning task (simulations, word processing, spreadsheets, databases, modeling) • Technology (computers, calculators, microscopes, probes, video, etc.) is used to enhance and extend capability for data collection, recording, analysis, and presentation • More time is spent on content than on decorative and extrinsic elements

Technology has now made its way into most of our schools. There is a huge variation in how that technology is used. In our experience, we have seen computers in the classroom used for fun when other work is completed, available to students for word processing, or only used by the teacher for administrative tasks. This section of DCO looks at how the available technology is being used in the service learning of facilitating or deepening student understanding of the content of a lesson.

Frequently, the teaching of technology is relegated to a "tech specialist" who may or may not be a teacher. DCO encourages every teacher to be a technology teacher and to use the school's information technology resources to deepen student learning. The Content section of DCO investigates the extent to which students are taught to use the tools of technology to gather and evaluate information. It also directs observers to note the other forms of technology used. (The ready availability of technology is assessed in the Classroom Culture section.)

Example 2.29

T-CO#7 and T-CO#8

WHAT DOES "STUDENTS USING ELECTRONIC RESOURCES TO SUPPORT LEARNING THE LESSON CONTENT" LOOK LIKE? WHAT DO UNDERSTANDING AND SELECTING APPROPRIATE TECHNOLOGY TOOLS LOOK LIKE?

A high school teacher teaching macroeconomics in a heterogeneously grouped class in a rural area has posed the essential question, "What is homelessness, and what can the government do to address this situation?" The class began with a video clip of a 1976 campaign speech by Jimmy Carter on welfare reform. The students were asked to analyze two questions in groups: "What was Jimmy Carter's message?" "Why do you think he delivered this message?" She introduced the students to Google Video and let them know that the number of quality clips available were limited but growing. An example given was National Geographic, which now has a wide assortment of quality video podcasts. (She noted that podcasts can also be downloaded so that teachers do not have to rely on streaming and the quality of the Internet connection.)

Next, students were asked to imagine they were looking at a photograph of a typical homeless person. Most students shared a description of a male, sleeping on a city bench, surrounded by his belongings, which were stored in plastic bags. The teacher then put up a photograph from Google Images that accurately matched this description. But wanting to move the class beyond the common belief that homelessness is a city problem, she then used a National Public Radio podcast that focused on homelessness in rural areas, a situation often classified as a "hidden problem." Providing a visual to support the radio segment, she put together a number of automatically timed PowerPoint slides of the rural homeless for background. This presentation was relevant, as rural homelessness has either touched the lives of students or someone that they know, with problems such as what to do with the colder weather approaching.

The final activity was to have students understand and graphically represent potential solutions to the housing shortages for low-income families in their area. They were presented with a set of hypothetical data representing low-income families' demand curve for housing. They also were given data for the number of homes that builders were willing to supply at the various prices. They then were asked to graph the information, find equilibrium, and analyze their findings. To check the accuracy of the graphs, the class was introduced to the use of TI Smartview, which allows the instructor to model the TI-84 calculator directly on the SMART Board. (The teacher noted that Microsoft's Excel can also be used for this same purpose.)

The teacher has accomplished several goals:

- Modeling the use of multiple technological tools, including both hardware and Internet technology.
- Tying the activities involving technology directly to the content that the students were learning.
- Discussing the technology options with the students.
- Assigning a related activity in which the students are required to use technology tools themselves to complete the task.

Box 2.30

Good Content Ideas That Go Bad (T-CO#7 and T-CO#8)

The idea: Technology should be integrated into instruction.
Having computer skills—word processing, spreadsheets, navigating the Web—can:

- expand the information that students are exposed to,
- inform the teacher as well as the students, and
- help students organize and manipulate information for better learning.

HAS IT GONE BAD?

Is technology class limited to learning basic computer skills, or are the skills used in the service of deepening learning? Can teachers distinguish between a student's own ideas and those "cut and pasted" from Internet sources, making assessment of understanding more difficult? Can students distinguish between reliable information and propaganda? Or are students collecting "junk information" that does not serve to promote better understanding of the topic?

Example 2.31

T-CO#7 and T-CO#8

WHAT DOES A CURRICULUM LOOK LIKE THAT TEACHES TECHNOLOGY SKILLS AS PART OF THE REGULAR CURRICULUM?

In an elementary school's curriculum, technology skills are integrated from Grades K through 6.

Kindergarten: Students are taught to manipulate the mouse and the keyboard in their writing program. Using KidPix, they create their own illustrations for their stories and, with assistance, type their sentences using appropriate invented spelling.

Grade 1: Students begin to use word processing and spell check and create illustrations in their science journals.

Grade 2: Students become familiar with the functions of word processing and editing for journals and reports.

Grade 3: Students learn keyboarding to gain comfort and speed at the computer. They are assigned e-mail accounts and begin to telecommunicate to group members about science projects.

Grade 4: Students learn how to set up and use databases as they learn about classifying animals, and they create a database of North American mammals. They begin to do guided research on the Internet.

Grade 5: Students are learning about various uses of graphs and learn how creating spreadsheets can assist them in organizing their data and creating readable graphs. They search the Internet for data on specific topics and learn about how to evaluate fact and opinion on the Web.

(Continued)

Grade 6: Students create animations of cell division as they learn about the reproductive system. They use the Internet and their e-mail to conduct a project with students from five other schools in the state.

Grades 7–12: Students responsibly use the Internet to research and develop projects from all subject areas.

THE CLASSROOM CULTURE CRITERIA: USING THE MATH/SCIENCE VERSION

Method 1: Scoring the Examples in Chapter 2

Using the scoring sheets as described in Chapter 7 and found in Appendix F, analyze the examples in this chapter and come to consensus with your study group about what score you would give each lesson for the indicators for which they were chosen. Note areas of agreement and disagreement for later reference. You may raise some questions to be resolved through professional development.

Method 2: Focused Discussions

With your administrative team or other appropriate group of peers, consider the following:

1. (MS-CO#4) Share some examples from your own teaching or supervisory practice of the neat activity syndrome. Do students actually get to investigate concepts, or are they participating in activities without having to understand what they are really doing?

2. (MS-CO#3) Discuss some of the activities that pass for assessment in classes that you observe, and discuss whether they actually assess the concepts in the lesson.

3. (MS-IM#5) Explore the idea of closure. How do teachers end lessons? Is there a time for students to reflect on or process what they have learned either together or in writing, or does the clock just run out on the lesson? Is it assumed that if the activity is completed, the object of the lesson has been learned?

4. (MS-IM#3, MS-IM#6) Analyze the direction of large-group discussions in classes that you observe. Does the conversation always go from teacher (question) to student (answer), or is there any student-to-student interaction? How many students participate in the discussion? Is there an opportunity for every student to think about the questions before they have to compete for "air time?"

Method 3: Classroom Co-observations

In your administrative team or supervisory support group, observe or walk through a math class or a science class in pairs. You will need to find teachers who will allow you and a colleague into their classes as you make it clear that this is not part of their evaluation, but rather for your own professional development. If it is not possible to co-observe an entire class, you can accompany each other on focused walk-throughs in which you decide to concentrate on one or two indicators that are readily observable in the space of a brief visit, or you can agree that everyone will visit one class and do a detailed write-up of what happened. This does not have to be a formal observation with an official write-up, but you can present your findings to the group. Consider together the following general discussion questions to analyze the effectiveness of each lesson.

DISCUSSION QUESTIONS

1. What were the math or science concepts that were at the center of the lesson?

   Note the difference between the topic of the lesson (A) and the concept (B):
   A. The lesson was about adding and subtracting fractions.
   B. Students explored the need for finding common denominators when adding and subtracting fractions.

2. What prior knowledge about the concepts did the teacher solicit?

3. What activities did the teacher set out for the students?

4. How did the teacher interact with the students? Who is doing most of the talking?

5. How did the students interact with each other? Who has their hands on the materials?

6. What evidence did you have of student understanding of the concept?

7. How did the teacher monitor the developing understanding of the students?

   Note the difference between assessment by wandering around (A) and keeping track of developing understanding (B).
   A. Students work separately or in groups on a worksheet while the teacher circulates checking on their work, making sure everyone is on task, correcting them when needed, or reminding them of the process with some questioning.
   B. The teacher circulates and notes on a clipboard which students are correctly working with the fractions and which ones need some probing, alternative models, or further instruction. The teacher collects student work at the end of the class for analysis of student understanding.

8. How did (or will) the teacher assess student understanding at the end of the teaching unit?

CONCLUDING THOUGHTS

Math and science instruction in this country has been so maligned, and intensive initiatives have been put in place on the national and state levels to address the shortcomings. Training principals in supervising these critical subjects has not been one of the focal points of these initiatives. While no book can teach you everything there is to know about math and science, DCO and the discussions that it generates among supervisory colleagues can sharpen your awareness and give you good questions to ask teachers. These questions, just by having been asked, will engage you and your teachers in a more substantive conversation around teaching and learning in math and science, regardless of your expertise in these areas.

Chapter 3

Learning to Read and Reading to Learn

Learning, as described now by a large body of research, is an active and interactive process in which a learner comes into contact with material in a particular context for a particular purpose. Reading is much the same as any other learning. It is a multilayered process that begins with a potential reader, presents that reader with material, and creates a context for learning that material (Billmeyer & Barton, 1998). Yet there is a distinct difference between reading and other things that we learn: Reading itself *is* the material, involving the mechanics of how to make meaning of letter and sound combinations that correspond to a spoken language that is usually familiar to the learner. It used to be assumed that the skills of putting those letter sounds together must first be mastered before any meaning could be substantively brought into the equation. This approach is familiar to those of us who learned about Dick, Jane, and Sally while memorizing letter combinations and sight words. Some children consistently stumbled over those words read in monotone. (It was really hard to put your heart into "See Spot run.") They were so focused on getting the words out right that the meaning became completely secondary. (Not that it mattered all that much; the depth of the "Dick and Jane" [Gray, Monroe, Artley, & Arbuthnot, 1956] passages hardly lent themselves to meaty discussions!)

When "whole language" approaches came into style, a new paradigm supplanting the first took the position that high interest in the content of the reading material, a rich literary environment, and plentiful opportunities to see and interact with words would create accomplished readers. The logic of the enthusiasm of a literacy-laden environment was hard to resist. Reading results were disappointing, however, as too many children were unable to crack the mysterious code of the written word without more explicit instruction. Just like the content versus process argument in math, new research has put this false dichotomy to bed (U.S. Department of Education, 2006). Children need to be provided with the phonetic awareness and skills to break into the words on the page, while *simultaneously* being encouraged to pierce the meaning of those words. Why are those words on this particular page? What do they mean to you? Do they remind you of something else you know, or do you need some background information to help assimilate the meaning?

Until recently, reading instruction was seen as a task of the primary grades. In one of the schools in which I served as principal, students in the early grades scored consistently well on standardized tests, but the phenomenon of ever-decreasing scores in comprehension as the students moved through the third, fourth, and fifth grades was troubling. Of course, the situation just worsened as these students progressed through middle school, until we were left with a split population: Some who could read with competence and some who barely could. The spillover to every other content discipline was predictable. Those who struggled with reading would struggle with textbooks and other reading material designed to teach science, social studies, and virtually everything else. In response to this phenomenon, which was national and not at all confined to our school, new research on reading above the third grade established a language about and norms for ongoing instruction (Billmeyer & Barton, 1998; Boke & Hewitt, 2004). These studies outline the strategies that accomplished readers use as they make their way through unfamiliar text and set standards for the use of metacognition as a tool for students to monitor their own reading and understand how they make meaning when they sit down to read.

Diagnostic Classroom Observation (DCO) asks the observer to look for both decoding and meaning-making strategies in the classroom regardless of the grade level. There are some special techniques to be noted in the earlier grades, but most of the indicators and examples of evidence apply across the grade levels. Writing is treated as an integral part of a total literacy program, with indicators and evidence provided to assess the extent to which students are becoming thoughtful writers as well as readers.

The Literacy Version of DCO has the same four sections as the Math/Science Version. There are two variations of the literacy instrument. The first evaluates the teaching and development of total literacy skills on the elementary level. The second looks specifically into middle and high school content-area classes, evaluating the use of literacy as a tool to learn subject matter. It examines the metacognitive role of reading and writing in the learning process. The elementary version follows a format similar to the Math/Science Version, but describes in depth the growth of literacy skills from phonemic awareness to meaning making. The Composite Version uses a general content-area approach similar to the Math/Science Version and includes elements of the use of reading and writing as a teaching and learning tool. Secondary teachers have not traditionally seen themselves as reading teachers. However, research studies from different quarters all suggest that emphasis on reading strategies and extensive use of writing to reflect on and explain thinking has a significant impact on student learning in the content areas (Amaral, Garrison, & Klentschy, 2002; Reeves, 2006; Santa, Havens, & Valdes, 2004).

This chapter presents the criteria, indicators, and examples of evidence of the Literacy Version of DCO (see Appendix D). Section 1 will describe direct instruction in reading and writing, illustrated by examples from Grades K through 5. Portions of the tool that deal exclusively with instruction of the writing process appear shaded in the boxes. Then, the chapter will introduce the Composite Version with examples of the use of literacy for teaching across content areas in Grades 6 through 12.

SECTION 1: LEARNING TO READ

The Literacy Version of DCO

The Implementation Criteria

The Implementation section of the Literacy Version focuses on instructional choices that produce comprehensive literacy skills. In reading, these range from decoding and fluency to deep comprehension. In writing, DCO emphasizes both the technical writing process and the use of writing as personal expression and metacognition. Observing a literacy block can be very challenging. Elementary teachers have been well-schooled in the general activities that should be part of competent literacy instruction. These include choral reading, phonetic awareness drills, read-alouds, guided reading groups, and reading centers. Writing has been stressed as an important component of literacy building, so an observer is likely to see students putting pencils to paper on a regular basis, but using writing as a metacognitive tool and being instructed in an effective writing process is rare. My classroom observations were frequently painful, as I watched teachers doing things that seemed on the surface to be engaging children in reading and writing, but were at their core empty of true literacy instruction. This sad commentary is passionately confirmed by a series of visits to literacy classrooms done by several experts who noted coloring, cutting, and pasting as the most frequent activities observed.

As in the Math/Science Version, both teacher and student activity is noted. The observer is directed to note teacher choices that reflect good pedagogical judgment, a deep understanding of the acquisition of literacy skills, and careful instruction in using those literary skills for further learning.

Box 3.1

Indicator L-IM#1	
Indicator	**Examples of Evidence**
L-IM#1. Teacher shows an understanding of how to use text to build reading fluency, comprehension, and writing skills in the students	• There is evidence of a balanced program including decoding skills, comprehension, and writing • The teacher models the skills of good readers and writers • Spelling and vocabulary are taught in context • Multiple decoding strategies (sounding out, beginning and ending sounds, blending sounds, using context or pictures, sight words, "word wall," etc.) are used in reading instruction • When teacher introduces a new phonogram, students have the opportunity to practice it (K–2) • Teacher reviews old phonograms, and students demonstrate recognition and mastery (K–2) • Teacher employs a variety of techniques and materials, including choral chanting, skywriting, use of chalkboard or chart (K–2) • Multiple reading strategies (pre-reading, making predictions, asking questions, identifying important themes, analyzing text structure, making connections and inferences, evaluating, summarizing, re-reading) are evident

Indicator	Examples of Evidence
	• Teacher builds students' independent use of all these strategies and provides opportunities to use them in appropriate contexts • Both meaning making and fluency building are the focus of these activities • There is evidence that writing is taught through a multiphase process, including prewriting, drafting, conferencing, revising, editing, and publishing • Teacher conducts direct instruction in writing skills (topic development, organization, sentence/paragraph creation and structure, developing tone, voice, purpose, etc.) • Instruction is given in the different writing genres (response to text, report, narrative, procedure, persuasive, reflective essay)

The first indicator (L-IM#1) centers on the teacher's understanding of the process by which students learn the mechanics of reading while attaining the skills and strategies to be lifelong readers and learners. Does the teacher address both the phonics and meaning-making aspects of early reading? Are skills being taught in context? Do students, as they mature as readers, receive from their teachers the strategies for higher level cognitive activities as illustrated by Bloom's Taxonomy (Bloom, 1984)? That is, are they being taught to apply, make inferences, evaluate, analyze, and synthesize what they read?

Writing is an integral part of a comprehensive literacy program. As obvious as that sounds, writing is frequently overlooked for its power to deepen learning, establish a habit of cognitive organization, and become a creative and thoughtful art form. DCO looks at the role of writing in the literacy program and breaks the steps of the writing process apart to ensure that they are all part of the instructional program.

The writing process is frequently not observed. Sometimes that is because when students are actively writing, it may be assumed that there is no lesson to be observed. In a literacy block, it is more likely to observe reading-related activities. Writing may be a part of them, but journal writing and other written activities that connect with the reading program are discussed in the Content section of the Literacy DCO. In the Implementation section, we focus on the writing process itself; writing that is produced as an art or a form of communication or persuasion. Evidence of a comprehensive, multiphase writing program in a classroom can be elusive. Many rooms identify a "writing corner" with signs that name the elements of the writing process (e.g., drafting, editing, rewriting, publishing). There may be writing portfolios or folders. However, it can be difficult to determine the extent to which a consistent writing program is in place, that is, the regularity of students' opportunities to write and the degree to which the steps of the writing process are actually taught.

What are some of the signs that a writing program is authentic? Is finished student work displayed? Is it current, or does it date back to September? Does it appear to be in final copy? Are the posted signs merely wall decorations, perhaps provided by the publisher of the literacy series? (A clue here is whether you can find identical signs in every room.) Whether these signs are homemade or published is, of course, secondary to the actual nature of the writing program. Are there signs of ongoing writing? Look through the writing folders of the students. Are there multiple pieces? How organized are they? Is there evidence of writing conferences, such as drafts with notes for edits from either their peers or the teacher? Are there rubrics or other criteria for students to gauge and therefore refine their work? Can students tell you what writing piece they are currently working on? Can they describe the process that they use when writing or show you examples? Finally, is the writing at a level of sophistication appropriate for the grade level? Do grade levels have benchmark pieces of writing of various genres that will guide teachers and their students?

Example 3.2

L-IM#1

WHAT DOES EVIDENCE OF A MULTIPHASE WRITING PROCESS LOOK LIKE?

A fifth-grade class is working on the genre of nonfiction. They have been reading different examples of nonfiction pieces and have the characteristics posted on the wall on chart paper, a list clearly generated by the class. Another wall is identified as "The Writing Center," and the steps of the writing process are identified and defined on student-made signs. Nearby is a bulletin board entitled "Our Finished Work." The pieces posted are all poems.

Each student is preparing his or her own nonfiction mini-book. Students have chosen their topics, have done some research, and are now at different phases of putting together their books. Some are working on a table of contents; some are already outlining the information in their chapters; others are writing their first draft of their introductions. One pair of students is sharing their drafts with each other.

The room has three computers. Two students are doing searches for their topics. The rest of the students are sitting at their desks or a comfortable writing spot. The teacher circulates around the room, which is very quiet. She carries with her a notebook. She spends five or more minutes with each student, conferencing. The students describe where they are in the process and show how they plan to use the class time to advance their project. She asks them some questions and chats comfortably with them as they consider options for the work. The teacher makes notes in her notebook, then passes on to the next student.

At the end of the period, students fill out a progress sheet, gather their resources into their writing folders, and store them in the file box.

Example 3.3

L-IM#1

WHAT DOES MODELING THE USE OF MULTIPLE DECODING STRATEGIES LOOK LIKE?

A first-grade teacher is working on fluency and meaning with her students. They have been using decoding strategies in their reading. She reviews those with the students: "I notice that you have been using the strategies of sounding out words, looking at pictures, and looking for parts of words that you know. But I still see some people getting stuck and stopping. So we're going to practice a new strategy. If you find a tricky word, skip that word and finish the sentence. When you get to the end of the sentence, you can go back and try to see what makes sense."

The students then take their independent reading books to their favorite reading spot. The teacher spends a few minutes with several of them doing running records and discussing their books as they read aloud to her. Ana struggles with the meaning of one sentence because she has read one word incorrectly. The teacher asks her to read the sentence again, and she again gets stuck on the problematic word. Without being prompted, she continues on to the end of the sentence and returns to the word, which she now correctly reads because she has figured out what the sentence was trying to say. The teacher praises her for using the new strategy.

When the students come back together, the teacher reviews the strategy again and asks Ana to share her experience. Ana reads the sentence she struggled with, tells how she skipped a word she didn't know, and was able to understand it when she got to the end of the sentence.

Example 3.4

L-IM#1

WHAT DOES EMPHASIZING BOTH MEANING MAKING AND FLUENCY WITH PHONEMIC AWARENESS LOOK LIKE?

A first-grade teacher is teaching the sound represented by *ou* or *ow* as in *foul* or *fowl*. In addition to the usual letters of the alphabet charts that are frequently posted in primary classrooms, there are also "sound cards" demonstrating letters or letter combinations that make certain sounds, with a representative word on the chart.

Today, students will be working on the *ow* sound as in *house*. The students locate the sound they are practicing on the wall, where one student notices that *ow* appears on two cards: the *house* card and the *snow* (long o) card. They talk about how some letter combinations could have two different sounds. The teacher puzzles, "So what would a good reader do if you didn't know which sound to use?" A girl answers, "You should try both." The teacher agrees that one should try both and see which one makes sense. They try it out with the word *cow*. Only one of the sounds yields a recognizable word, so they decide that the long o sound would not work.

Now they begin their practice with the *ou* sound. The teacher slowly writes words on chart paper, having the students make the sound, hold the sound, and blend the sounds as the word appears: *out, owl, down, crowd, growl, shout, stout, our, sour, fowl, foul*. (As she writes down the word *stout*, she puts a star next to it so she will remember to come back to it for meaning.) After the words have been read and repeated several times, she asks students to turn to a partner and practice reading the list of words to each other. She returns to the word *stout* to give its meaning. She relates it to the poem that they have learned: "I'm a little teapot, short and stout." The students remember that it meant short and round or fat. They discuss the case of *foul* and *fowl*, which sound the same but have different meanings. One student knows that *fowl* means a bird; another identifies *foul* ball.

(Continued)

Next, she plays a game with the students. She asks each student to pick a word from the list and think of a clue to help the others guess the word. She begins with the clue, "The word I'm thinking of is the opposite of *in*." A student guesses *out*. She now comes up to the front and gives her clue: "The opposite of *up*."

She chooses a student who guesses *down*, and that girl comes to the front. A boy guesses her clue ("opposite of *sweet*") and gives his clue ("this animal only comes out at night"). The game continues until at least half of the students have had a turn. The students leave the session with lots of practice reading the sound, hearing the letter-sound correspondence, and playing around with the meaning of each of the words.

Box 3.5

Good Implementation Ideas That Go Bad (L-IM#1)

The idea: Teacher introduces new phonograms or reviews old ones using choral chanting.

CHORAL CHANTING

Choral chanting:

- uses the elements of music, rhythm, and rhyme, which enhance memory,
- uses repetition and patterns to reinforce learning, and
- creates an engaging group activity that sets the stage for the rest of the lesson.

HAS IT GONE WRONG?

A first-grade teacher begins her lesson on the rug area with a workout. She recites rhymes and cute sayings that describe phonetic blends and tricky letter combinations. The poems are coordinated with karate chops and calisthenics that get the children moving and engaged.

The problem is that the rhymes are too long and complex to keep pace with the chops and jumps. They all have a similar cadence, jumbling them together instead of distinguishing themselves from each other. The students follow the teacher's motions and try to follow her chants. The amount of mumbling and mouthing the words increases as the activity progresses. The teacher, herself engaged in physical movement, does not catch who is repeating the sounds and who is not.

HOW CAN IT BE BETTER?

- This technique should be used selectively and not for every letter combination taught to avoid their all running together in the students' minds.
- The chants should be short and catchy, not so long and complex that the students are lost before the end of the first chant.
- The teacher needs to be able to watch the children to ensure that everyone is keeping up and saying the sounds.
- An opportunity for students to perform the exercise individually should be added so that the students get the benefit of both the security of the group and a chance to be heard (and assessed) separately.

Box 3.6

Indicator L-IM#2	
Indicator	**Examples of Evidence**
L-IM#2. Teacher's instructional choices are effective in engaging students in literacy activities	• Assignments are varied in nature and difficulty so that all students are engaged in the activity • Lesson construction has been purposefully planned for active engagement of all students • During read-alouds, teacher reads with animation and stops to ask questions, involve students, and describe new or relevant vocabulary without interrupting the flow of the story • Students have text or reading response journals to follow along with during read-alouds • Books used are appropriate, and the students are engaged in reading or listening **Prewriting Phase** • Teacher clearly defines the purpose of the writing • Teacher activates background knowledge about the topic • Students are encouraged to use a graphic organizer • Teacher helps students generate possible language for their writing • Teacher gives feedback on students' prewriting

Indicator L-IM#2 is the invitation to read and write. How does the teacher draw the students in and make them excited about what they may learn from the next book they pick up, or what inner thoughts they might get to turn into a story, a poem, or persuasive essay? Once again, the Examples of Evidence column in the DCO is just that: examples. There are dozens of ways teachers underscore the importance of literacy and engage students in the worlds that open up for them when their reading and writing skills unfold. Examples 3.7 and 3.8 demonstrate two ways that teachers use reading and writing to build skills while building a literate community in their classrooms.

Constructing one's knowledge means owning one's learning. In literacy, it takes the form of developing internal cognitive strategies for understanding what you read and organizing your thoughts for what you are planning to write. Too frequently, literacy

Example 3.7

L-IM#2

WHAT DO PLANNING ACTIVITIES THAT WILL ENGAGE ALL STUDENTS IN READING LOOK LIKE?

A second-grade teacher has created a literacy-rich classroom with a library stocked with books of varying appropriate reading and interest levels. In a "reading workshop" atmosphere, students have a guided selection for their independent reading, and each student carries a reading journal to the chosen reading spot. As they read their book, they choose a venue to showcase their reading. Some students who are reading the same book may choose "reading theater," in which they will dramatize their favorite scene in the story. Others

(Continued)

may join a discussion group, which has guidelines for sharing main ideas, reading challenges, interesting characters or settings, and so forth, whether they are reading the same book or not. Others may share one on one with a reading buddy. Some students find a cozy reading spot and read alone. The teacher makes sure to touch base with those students so they can articulate what they are reading about and develop some thoughts about their reading. Each student feels a strong sense of ownership of their book choice and demonstrates pride in the way in which they have chosen to process and share those books. Every child has an audience of at least one for his or her responses to the literature and a place to record thoughts and progress, regardless of the child's reading level.

Example 3.8

L-IM#2

WHAT DOES PREWRITING LOOK LIKE?

A fourth-grade teacher has assigned a writing piece for students to practice constructing rich details around a clear main idea. Each student is allowed free choice in selecting a topic to write about. The teacher gives them a brief period to write down their main idea and then to jot down some details that will help bring life to their main idea for their readers. Typically, students have trouble expounding on their ideas. Alternatively, they crowd their writing with endless details that do not support a central point.

After about five minutes, the teacher asks them to turn to their writing buddies and share their topics and details. As the students begin their discussions, she visits each group to listen. As the students share their ideas with her, she probes them with questions that will yield relevant details. As she leaves each group and moves on to the next, each set of partners continues their discussion visibly more excited and raring to get on to the drafting phase.

Box 3.9

Good Implementation Ideas That Go Bad (L-IM#2)

The idea: Reading aloud to students on a regular basis invites students into the world of reading. Read-alouds can:

- engage students and model the fluency of accomplished readers,
- expose students to stories that they may enjoy but that may be a bit above their reading level, and
- build a community of readers, giving all students a common literary experience.

HAS IT GONE BAD?

Common mistakes committed during well-intentioned read-alouds:

- Teacher reads complex material without stopping to check for understanding of content or vocabulary.
- There is no accountability for student listening, allowing students to "space out" and not pay attention.

- Teacher continues to read while some students either wander about or talk to or distract other students.
- Teacher finishes reading the section of the day and moves to the next activity with no opportunity for discussion or reflection.

EASY TIPS FOR GETTING THE MOST OUT OF READ-ALOUDS

- Begin the section of the day by reviewing the story so far (frequently done by teachers).
- Stop intermittently to discuss points of interest, unusual phrases, new vocabulary, and relevant connections.
- Provide each student with a copy of the text so they can follow along and circle words or expressions that they are unfamiliar with to ask about or look up later.
- Pair students for a short structured conversation in the middle or at the end of the reading, allowing each student an audience for his or her thoughts.
- Have students keep a reading journal for read-alouds as well as for their own reading. At the end of the reading, students can jot down thoughts or questions that they can bring to the next day's reading.
- End the reading with either a short discussion or question or prediction to think about for the next day.
- Keep a teacher's notebook to monitor student participation during the discussion phase. This will help make sure that all students get a chance to express their thoughts and allow you to track the kinds of thinking being exhibited by each student.

Box 3.10

Indicator L-IM#3	
Indicator	**Examples of Evidence**
L-IM#3. Students have opportunities to construct their own meaning	• Students write or tell their reactions and connections to the reading selection • Students can discuss strategies they use for understanding text • Activities are used to help students "own" their new learning; elements of choice are part of the lesson strategies • Students write frequently and can discuss the writing process **Drafting phase** • Teacher encourages students to get ideas down without focusing too intently on spelling, grammar, or editing (Note: If this is not directly observed in the lesson, teacher can identify when and how in the unit this will occur) • Students write their ideas easily and freely, knowing they can edit, correct, or change things later (Note: If this is not directly observed in the lesson, teacher can identify when and how in the unit this will occur)

comes at students from the outside in the form of required reading, basal readers, and assigned writing. Engaging students is the first step; following close on its heels is the internalizing of the ability to read and express oneself in writing. Choice is one element that encourages this, but not every book or writing project needs to be chosen. The strategies and activities around the reading or writing allow students to activate their hearts and minds and become accomplished participants in literacy.

Writing is one way that we process what we are learning. It helps us organize our thoughts and think about things in different ways. The various writing genres all have a point of view that can affect the way we see the world. Fiction or creative writing allows children to imagine a new world, either proximate to or vastly different from their own. Nonfiction requires research and a commitment to finding and verifying facts. Personal journaling teaches us about author's point of view. Both history and empathy can be taught by having children write from someone else's personal point of view.

Example 3.11

L-IM#3

WHAT DOES CONSTRUCTING OR OWNING ONE'S KNOWLEDGE LOOK LIKE IN LITERACY?

Example A

A first-grade teacher is using a basal reading program. The chapter begins with a reading selection. It is a fable about a hungry bird in a garden that needs to problem solve to retrieve a piece of cheese from a glass bottle. The teacher asks the students to close their eyes as she reads the selection to them and instructs them to "paint a picture in their mind" as they listen. She occasionally stops reading to ask them what their picture looks like, what color their bird is, what the garden looks like, and so forth. When she is done, they open their eyes and she shows them the illustrations from the book and asks them how their pictures differed from the ones drawn by the illustrator. They then re-read the story together.

After they have read the story, the students go to their tables, where they have paper, crayons, and markers. They now are asked to draw one of the pictures they had in their mind during the read-aloud. They will all draw a bird that needs to solve a problem. It can be the "cheese in the bottle" problem or another problem if they wish. When they are done drawing, they will each write a sentence below the picture describing what they have drawn, using "inventive spelling." Finally, the students will share their pictures and their sentences with a partner. This activity combines the prewriting (visualization) and drafting phases.

The teacher has done more than practice reading with these students. She has encouraged them to use visualization as they listen and read and then to translate that visualization into an original product that they can share with others. Visualization mobilizes the metacognitive function and allows the students to experience using their minds as an integral part of the reading experience.

Example B

A fourth-grade teacher is reading a chapter book aloud with her class, which is organized into table groups of four. Each table has a team facilitator. After reviewing the events in the book from the previous day, the teacher reads on, stopping occasionally to check on vocabulary and ask questions to make sure that everyone is following the story.

She then gives them a graphic organizer on which they write four discussion questions. There are two factual recall questions, one interpretive question, and one prediction question. Each student has a few minutes to write down his or her own thoughts. Students then begin to discuss their answers with the group. The facilitator keeps a sheet for the group. The teacher explicitly directs them to come to consensus on their group answers, but then adds, "If you do not agree with your group, you may put down your own answer." Students earnestly discuss their thoughts and agree about what answers to register on the group sheet. All students are reassured that at the end of the discussion, they may submit their own interpretations if they feel they have not been represented in the group answer. Each student is given permission to own his or her own thoughts, while at the same time being encouraged to share, listen, and come to consensus.

Box 3.12

Indicator L-IM#4	
Indicator	**Examples of Evidence**
L-IM#4. The pace of the lesson is appropriate for the developmental level of the students	<ul><li>Students have time to complete work</li><li>Some activities allow for students to work at their own pace</li><li>Adequate time is provided for discussion and processing of learning</li><li>When appropriate, teacher holds whole-class discussions to clarify expectations or provide direction</li><li>All students have opportunities to participate</li><li>Pace is adjusted as necessary</li><li>There is closure at the end of the lesson</li></ul>

Writing is difficult to teach well. A first-grade teacher once asked me how she could be expected to teach children to write when they were not yet able to spell. Fortunately, this question was asked of me many years ago. DCO honors the complete writing process by outlining each of the individual steps. After prewriting comes drafting. Observers should see students getting their ideas down, sharing their thoughts, and getting a sense of what the finished product will be well before they are asked to produce it. Once a student has drafted a piece of writing; made a beginning, a middle, and an end; and then shared it with another person, either a peer or the teacher, that students owns that writing.

Pacing in a literacy classroom is particularly challenging, as students are liable to be rotating between whole-class and independent work, and each student has differing reading levels and abilities to work independently. Frequently, multiple activities are planned during the reading block, some simultaneous and some consecutive. In other observation instruments, pacing becomes the handling of transitions and time management. DCO places those more mechanical aspects critical to smooth running classrooms in the Classroom Culture section. What we look for in L-IM#4 is the balancing of instructional activities so that all students have opportunities to participate, can finish or manage their workload, and have time to process their learning. This means that thinking and "digesting" time is provided and that the end of the lesson, rather than running right up to the end of the time period, builds in a reflective activity. This can take the form of students gathering to share what was accomplished, a short freewriting session in which students leave their final thoughts in a journal or "exit notes," or the teacher helping students summarize where they are and where they are going.

Example 3.13

L-IM#4

WHAT DOES HAVING TIME TO PROCESS LEARNING AND CLOSURE LOOK LIKE?

Example A

A first-grade teacher is reading a chapter book to her class on the rug, a process that will take a few days. At the end of the reading for that day, she asks the children to go back to their desks, predict what they think will happen next in the story, and write a sentence describing their prediction. After a few minutes of writing, the students gather on the rug again. Five students are chosen to read their prediction to the class. Then, each student turns to a partner and shares his or her prediction. They have all now had the opportunity to evaluate where the story left off and where it might be going. In addition, they have each now had an audience for their thoughts. They leave the session excited for tomorrow, when they will find out what actually happens.

Example B

A fifth-grade class has just completed reading a book together. They are going to do a review of the book, which will have several portions. They will first divide the book into chapters, with a pair of students responsible for each chapter. They will rename their chapter to give their own spin on its main idea, summarize the events that occur in the chapter, illustrate a key event, and create a poster with all those elements. The class will then hang the posters in chapter order and take a walk-around to review the book from beginning to end. This project will take a few days. At the end of the first day, they have reviewed the events of their chapter with their partners and have renamed the chapter. After spending about twenty minutes in this activity, the teacher calls them back together, where they share, in order of chapter number, their new title and what events in the chapter caused them to choose that title. Taking the time for this step allows students to hear how others handled the task and has them articulate their thinking of the last twenty minutes before continuing on with the other parts of the task.

Box 3.14

Indicator L-IM#5	
Indicator	**Examples of Evidence**
L-IM#5. Periods of student-student interaction are productive and enhance individual understanding of the lesson	• Tasks for each reading group or center are clear for students to engage in productive learning at all times • Students use reading group or center time when teacher is not with group to support each other and continue to build their reading skills • Students working with the teacher engage in cross-talk with and respond to each other and not just the teacher • Students are encouraged to have peer conferences during drafting and editing stages • Student peer conferences add to the quality of student writing products • Teacher provides opportunities for students to share their writing with each other

Literacy blocks are challenging to manage. One strategy is known as "learning centers," or some variation thereof. It divides students into reading-level groups so that the teacher can work intensively with a small group while the others are ostensibly involved in literacy-building activities. This is a sound strategy, but because of its complexity, it can turn a literacy block into a free-for-all with little happening during much of that coveted element of teaching: instructional time. Well-run learning or literacy centers are a valuable way to differentiate instruction, reach all students, provide an extended period of literacy work, and allow the teacher to work intensively with individuals in small groups, in instruction, assessment, or conferencing. DCO gives a supervisor specific outcomes to look for. See Box 3.15 for the red flags indicating that this "good idea has gone bad."

When students are not working with the teacher, what are they doing? If they are assigned in groups, is there productive learning going on or is the work incidental to other conversations or interactions? When the teacher is with the large or small group, note which direction the conversation flows. Is it always teacher-student-teacher-student? Does the teacher encourage cross-talk or active listening? Is there lively discussion and debate as students grapple with the motivations of a character in their story or give each other feedback on a writing piece? Productive student-to-student interaction, when it occurs as a matter of course in a classroom, is the work of a skilled teacher who knows that the social aspect of learning requires that the students interact with more than just the authority figure. This simply does not happen on its own in a classroom setting. The conversation may be facilitated to be kept on track, but talk should include adults and learners who are all striving for understanding and interpretation of the reading at hand. Good student interactions can be observed during large-class discussions, during small-group work, or without the teacher during independent working times.

Box 3.15

When Good Implementation Ideas Go Bad (L-IM#4 and L-IM#5)

The idea: Literacy centers engage all students for an entire block of time dedicated to literacy. The literacy center structure allows students to:

- engage in literacy activities at their own pace,
- choose books appropriate to their reading level, and
- interact with each other in literacy (read to each other, peer edit writing, and cooperate to complete tasks).

HAS IT GONE BAD?

Frequent Mistakes That Leave This Structure Merely a Time-Filler

- Center activities are poorly structured. Either the activities are mostly games with little real instructional benefit, or there are rote worksheets to fill out.
- The students move from center to center in groups, although the activities do not require any collaboration to complete, thus negating the "student-to-student" advantage.

(Continued)

(Continued)

- Pacing is poor. The time at each center is insufficient to complete the task, not taking into account the ways the children make independent transitions. Students are rushed from center to center with timers, bells, or other signals, potentially leaving each task incomplete and getting them used to not having to finish anything. There is no closure for any of the center activities.
- Whatever work is done at centers does not receive immediate feedback from a teacher, leaving the student without the ability to know how he or she has done or how to correct misunderstandings.

HOW CAN IT BE BETTER?

- Fewer, well-thought-out activities are better than multiple, superficial ones.
- Activities that are integrated into other class learning and that can be followed up on are better than random "neat activities."
- Independent reading with required reading journal entries keeps students reading on their own level and reflecting on their reading. It also provides a forum for the teacher to respond to each child and track his or her reading daily.
- Independent or class-assigned writing projects are good center-time activities. They keep students writing regularly at their own pace and allow teachers to respond to students' writing daily.
- Take into account the ability of the group to work independently. Try short periods with one activity until students have learned the routine and can sustain their efforts and make transitions. Make plans for students who will have difficulty with this structure.
- Always follow up on any work assigned during center time.

The Content Criteria

There are several levels of conceptual content inherent in literacy instruction. One is the structure of language with its phonetic idiosyncrasies, parts of speech, and structures of text, including the genres of fiction, nonfiction, poetry, and prose. There are the purposes of writing, such as persuasive, procedural, communication of knowledge and feelings, and creative art. There is the building of word skills, such as increasing vocabulary, understanding and using figures of speech, and appreciating the power of language. These all represent information that teachers need to not only know, but know how to teach. In addition, while reading various pieces of text, it is incumbent on the teacher to have some background knowledge of the subject matter contained within. This requires a broad knowledge base and a readiness to read and learn before and along with the students.

Box 3.16

Indicator L-CO#1	
Indicator	**Examples of Evidence**
L-CO#1. Academic standards and assessments are central to the literacy program	• The content is aligned with state or national standards • Rubrics and processes used in reading and writing are clearly established and are understood by all students • Agreed-on processes of reading, writing, and other literacy skills are used to judge the quality of student products and performances

At this point in time, there is no excuse for teachers to be unaware of national standards and the new research on reading, whether from the National Reading Panel (2000), the Reading First program (U.S. Department of Education, 2006), or any of the studies that have shown that reading ability is closely linked with overall student success (e.g., Amaral et al., 2002; Reeves, 2006). Many schools have adopted basal reading programs that have incorporated many of the recommended practices, including linking reading and writing. Some classrooms have attractively colored and laminated signs over their reading or writing centers, outlining what good readers and writers do. These signs tend to appear in every class in a school, signaling that there has been a schoolwide adoption of this program or approach. They may or may not be a reliable indicator these approaches are truly used or even understood in every class. In the end, it still comes down to instruction, and consistency in instruction will not be achieved unless the building principal is well-enough informed as to what the platitudes proclaiming "Good readers make connections" look like in action. Thus, while indicator L-CO#1 (the alignment of the curriculum and assessment with appropriate standards) is essential, it is not sufficient to ensure that students receive the instruction they will need.

Box 3.17

Indicator L-CO#2	
Indicator	**Examples of Evidence**
L-CO#2. Teacher has depth of knowledge of the content and concepts, and he or she is skilled in using text to build meaning	• Teacher clearly connects the learning activities with the skills they are intentionally designed to elicit • Teacher models appropriate reading and writing strategies • Information provided is clear and accurate • Teacher takes advantage of reading material to discuss background knowledge or vocabulary • Teacher refers directly to the text to build understanding • Teacher asks a variety of types of questions (probing for meaning, clarification, inference, evaluation) • Teacher has students justify answers by referring to text • Teacher addresses misconceptions and misunderstandings • Teacher connects content in reading selection to previously learned material in this unit or others • Teacher reads difficult passages and helps students understand the material (students follow with finger if necessary; K–2) (Note: If this is not directly observed in the lesson, teacher can identify when and how in the unit this will occur)

When talking about literacy instruction, our conversations tend to center on implementation strategies: read-alouds, choral chanting, techniques for blending phonemes, reading centers, and so forth. It may be that we are treating reading simply as a skill, assuming that a certified teacher should be able to succeed as long as he or she is skilled in these techniques. But there is content knowledge that is critical to student learning as well. A teacher poorly informed about the topic being studied, whether it is in the structure of language or any content related to a class reading, can create misconceptions that could stay with students forever. "A Private

Universe" (Annenberg Foundation/CPB, 1987) demonstrated that when students acquire misconceptions, it is very difficult to uproot them. Teachers are well advised to be open with students about what they know and what they need to find out, but it is not acceptable for a teacher to be unsure about what a main idea is or how to distinguish nouns from adjectives. Once again, this seems hardly worth mentioning, as patently obvious as it seems. Box 3.18 gives two examples of teachers who, charged with educating second graders, were unable to provide them with the most basic information.

Box 3.18

Good Content Ideas That Go Bad (L-CO#2)

The idea: Information provided to students is accurate.

EXAMPLE 1

A second-grade teacher in Florida is teaching students to read nonfiction. The piece they are reading is about maps and includes much information about land forms and bodies of water. The word *peninsula* is in one of the chapters and is described in the piece as a "piece of land jutting out into the water." Hanging on the front board is a large map of the United States. The teacher, mispronouncing the word *peninsula* as she goes, covers the U.S. map by pulling down a map of the world that is above it. It all but covers the U.S. map, but the bottom section is still visible. The teacher and the students search the world for a peninsula, pointing out many non-peninsulas in the process. Sticking out below the world map is the state of Florida, our country's most obvious peninsula and the home of the teacher and students in the class. The chance to give the students a clear visual picture of what a peninsula is has disappeared, along with the knowledge that this odd land form is the state in which they live.

EXAMPLE 2

Another second-grade teacher is introducing the concept of adjectives. She has called them "describing words" and has a large chart divided into six columns. Her plan is to fill up the columns and then have the students write a paragraph with lots of adjectives. The headings for the columns are: how many, shape, size, texture, feelings, and what kind. Gathered on the rug, she asks the students to begin to fill in the chart. As the chart gets filled in, nouns begin to mix imperceptibly with the adjectives. In the "how many" column, numbers abound. After the first student mentions "a hundred," words like *many* and *few* are overwhelmed by every number the children can think of. And, while a number can serve as an adjective, a number in and of itself is not one.

The activity worsens as they move through the columns. In the shape category, words like *round* cede their place to *circle*, *triangle*, and *hexagon*. The size column doesn't have nouns in it, but the students get on the *big* kick and the list begins to take on words that may not be technically words, like *gigundo* and *humungus,* as the students try to outdo each other.

When they are done, there is a chart with at least 50 words on it in six columns. The words are crunched together, the adjectives mixing with the nouns and the words that are not words. That which distinguishes an adjective is completely obscured and is certainly not learned by the second graders.

Example 3.19

L-CO#2

WHAT DOES USING TEXT TO BUILD MEANING LOOK LIKE?

A sophomore class is reading excerpts from Homer's *The Odyssey*. The class is heterogeneously grouped, containing students of all reading levels and future plans. Each student has a photocopied portion of the text and a colored highlighter. The teacher reads a long passage out loud while the students follow along, highlighting any words or phrases that they do not understand or have questions about. The teacher reads with great expression, making the story come alive. Students listen intently and silently use their highlighters. The teacher stops from time to time to ask questions, clarify motives and relationships, make connections to previous sections, and answer questions from students.

After the selection of the day, the teacher asks students to share the words or phrases that they highlighted. A long list is compiled on a piece of chart paper. The teacher then divides the list into chunks of five words and assigns pairs of students to look up the word, use it in an original sentence, draw a picture illustrating the meaning, and make the connection of meaning as the word appears in the *Odyssey* text. This is made into a small poster with the word appearing in the heading.

Each group presents their words, and the posters are put up around the room. They will remain there for a while and will eventually become part of the students' individual "*Odyssey* Notes," which each student will develop using the words and phrases that he or she did not originally know. They will also become integrated into an assessment that evaluates understanding of the text.

Finally, students are given a brief writing assignment for homework. They are to summarize the section in their reading journals and incorporate into their written summary a minimum of five of the vocabulary words that they were *not* responsible for researching during the day's activity.

Box 3.20

Indicator L-CO#3	
Indicator	**Examples of Evidence**
L-CO#3. Teacher collects and assesses evidence of student progress to enhance teaching and learning	• Assessment is systematic and ongoing so that teacher can track student progress and adapt instruction • Clear criteria are used to judge student work • Student misconceptions are identified through formative assessment so that students can adjust their thinking • Assessments clearly target concepts *and* skills • Assessments are varied in the kind of tasks required • Teacher gives oral and written feedback • Assessments test spelling and vocabulary with an emphasis on context • Teacher guides students to focus on criteria or rubrics to edit writing for final copy • There is evidence that teacher conducts both informal and scheduled reading and writing conferences that are focused and positive • Assessments clearly indicate conceptual closure

In Chapter 2, I refer to Black et al. (2003) and Wiggins and McTighe (1998) to make the point of the importance of both formative and summative assessments to student outcomes. Literacy has its own methods of assessment. There are "running records," which help primary-level teachers monitor and guide emerging literary skills such as phonetic awareness and fluency. There are a multitude of assessments that measure growth in comprehension and word skills. Many states, districts, or commercial programs have developed rubrics for assessing writing and speaking skills. From day to day, however, teachers are responsible for tracking student progress on all the levels that have been mentioned. As in mathematics, the teacher must fully understand the knowledge or skills contained in the many "neat activities" that come with reading programs. Sometimes published programs come with assessments, but frequently teachers are reading literature with no supports from a literature program. Teachers on different grade levels are required to assess different skills, and frequently they have not been trained to do so. DCO asks the observer to note the extent to which assessment is happening on an ongoing basis and whether there is a systematic approach to tracking student progress. I have already discussed how assessments at learning centers range from quality assessment to busy work with little feedback. In a total literacy program, one should be able to observe peer and teacher conferencing for reading and writing, the establishment of criteria or rubrics that are understood by all, and a system demonstrating that as the teacher circulates or rotates with small groups, he or she has some method of keeping track of what and how the students are doing.

As important as the monitoring of student progress is, so is the use of the information gained when one does so. If the students are unsure, does the teacher alter the plan and investigate ways to reteach? Can the teacher differentiate so that the needs of all students are met? Is there a structure available to reteach for those who need it while not repeating for others that which they already know? Teachers sometime complain that assessment robs instructional time. When results of assessments are not immediately fed back into the instructional process, that certainly is the case.

Example 3.21

L-CO#3

WHAT DOES ASSESSMENT THAT IS ONGOING AND SYSTEMATIC LOOK LIKE?

Example A

A fourth-grade teacher is leading a read-aloud, which is part of his daily routine. The class is working on the literary device of metaphor and using text to make predictions. The teacher sits on the floor among the students, who all have reading response journals open with pens in their hands. He has a clipboard on his lap. As the discussion unfolds, he makes notes on his clipboard, jotting down who is participating and briefly what they are saying. Later he will be able to review the level of participation and the depth of insights shared by each student. He will be able to make sure to give opportunities for sharing to those who did not get a chance to share the day before.

At a point in the middle of the discussion, he poses a thought-provoking question involving a particularly rich metaphor and asks students to think and write for a few minutes about what they think it means and why the author chose to use that image. They will share with a partner and then offer their thoughts to the larger group. In any case, the teacher will have not only his notes from the discussion, but a journal entry from every student, indicating his or her level of understanding of the specific metaphor and the power of metaphor as a literary tool.

Example B

A first-grade teacher is working with a small reading group on the "silent 'e,'" which is featured in their story. They review a catchy mnemonic device designed to help them remember that an "e" at the end of a word can make the inside vowel "say its name." They practice with words like *bake*, *cake*, *hole*, and *side*. The children seem to be able to read the words one at a time, so they move on to the story.

As they take turns reading, all of the students falter on the words with the silent "e." The teacher is surprised, but makes a note to change her plan for tomorrow. They will not move on to the next story or letter combination, but will spend another day on "silent 'e.'" She will be going back to the drawing board to look for other ways to help them understand, remember, and apply this basic rule of English reading and spelling.

Box 3.22

Indicator L-CO#4	
Indicator	**Examples of Evidence**
L-CO#4. Students demonstrate the building of their literacy skills	• Students demonstrate building fluency by reading aloud with expression, accuracy, and appropriate pace, and by following text (with their fingers if needed at the K–2 level) • Sound symbol patterns previously taught are recognized and used correctly in new reading and writing situations • Students demonstrate building vocabulary by using new words in their speech and writing • Students engage in literature discussions to reflect on and react to reading selections, and they directly refer to the text to demonstrate and improve comprehension • Students are developing a metacognitive understanding of the skills and strategies they are using so that they fully understand the processes of reading and writing • Students are building their writing ability—using invented spelling that demonstrates grade-appropriate sound-symbol correspondence at the K–2 level—using writing resources as necessary (dictionary, thesaurus, etc.) • Students have many opportunities to practice writing

Indicator L-CO#4 directs the observer to watch and listen to the students. As mentioned in Chapter 1, classroom observations have focused on teacher content knowledge (Ball, Lubienski, & Mewborn, 2001), teacher pedagogical knowledge (Shulman, 1987), teacher skill (Danielson, 1986; Saphier & Gower, 1997), and adult development (Glickman, 1990). DCO is an active observation requiring not only circulating around the room to watch students, but stopping to discuss with students what they are doing and how they understand what they are learning. In a literacy class, you might ask a child to read a passage to you and describe the book he or she is reading. You might ask to read the draft of the student's writing and even conference with him or her a bit to see how the student is approaching the writing piece. You might wonder about the "experimenter effect," or the extent to which your interaction is impacting the class. The fact is that it is, but that has always been so. In the days when the principal came in to observe and sat as inconspicuously as possible in the back of the room, the impact was substantial. The teacher had prepared his or her best or most likely to succeed lesson. Perhaps the students had been prepped. Even if not explicitly instructed on how to behave, the principal's presence was usually duly noted with some measurable effect. In other words, any formal observation was always likely to produce artifice. Rather than duck out on that, DCO embraces it. If you're going to be in there, it is best you get in close and get a real sense of what is going on. Students are capable of behaving differently when the principal is near, but they are not capable of feigning literacy skills that they do not possess, so approach them and see. Do they seem to be doing the sort of work that they are accustomed to? Are they demonstrating the independent use of the skills of the lesson? Can they tell you what they are learning, describe their reading, share their plan for their writing, and self-correct? Are their discussions sophisticated for their age? How do they use language? Do they grab a book automatically when their assignments are completed? Do they use graphic organizers to help plan writing and map concepts or events in their reading to assist in their understanding of how they are becoming strategic in their reading and writing? In essence, are they becoming readers and writers who will enjoy using these skills for the rest of their lives? The only way you will be able to assess their metacognitive understanding is to get them to describe it to you.

Box 3.23

Indicator L-CO#5	
Indicator	**Examples of Evidence**
L-CO#5. Connections are made between reading and writing and other subjects and have applications to the real world	• Teacher makes connections between writing assignments and reading selections • Students have opportunities to write about what they are reading • Teacher connects reading and writing to other texts and other content areas • Teacher asks students to make these connections • Student activities and discussions further lead to having them make connections • Teacher uses reading and writing assignments to point out vocabulary, syntax, and usage • Reading and writing skills are taught in a context and have relevance to students • Students discuss real-world applications • Students are provided with opportunities to actually apply new learning in the real world

Finally, in the content section, L-CO#5 seeks to put an end to the days when first it is reading time, then spelling time, then language arts skills, and last (if there is any time left) writing time. Literacy, being a complex mesh of speaking, listening, reading, and writing, must be taught that way. Best practices as expressed through the current research (National Reading Panel, 2000) clearly set the compass in the direction of the integrating of the pieces of literacy. How does this look in the classroom?

It doesn't preclude a spelling lesson or require that every piece of writing grows out of a reading assignment. To the extent possible, however, students should have multiple opportunities to speak and write about what they are reading, read their writing, listen to reading, and write about what they have heard.

SECTION 2: READING TO LEARN

The Composite Version: Integrating Literacy Into Content-Area Instruction

Secondary teachers protest that they are not trained literacy teachers. And, indeed, they are not. Yet they assign reading and writing all the time, and when they are not assigning reading or writing per se, they are assuming that it is being done. All content areas have textbooks or texts of some sort to read, interpret, understand, and use in the service of learning. Traditionally, textbooks in the social sciences have been most explicitly assigned as reading assignments, with essay questions frequently included. But science texts are laden with explanations and new vocabulary, and today's standards-based math texts stress context and require student oral and written justification or explication of approach and proof. It is not possible to navigate a high school curriculum if one cannot read and write, and those who struggle potentially struggle in every class.

Various researchers and experts have noted that the ability to read and to organize one's thoughts in writing across the curriculum may be among the most powerful ways to elevate student achievement (Amaral et al., 2002; Reeves, 2006). In his address to a group of school administrators in May 2000, Willard Daggett responded to a question regarding the most essential change that schools could make that would have the biggest impact on student performance. Without hesitating, he responded, "Make every eighth-grade teacher a reading teacher." But research and the positive experience of others have never been enough to overcome the skepticism of secondary teachers and their administrators, who would be asked to seriously rethink their entire approach to instruction. Secondary schools have been willing to tinker around the edges with reforms such as block scheduling, advisories, expanded electives, and the occasional interdisciplinary course such as American Studies, which can combine history and the literature of the same era. Other schools, more bold and forward thinking, have adopted more fundamental changes such as professional learning communities (DuFour & Eaker, 1998), in which teachers actually meet to create common assessments and analyze student work with the purpose of helping each other maximize successful instructional strategies. Others have dived headlong into differentiated instruction (Tomlinson, 1999), readjusting their understanding of learning and learners and applying that new understanding to an instructional approach that meets students on their level and pushes them to stretch their limits. Still others have had their faculties trained in the CRISS program (Santa et al., 2004), which is predicated on the assumption that incorporating reading and writing strategies in the content areas boosts metacognition and the learning of concepts. This program trains content-area teachers to become literacy teachers so they can use the techniques that elementary teachers use to help students work through challenging texts. And yes, this does compete for instructional time, but it ends up saving both time and the anguish of failure by helping students process the new learning the first time around.

Let's look at the problem by examining an excerpt from a freshman-level math text that is focusing on data represented on scattergrams to help make decisions.

This series (Berlinghoff, Sloyer, & Hayden, 2000) is part of the new generation of math texts committed to the National Council for Teachers of Mathematics standards, incorporating communication and the use of language to impart and internalize mathematical ideas. Here, blood pressure is being used in an example of the use of graphs to interpret data. Several paragraphs, charts, and graphs in the chapter are dedicated to explaining diastolic and systolic blood pressure, normal levels for various age groups, and effects of resting or physical activity on blood pressure. There are several questions to answer by reading a chart and a scattergram, and the section concludes by asking students to write a paragraph about whether the chart or the scattergram was easier to use in answering the questions. If the teacher were to use every piece of this section, it would take more time than she perceives that she has to teach the use of scattergrams in linear relationships. She skips the reading of the information on blood pressure and does not assign the paragraph writing. The students are sent home with homework to answer the following questions:

1. In terms of systolic blood pressure, would you say that a majority of these patients are low, normal, or high, as compared to healthy adults?

2. In terms of diastolic blood pressure, would you say that a majority of these patients are low, normal, or high, as compared to healthy adults? (Berlinghoff et al., 2000)

Without having read and processed the background information, one of two things will happen. Students who find it easy to read graphs will answer the questions correctly. Those who do not may get stymied by the language and look at the tables and graphs as if they were written in a foreign language (which, essentially, they are). They will either struggle with the homework or simply not do it. This sort of learning versus nonlearning is a staple of high school instruction, so much so that we have become complacent about the failure of too many of our students. We may institute stringent homework policies that require zeroes of those who do not hand homework in, or who have to stay after school to complete work, but these overlook the possibilities of preventing failure by using the better practices of literacy integration in the initial teaching of the intended concepts.

DCO's Composite Version is applicable to any content area. It is essentially identical to the Math/Science Version, differing in two fundamental ways: (1) the specific references to math and science are removed and (2) there are three indicators added to the Implementation section that integrate the explicit teaching of reading and writing as a strategy to increase student learning. In this section of the chapter, we will explore the observation of the integration of teaching reading and writing in the content areas. All the examples cited are from secondary classrooms.

READING AND WRITING IN THE CONTENT AREAS

There are many reasons, some of them having nothing to do with a lack of ability, why high school students do not do their homework or passively sit in class producing little. A classic scene from the movie *Ferris Bueller's Day Off* depicts a social studies class, with the teacher portrayed by actor Ben Stein. He addresses the class with deadpan delivery, discussing and asking factual questions about an arcane labor law.

Each question is followed by the exhortation, "Anyone? Anyone?" No one, of course, responds, and the manner in which he asks suggests that he neither expects for a minute that anyone will, nor frankly cares. He answers each question himself and leaves the students completely out of the discussion, literally drooling on the desks. These students clearly have not read the chapter, although it is not implied that they were incapable of doing so—just unwilling. While this scene leaves us laughing, the real-life classrooms that it parodies do not.

The CRISS project (Santa et al., 2004) is composed of key strategies to engage students' metacognitive processes, build literacy capabilities, and harness those in the service of learning any subject area. How could this approach have helped our ill-fated social studies teacher in the movie? What would have happened if, knowing that the students would not read the chapter and know any of the answers, the teacher made an exercise of reading the chapter together? Here are some ideas that could have created a lively discussion with full participation and increased the numbers of students who would be able to do their work, regardless of their reading level:

- Assign pairs of students to read the chapter together and determine the main idea and key facts that would be important to know. Ask them to come up with something happening in today's economy that would be different if the law being discussed hadn't been passed. Allow the final ten to fifteen minutes of the period for groups to share. Have each group hand in their papers at the end of the period. Instead of a handful of students who have read or understood the chapter, everyone now has. The conversation has been led by the students, and the same facts have been reviewed, with a reasonable likelihood of being remembered for Friday's quiz.
- Together, ask the class to look at the chapter. Ask the students to read the section titles and have them predict what the chapter will be about. (In elementary school, we call this "pre-reading" and "predicting." High schoolers can do it too!) Ask them to skim the sections and identify any words that pop out at them that they do not know. Then assign the chapter for homework with a written summary.
- If the class has a lower reading ability, read the chapter to them like a read-aloud, stopping occasionally to review new or difficult vocabulary. Provide the students with a printed copy of the text, have them highlight words they do not understand, and have them hand it in at the end. Homework is now to look up those words and come up with an example for each. Friday's quiz will be a composite of the words that the students were struggling with during the reading. Does this seem like a waste of a class period? Weigh it against a class spent reviewing a history of something that few students have read or understood.
- Do a "word search" through the chapter. Have pairs of students find key selected words and see if they can determine the meaning from the context of the paragraph containing them. Use the words, once defined, to weave together the story of the law that was passed, what it meant at the time, and what effect it has had on the present economy.

The Composite Version has three added Implementation indicators and one Content indicator. These indicators can be added directly to the Math/Science Version or the more general content-area version referred to in Chapter 2. I present these in the following, each with an example from actual classrooms.

Box 3.24

Indicator Composite-IM#4	
Indicator	**Examples of Evidence**
Composite-IM#4. Students have opportunities to construct their own knowledge	• Investigative tasks are essential elements of the lesson • Curiosity and perseverance are encouraged • Students apply existing knowledge and skills to new situations and integrate new and prior knowledge • Students make notes, drawings, or summaries in a journal or lab book that becomes part of their ongoing resources • Students have opportunities to do more than follow procedures; they ask their own questions, choose their own strategies, or design investigations • Elements of choice are part of the lesson strategies. • Students manipulate materials and equipment • Students select and use appropriate reading strategies and can articulate how the strategies help them learn the concepts

Box 3.25

Indicator Composite-IM#7	
Indicator	**Examples of Evidence**
Composite-IM#7. Use of reading as a learning tool is evident	• Reading is routinely used as a learning tool • Teacher models the skills of good readers • Multiple reading strategies (pre-reading, making predictions, asking questions, identifying important themes, analyzing text structure, making connections and inferences, evaluating, summarizing, re-reading) are used • Teacher builds students' independent use of these strategies and provides opportunities to use them in appropriate contexts • Students discuss strategies they use for understanding text, demonstrating a metacognitive grasp and ownership of the strategies • Context is used to enhance learning of vocabulary and spelling • Students write or tell their reactions and connections to the reading or answer questions about the reading selection

Example 3.26

Composite-IM#7

WHAT DOES USING READING AS A LEARNING TOOL LOOK LIKE?

A tenth-grade math teacher is teaching exponents and scientific notation. The students are working with the concept of using powers of two and ten to scale up or down. They have been working on several examples of fitting small values into much larger ones, such as Earths in the sun or atoms in a given volume of a compound. The textbook uses a metaphor from *Alice's Adventures in Wonderland* to illustrate the point. Alice finds cakes and liquids entreating her to "Eat me" or "Drink me." When she does, she grows or shrinks alarmingly, while keeping her proportions intact.

This is a heterogeneously grouped math class, unlike many tracked high school classes. Most of the students have not read *Alice's Adventures in Wonderland*, although some are familiar with the general story, having seen the Disney version of it as children. The teacher begins using text directly from the novel, as well as explanations and problems from the textbook based on the novel. They read the text in pairs first. Then the teacher takes turns with the students reading portions of the text, which has Alice closing up like a telescope as she drinks the potion designed to allow her to fit through the tiny door through which the White Rabbit had passed, then growing to a huge size as she eats the cake in an effort to retrieve the key to the door that she has left on the table.

They now have a challenge in the form of a word problem in their textbook: Given Alice's normal height and the distance from the Earth to the moon, if every time Alice ate a piece of cake, she grew tenfold, how many pieces of cake would it take for her to reach the moon? Using the powers of ten, they will compute the answer. Instead of simply assigning the problem for homework, the teacher has the students read the problem aloud in their groups. Groups report in their own words what the task is, tell what the relationship the task has to the original *Alice* text, and review with the teacher the use of the graphing calculator, which will help them with their exponential computations. They finish the period with a written reflection, each student writing what was learned about using exponents in place of repeated multiplications. Again, they share their writing with their table mates and turn their journals in for a response from the teacher. The reflection, which appears to be a part of their daily routine, becomes a metacognitive review of the concepts just learned.

Box 3.27

Indicator Composite-IM#8	
Indicator	**Examples of Evidence**
Composite-IM#8. Use of writing as a learning tool is evident	• Teacher models the skills of good writers (organizing, drafting, revising, etc.) • Journals, lab notes, notebooks, graphic organizers, and so forth are used to enhance learning • Writing is conducted through a multiphase process including prewriting, drafting, conferencing, revising, editing, and publishing • Students write frequently and can discuss how it helps them learn • Teacher conducts direct instruction in writing skills (topic development, organization, sentence/paragraph creation, and structure) • Students are learning to distinguish the purposes of writing (tone, voice, point of view, fact versus opinion)

Example 3.28

An Example Composite-IM#8

WHAT DOES USING WRITING AS A LEARNING TOOL LOOK LIKE?

An eighth-grade science teacher in a small rural school with heterogeneously grouped students is teaching the composition of the Earth and its systems. The students are learning about the layers that make up the Earth, theories about the formation of land forms,

(Continued)

and the forces that create changes in the Earth. The unit takes the better part of a month and contains many opportunities to explore the concepts behind "our ever-changing Earth." The students read a textbook, research using the Internet, make models and diagrams, and even correspond with a volcanologist who works with middle school students to excite their interest in the sciences. In short, they do many of the same things that students have always done when learning a new set of concepts in science.

But they have an additional challenge. Working in small teams, they take on the characters of a research team attempting to reach the Earth's core with the assignment of coming up with a theory about why there has been a spate of volcanic eruptions and earthquakes recently. Along with much of the scientific data that they research, diagram, and explain, they are to write a log of the team's progress in this daring adventure. In these logs, they take on the fictitious personalities of a team of geologists and each write journals in the voice of their particular character. This genre of writing asks students to explore the concept of author's point of view. The journey is fiction, and the characters can take on any personality the students choose, but the facts they cite must be accurate. They are also asked to write a traditional report, gather and display their data, and draw conclusions supported by the data. Their final product ultimately contains several genres of writing and is assessed in part according to statewide writing rubrics. By expressing their learning in both scientific and inventive written pieces, the students own their learning in ways that they wouldn't have if they had only produced a traditional report.

Observing this classroom at any point during the unit, you will typically see students intent and purposefully pursuing whatever task they are on at the moment, whether it is reading the text for information on the layers of the Earth, searching the Internet for weather and earthquake data, or designing the expeditionary vehicles that will carry them to the Earth's core. This unit takes advantage of the best part of the neat activity syndrome by actively engaging students over an extended time, and it finishes by requiring them to integrate their learning in multiple ways.

Box 3.29

Indicator Composite-IM#9	
Indicator	**Examples of Evidence**
Composite-IM#9. Connections are made between reading and writing	• Teacher makes connections between reading selections and writing assignments • Students have multiple opportunities to write about what they are reading or learning • Students have opportunities to read their own writing or work to an audience • Teacher uses reading and writing assignments to point out meaning and structure (content, vocabulary, syntax, usage)

Example 3.30

An Example Composite-IM#9

WHAT DOES CONNECTING READING AND WRITING LOOK LIKE?

A freshman English class is reading its first Shakespeare play: *Romeo and Juliet*. Some of the students had some experience with Shakespeare in middle school, but not all of them have. The teacher has the challenge of teaching them about Shakespeare and his time, exposing them to unfamiliar vocabulary and linguistic patterns, and teaching the play itself. During the course of the study, they will be listening to readings by the teacher, reading sections aloud in class, and acting out several scenes.

One of the assignments is to choose a scene and to rewrite it in modern language. Students will do this in groups of size appropriate to the selected scene. Each of them will assume a character, rewrite the dialogue for that character, and take that part in the group's presentation of the scene. Having written an original adaptation of a scene gives students ownership of something that they have read and creates an intimate familiarity with that section that will last a lifetime. The most popular scenes chosen are the balcony scene (where students appreciate what the question, "Wherefore art thou Romeo?" actually means) and the fight scene where Tybalt and Mercutio die.

As a final assignment, students are asked to choose among a set of focus questions to write an essay on elements in the play. Some examples are: (a) presenting arguments about the ethical responsibilities of the nurse and Friar Lawrence, who have abetted the plans of the young lovers, but have not properly protected them from the disastrous results and (b) likening the family feud to ethnic rivalries in past and current history, in which students imagine comparable stories (such as *West Side Story*) in which two members of rival groups have fallen in love.

Having written both the words of the play and philosophical thoughts about ideas contained in the play, students will forever remember this play and will have no fear of approaching Shakespeare in the future.

Box 3.31

Indicator Composite-CO#2	
Indicator	**Examples of Evidence**
Composite-CO#2. Teacher shows an understanding of how to use text to build comprehension of the content	• Teacher takes advantage of reading material to discuss background knowledge or vocabulary • Teacher refers directly to the text to probe and to build understanding • Teacher asks a variety of types of questions (probing for meaning, clarification, inference, evaluation) • Teacher has students justify answers by referring to text • Teacher reads difficult passages and helps students understand the material • Teacher uses graphics in the text as well as written words to build understanding

Example 3.32

An Example Composite-CO#2

WHAT DOES USING TEXT TO BUILD CONTENT KNOWLEDGE LOOK LIKE?

A tenth-grade social studies teacher is teaching an elective course in macroeconomics. The class is studying the effects of poverty on society and is debating the role of government in addressing the issue. As part of this discussion, they are considering the views of Thomas Malthus, who, along with many of his contemporaries in the eighteenth century, debated the proper role of the government in the economy. Malthus believed that the government's attempt to address poverty through the poor laws would only exacerbate the condition of the lower class. He thought, instead, that the poor must exhibit moral restraint by putting a check on population growth. The teacher projects excerpts from Malthus's writing, *An Essay on the Principle of Population (1798)* up on the SMART Board. The class reads a selection from the essay together and is asked to examine it to identify the key aspects of Malthus's argument, justifying their thoughts by referring to the text. They have the opportunity to not only read the text right there in class, but to discuss the various aspects, using skills of interpretation, inference, and personal connections.

Example 3.33

What Does It Look Like When It Goes Wrong? (All Composite Indicators)

WHAT HAPPENS WHEN READING AND WRITING ARE NOT USED ACTIVELY?

Example A

A math teacher assigns a series of examples from a section of the textbook for homework. The book lays out a complex situation. The student doesn't do the homework because the text of the example was too difficult to read and she didn't understand what she was supposed to do. The next day, the first half of class is spent going over the homework examples. The student receives a zero for not having done her homework and then sits doodling in her notebook while the teacher goes over the answers. For more than twenty minutes, the student does no work.

Example B

A social studies teacher is teaching an economics lesson on supply and demand. The chapter had been assigned for homework. Most students didn't read the assignment. The teacher discusses the content of the chapter, asking questions as she goes along. As she asks a question, one or two students who have read and understood the chapter either raise their hands or call out the answers. The teacher, hearing an appropriate response, seems satisfied and moves along, essentially having a stimulating conversation with herself.

Example 3

A science teacher assigns a lab. Students are provided with written directions and are expected to follow them, observe and record results, and write up their conclusions. Those who have reading challenges will find themselves unsure about what to do and will again run into difficulty as they have to write up their conclusions, even if they complete the experiment properly. They may fail the lab even if they might have been able to understand the scientific concepts being investigated.

SECTION 3: USING THE LITERACY AND COMPOSITE VERSIONS

Method 1: Scoring the Examples in Chapter 3

Using the scoring sheets as described in Chapter 7 and found in Appendix F, analyze the examples in this chapter and come to consensus with your study group about what score you would give each lesson for selected indicators. Try first with the indicators that the example was chosen for. Then try another indicator that you have enough information on to make a judgment.

Method 2: Focused Discussions

With your administrative team or other appropriate group of peers, consider the following:

1. (L-IM#1) Discuss the various formats your group has seen involving the teaching of literacy skills to young children. Consider the pros and cons of leveled reading groups versus whole-class instruction, and give examples of how different teachers you have seen have attempted to build comprehensive literacy skills.

2. (L-CO#2) How effectively do teachers use context and background knowledge to build understanding of vocabulary, literary devices, and content of material read in class?

3. (L-CO#4, L-IM#1) Explore the idea of metacognition. How are students becoming aware of the strategies they use to process reading material? What techniques do teachers use to model the metacognitive approach to reading development?

4. (L-IM#3, L-IM#6) Analyze the direction of large-group discussions in classes that you observe. Does the conversation always go from teacher (question) to student (answer), or is there any student-to-student interaction? How many students participate in the discussion? Is there a chance for each student to think about the questions before having to compete for "air time?"

5. (L-CO#5) What examples have you seen of creating opportunities to connect reading and writing? Have you seen examples of the use of writing to reinforce reading skills or the learning of content that has been read?

6. (Composite-IM#7, Composite-IM#8) What evidence have you seen in classes of reading text or student writing being used to reinforce or develop student understanding of subject matter?

Method 3: Classroom Co-observations or Walk-Throughs

In your administrative team or supervisory support group, visit a literacy class or a content-area class together. As with the Math/Science Version, you will be looking for teachers confident enough to open their classrooms for your professional development. Caution: This does not guarantee (although it does increase the possibility) that the instruction you find will be of the highest caliber, but it does mean that you will find a teacher comfortable with and open to feedback. In the absence of being able to co-observe, bring write-ups of individual observations done. Consider together the following discussion questions to analyze the effectiveness of each lesson.

DISCUSSION QUESTIONS

1. In primary grades, were there opportunities for the building of both fluency and comprehension? In upper elementary through high school classes, did the lesson focus on making meaning from text? Did the students and teacher refer directly to text to support the elements of their discussion?

2. What accommodations were made for students of differing reading ability?

3. How did the teacher interact with the students? Who did most of the talking?

4. How did students interact with each other? Did students all have an audience for their ideas?

5. Did students engage in writing? Were there lost opportunities to write about what they were reading or learning? Was there evidence of the use of a clear writing process with frequent opportunities to write?

6. How did (or will) the teacher assess student understanding at the end of the teaching unit? Was a consistent approach to assessing writing pieces evident?

CONCLUDING THOUGHTS

Literacy is the key that opens the door to all future learning. We have closed this door far too early on far too many students. We have too much research coupled with mounds of anecdotal examples demonstrating successful practices that make a serious difference. It is incumbent on all of us to make use of what we know, make no more excuses, and move forward with instruction that ends the discrepancy in what we teach and what is learned.

Chapter 4

Classroom Culture

Treating Everyone as You Would Be Treated

We live in a world of self generating beliefs which remain largely untested. We adopt those beliefs because they are based on conclusions, which are inferred from what we observe, plus our past experience. Our ability to achieve the results we truly desire is eroded by our feelings that:

- *Our beliefs are the truth.*
- *The truth is obvious.*
- *Our beliefs are based on real data.*
- *The data we select are the real data. (Senge, Kleiner, Roberts, Ross, & Smith, 1994, p. 242).*

This quote leads us to the "ladder of inference" (Senge et al., 1994, p. 243) beginning with our personal observable experiences from which we select the data to use as a framework for our beliefs. We create meaning, assumptions, and conclusions from these data. The resulting beliefs cause us to act in accordance with those conclusions and control which further data we pay attention to. As this illustrates, we are all a product of our cultures, environment, and experiences. Our assumptions, whether they are conscious or not, affect our actions. In schools, our beliefs come out in the form of the expectations that we hold for our students. Because these expectations have a direct impact on student learning (Bamburg, 1994), it is worth taking a long look at how they appear in classroom settings. Few teachers set out to discriminate against their students based on race, ethnicity, gender, or economic class. I don't believe that there is a teacher who wakes up in the morning with the intention of excluding any child or class of children, but it happens inadvertently, and the effect is withering. Privilege is invisible to those who have it (McIntosh, 1988). Therefore, to the extent that any of us does have it, it is only by making it visible to ourselves so that we can eradicate its effects—no matter how unintentional—on others.

Teachers' experiences with children of any particular group may be the "data" affecting their behavior toward those children. It is pro forma to profess to the belief that all children can learn, but DuFour and Eaker (1998) speaks of four subtexts to that belief:

1. We believe all children can learn . . . based on their ability.

2. We believe all children can learn . . . if they take advantage of the opportunity to learn.

3. We believe all children can learn . . . and we will take responsibility for their growth.

4. We believe all children can learn . . . and we will establish high standards of learning that we expect all students to achieve. (pp. 59–60)

The first applies a "survival of the fittest" model, blaming failures to learn on genetics—something certainly beyond the control of schools. Number 2 implies the "I taught it; I can't help it if they didn't learn it" approach, which allows teachers to wash their hands of responsibility after the lesson is over. The third expresses a caring for individual students, but allows for low expectations to be satisfied as long as any progress at all is made. Only the fourth takes on the challenge of actually reaching all students, using the words, "We will take responsibility." This last statement reflects the approach that has taken schools such as those in the 90-90-90 study (Reeves, 2006) and other high-performing schools with significant challenges to the point where they were able to turn their results around.

"I was taught to see racism only in individual acts of meanness, not in invisible systems conferring dominance on my group" (McIntosh, 1988).

Differing expectations can leak out without ill intent. An example of this comes from the presidential political campaign season that began prematurely in 2006. A longtime senator was embarrassed by his own comments in which he referred to one of the rival candidates, an African American senator, as "articulate." While it was widely acknowledged that the record of the speaker of this comment reflected a real commitment to equity and that his intentions were not intentionally racist, the insult was keenly felt. By choosing the word *articulate*, he made an unconscious reference to negative stereotypes that produce surprise when an African American expresses himself or herself with grace and eloquence. The problem was not that the clumsy reference was intentionally racist; it was specifically that it was *unintentionally* racist. While many debated whether or not the senator meant to insult, the argument was irrelevant. It did not matter that he did not set out to devalue anyone; the standard is not set by the speaker of the comment, but rather by the recipient of its impact. This is the same whether you are deciding if a sports team's "Indian" mascot is racist, or if a joke was anti-Semitic. The insult is in the eye of the beholder. If it hurts someone, it's unacceptable. (This particular presidential contest went on to showcase multiple examples of race being intentionally and unintentionally used as a wedge. At the printing of this book, the outcome of this election is still unsure.)

When comments like this are spoken in a classroom, learning is affected, as learning is a highly social activity. The Classroom Culture section is an expression of Assumptions 3 (learning is a social activity) and 4 (technology enhances instruction). It addresses a range of interpersonal issues ranging from classroom management and behavior to the level of respect and free flow of ideas from both teacher and students. Issues of equity of access and the degree to which diversity is honored hold a prominent place when observing the climate, which should be free of harassment, both overt and covert. This section also includes equity of access to technology and the ethical use of our new technological resources. The Math/Science and Literacy Versions are closely related, with many indicators virtually identical. This chapter will present the Math/Science Version, noting where there are outstanding differences with the Literacy Version. Examples from both types of classrooms will be presented.

THE CLASSROOM CULTURE CRITERIA

The culture criteria begin with three indicators that paint a portrait of a classroom environment that is orderly but dynamic and in which vibrant learning is apparent through the purposeful work of both teacher and students and evidence of a collaborative learning community. There is much work on classroom management that describes and justifies these indicators, so they do not need repetition (Danielson, 1986; Kohn, 1996; Marzano, Pickering, & Marzano, 2003). The examples of evidence provide an additional emphasis to the extent to which "relevant and important" work is happening at all times, whether the students are working directly with the teacher or not. While the indicators and examples of evidence speak for themselves, falling well within the parameters of the aforementioned work, it is worth noting how some good ideas of behavior management can go bad.

Box 4.1

Indicators CU#1, CU#2, and CU#3	
Indicators	**Examples of Evidence**
CU#1. Classroom management maximizes learning opportunities	• Teacher maintains a level of order conducive to learning (students are attending to the teacher and the activity) • There is an atmosphere of freedom and flexibility within that order • Classroom norms emphasize personal and collective responsibility to create a learning community • Directions to students are clear to avoid confusion and constant questions, which interrupt the flow of the activity • During group times, students not working with teacher are engaged in relevant and important work
CU#2. Classroom routines are clear and consistent	• There are clearly stated classroom norms • There is a minimum of disruption and inappropriate interruptions; transition times are seamless • Routines for noninstructional duties are clearly established, and students follow them consistently
CU#3. Behavior is respectful and appropriate	• Teacher manages classroom control preventively and with respect • If correction is needed, teacher handles the situation with respectful control and minimum disruption • There are clearly stated consequences for specific behaviors, and they are applied consistently • The atmosphere of the classroom feels safe, and there is an absence of bullying, harassment, and inappropriate language • Students are provided with strategies for self-monitoring and correction

Box 4.2

Good Classroom Culture Ideas
That Go Bad (CU#1, CU#2, and CU#3)

The idea: Classroom rules and a behavior system should be implemented.
A good set of commonly understood rules with a behavior system:

- sets a tone of civility in the classroom,
- creates a basis for routines that students understand, and
- gives the teacher tools for managing behavior with consistency.

HAS IT GONE BAD?

Do the classroom rules look like they were arrived at collaboratively or imposed on both teacher and students? Are teacher signals for quiet (lights out, two fingers raised, claps or responsive phrases) responded to or ignored by students? How frequently does the teacher need to use those? Are behavior systems (color codes, warnings, names on board) handled respectfully? Are they actually connected to consequences or is the threat, "You'll lose your recess" an empty one?

The idea: Group work helps students learn math and science.
Assigning work to groups:

- allows teachers to work individually with students,
- takes advantage of the social aspect of learning and helps students process learning through dialogue and mathematical discourse, and
- provides opportunities for students to conduct investigations and construct their own knowledge.

HAS IT GONE BAD?

Is the classroom climate safe and industrious? Does the teacher have to continually interrupt his or her work with individuals or groups to remind students to "use their indoor voices?" Does every group activity have some sort of product required from each student to ensure the sense of accountability for assigned tasks? Is the activity in the classroom mostly on task, or is there undue wandering about and procrastination by some students? Most important, have teacher comments about behavior begun to overshadow substantive math or science conversations with student groups?

The giving of directions is not routinely associated with classroom behavior. But when you are looking at a class in chaos with poorly focused students and wondering what went wrong, ask yourself how the activity began. Just like predictable and sensible routines, the giving of directions for an activity can set up productivity or confusion. Since lack of focus of a few students can derail the activities of others, it is worth taking a look at how to diagnose whether poor direction giving is at the root. In literacy classes, the clear giving of directions may be the key to success or failure of the reading center approach. In math or science classes, good directions make the difference between productive inquiry and the mere playing with materials.

Box 4.3

Good Classroom Culture Ideas That Go Bad (L-CU#1)

**HOW GIVING POOR DIRECTIONS CAUSES BEHAVIOR
PROBLEMS, CONFUSION, AND LACK OF PRODUCTIVE WORK**

A first-grade teacher is planning a lesson that will use reading centers so that she can work with her reading groups, which have been established on the basis of reading assessments. There are five activities that will need to be completed during center time. At the beginning of class, each student has in his or her reading folder five sheets of directions. Each sheet corresponds to one of the centers. She asks students to open their folders and take out the papers.

She begins with Sheet 1. She holds it up to show the students which sheet she is reading from. Since the sheets have typed directions in normal font, the sheet she holds does not differ greatly from the others. The sheets are not numbered, color coded, or otherwise visually distinctive. She does not move around the room to make sure that everyone is following along with the correct sheet.

She begins to read the directions and describe the activity that students are supposed to do at each station. As she goes through the five sets of directions, she sets up the likelihood that center time will be a mess. Here are some of the mistakes:

- Each activity is somewhat complicated. The directions include which part of the room to go to, what materials students will find there, and how they are to fill out their papers.
- Because there are five centers and five separate, complex set of directions, the chances that a classroom of first graders will retain all of them until they reach the centers (which they will do after a complex whole-group activity) are remote.
- The teacher describes the planned activities in varying detail. Some include far more detail than is necessary. One of the centers will reinforce the concept of nouns, the part of speech they will be working on as a whole class. The sheet asks the students to write as many nouns as they can think of. Although the lesson they are about to have will go into what a noun is, she asks the students to give some examples of nouns. Students begin to throw out words. As can sometimes be the case, children go for "sound-alikes." The first student offers the word *light* (which can be a noun or adjective), and the teacher accepts it. The next word offered is *bright*. Now she has the problem of explaining that *bright* isn't a noun, it's an adjective. She has gotten herself into a tangle which will only get worse when the next word offered is *fight*. The purpose of giving directions has been completely obscured.
- Not deterred, she goes on to the next sheet. This one requires the use of a dictionary. She asks students to point to the section of the room where the dictionaries can be found. The students all point to the teacher, none of them seeming familiar with where the dictionaries are. One wonders whether if they don't know where the dictionaries are, have they learned the skills needed to use them?
- The final center will have the students using word cubes to construct sentences. The teacher was encouraging the students to use nice, long sentences, not short ones like "I like the cat." The directions were so complex that I was unable to determine whether this activity was an individual or group one, if they were to copy the sentence after they had constructed it (otherwise, how would she be able to monitor how they'd done?), or if there was any way that the concept of nouns was going to be highlighted.

So, how does center time go? The teacher's reading groups are interrupted frequently with students asking for help. They are told that she cannot help them while she is with a reading group. There is considerable background noise, making concentrating in the reading group difficult. At one point in between two reading groups, she circulates to quiet things down and assist students. Many of the students have gotten little done, having gotten stymied at an early phase. Some have skated on the edge of bothering other students, but no adult has responded and no consequences have been applied. The end of the reading block comes. The students return their folders to the box, the word cubes are put away, and the students line up for recess. The teacher will be faced with twenty folders of five papers each. It is unclear when the teacher will return the papers to the students, what they will do next with them, if there is any accountability for completion of work, or if she will address the level of understanding of each of the concepts contained in those well-intentioned activities.

Box 4.4

Indicators MS-CU#4 and L-CU#4	
Indicators	**Examples of Evidence**
MS-CU#4. The classroom culture generates enthusiasm for the exploration of mathematical and scientific ideas	• Many mathematical and scientific tools and resources are prominent and frequently used • Students generate ideas, questions, propositions, and solutions • Students are encouraged to use multiple approaches to solve problems (numeric, algebraic, and graphic in math; open-ended inquiry in science) • Students are engaged and motivated to participate • There is student math and science work displayed
L-CU#4. Literacy is valued, and reading and writing are enthusiastically promoted	• Literacy is approached with enthusiasm by teacher and students • Student work displayed is connected to curriculum or in some way used by children or teacher • Writing is valued and enthusiastically promoted • Many types of authentic reading materials are displayed and are available to students for reference during class • Dictionaries, thesaurus, style manuals, and literacy resources are available for students to use at all times; teacher encourages students to use these when reading and writing

When answers all reside in the mind of the teacher, students see math and science as a guessing game or a magic trick that mysteriously works out in the end when someone either correctly answers the teacher or the teacher reveals the secret. Diagnostic Classroom Observation (DCO) asks that the culture of the classroom generate students' enthusiasm by letting them know that *they* can do the thinking. Is there ever room for teacher lectures and demonstrations? Yes, but only under certain conditions. A general rule of thumb for when to conduct teacher demonstrations is: (1) when the materials are dangerous and (2) when the materials are too expensive for everyone to have them. Teacher lectures should be confined to mini-lessons prior to an investigation and, at the end, helping the students tie the pieces together. Other than those circumstances, the classroom culture should exude a sense of curiosity and perseverance as students have multiple opportunities to handle materials and figure things out. The classroom should be student centered (we'll take a look at what that *really* means), with student projects prominently displayed, and there should be a variety of materials in the room that feel accessible to all (within the bounds of safety). One correct answer is appropriate when, in fact, there is one correct answer. However, there are multiple strategies for reaching that answer, and when students have opportunities to find their own solutions, they can often surprise the teacher with new insights. The sense of enthusiasm is palpable when students are excited and focused.

Example 4.5

MS-CU#4

WHAT DOES A STUDENT-CENTERED CLASSROOM GENERATING EXCITEMENT LOOK LIKE?

A fourth-grade teacher is leading a lesson on complete circuits through an investigation using batteries, wires, and small motors in a class with ethnic, socioeconomic, and gender diversity. She creates a challenge: How many ways can you get the motors to spin? She directs students to draw in their science journals ways in which they get the motors to work *and* ways in which they don't work. With few other directions, the students eagerly get to work. She has assigned the students to samesex pairs for the activity. She notes that she had found through experience that in mixed-gender pairs, the boys tended to manipulate the materials, and the girls tended to take the notes. As each pair carries out the investigation, the teacher circulates, and when she notes that one person is doing the "heavy lifting," she suggests that the partners switch roles. She briefly stops the group to remind them to include the configurations that do not work as well as the ones that do.

Toward the end of the lesson, before they share any results, the teacher directs the students to find someone in the room whom they have not worked with and share what they found in their explorations. She notes that pushing each student to articulate what it is they have been learning to someone new forces them to have to rethink what they actually did. This also makes sure that all students have an audience for their independent thoughts. Every student has been engaged, and everyone has something to share.

What Makes This Class so Engaging?

- The challenge is open ended.
- Every student has an equal shot at the materials, hence the learning.
- There is accountability for the learning in the form of the journals and ownership in the form of sharing.
- Real learning will be extracted from the activity as the students analyze which configurations worked and which ones didn't, thus building the understanding of complete circuits from the ground up.

From the Annenberg/CPB Math and Science Collection (1995).

Box 4.6

Good Classroom Culture Ideas That Go Bad (MS-CU#4)

The idea: Activities should generate enthusiasm and be hands on.
Hands-on activities:

- engage students both physically and intellectually;
- allow the manipulation of materials, which enhances learning; and
- make concepts come alive by having them play themselves out in front of students.

(Continued)

(Continued)

HAS IT GONE BAD?

Who owns the learning? Who asks the questions? Who handles the materials? Has the teacher *really* turned over the discovery of the concepts to the students? Some ways to tell are by answering these questions:

- Is the teacher demonstrating the activity first or handing out a detailed instruction sheet, expecting that the students will follow a step-by-step process?
- Does every student have access to the materials, or are the groups too large to allow everyone to handle them?
- Is the activity posed as a challenge with a question to be answered, or are the results predetermined and identified so that students are merely looking for something specific to occur?
- Is the concept to be learned disclosed prior to the activity, or are the students called together at the end to make sense together of what they observed and build their conceptual understanding?
- Are the students talking about the activity? Are they problem solving? How often do they call on the teacher to direct them in their next steps?
- Are the students confused and timid about taking the next steps, or are they excited, focused, and purposeful, taking notes, making guesses, and listening to each other?

Indicator L-CU#4 asks, "What does a literacy-rich environment look like?" We know that it takes more than an attractively set-up room with colorful and decorative wall posters. Are the books plentiful, organized, and accessible? Are the reference books present and used on a regular basis? If there are word walls or guidelines for reading and writing posted, are they referred to or used by students? Are the classroom displays student made or prefabricated? Is there an excitement about the activities of the day? Do students show pride in their writing and enthusiastically dive into their reading? Do they, without being told to, frequently jot notes in a reading journal? Does the teacher model the enthusiasm and show himself or herself to be a reader and a writer?

Example 4.7

L-CU#4

WHAT DOES A LITERACY-RICH ENVIRONMENT LOOK LIKE?

A sixth-grade teacher is working on the mystery genre with her students. They have begun with a read-aloud of Agatha Christie's *And Then There Were None*. They read a chapter a day. As the teacher reads with suspense building in her voice, the room is silent, the students leaning slightly forward. Occasional audible gasps are heard. On the wall are student-drawn portraits of each of the ten characters. Some of the portraits have been moved to the bottom of the bulletin board. They represent the ones who have already been murdered. The teacher pauses occasionally at appropriate stopping points to review some of the more unusual vocabulary and sentence structures, because this book was written in another era and another country.

Also on the wall is a student-generated chart of elements of mystery stories. The list includes "twists and turns in the plot" and "scary characters." After the chapter has been read, the students get their writing folders. They are each creating a mystery story. They have been mapping out their plots and identifying their characters with a brief "bio" of each. Some of the storylines include theft of rare and valuable items or stories involving national and international security, but the majority of them are murder mysteries. Some students are reading a draft of a chapter to a peer. Others are working alone. There is a shelf of dictionaries, enough for everyone in the class. Some are off the shelf and in full use. There is a purposeful sense in the room, and discussions appear enthusiastic but respectfully quiet. The teacher sits with some students, a clipboard in her hands. She makes notes as she conferences with these students to monitor their progress.

Another bulletin board has published quality student writing displayed. The title of the bulletin board is "Black History Month." Each piece is a biography of a noted African American. There are also bookshelves with many reading choices and varying reading levels. One shelf is designated "Mystery Novels." Each student is simultaneously reading a mystery while they are writing one.

WHAT MAKES THIS CLASS SO ENGAGING?

- The read-aloud is high interest, and the environment is rich with resources and student work.
- Students have been engaged in the read-aloud by creating visual images of the characters who will disappear one by one; they will be guessing who the murderer is and who will be the next to go.
- Their writing is connected with the reading.
- They have generated themselves the elements of the genre and will own them as they incorporate them into their original pieces.
- There is accountability as well as sharing, as the students read their pieces to their peers as well as the teacher.

Box 4.8

Indicators CU#5 and CU#6	
Indicators	**Examples of Evidence**
CU#5. Teacher shows respect for students' ideas, questions, and contributions to the lesson and works collaboratively with students	• Teacher has routines that encourage all students to participate • Adequate time is provided for discussion • Teacher listens carefully to student responses, not always looking for a predetermined answer • Teacher accepts ideas without judging and respectfully helps students untangle their misconceptions • Teacher supports and facilitates work of students as individuals and in small and large groups
CU#6. Students show respect for and value each others' ideas, questions, and contributions to the lesson; students work collaboratively	• Students readily share ideas and listen to each other in large and small groups • No student dominates • Students discuss alternative ideas • Students challenge and question each other respectfully • Students coordinate efforts and share responsibility for group results

When a teacher is confident in his or her knowledge of the content and comfortable with the activities that he or she has set up, the teacher is freed up to really listen to student thinking. Contained within their answers to questions are the keys to students' developing understanding. Potentially among them are nascent misconceptions that could follow them for the rest of their lives. Respecting student thinking does not mean accepting all ideas as equally valid. The teacher must help the students sort out the promising ideas from the erroneous ones, but he or she must do so thoughtfully so as to not discourage any student from sharing those thoughts publicly. The culture must stress that all sorts of theories may be proposed but only some will be useful in the concepts being pursued. A lack of embarrassment, a sense that predictions frequently don't pan out, and an acceptance of not knowing the answer right away must be cultivated. A sense of trust must be created so that all thinking can be shared, with the agreement that in the end, all will share in the collective wisdom. This, again, is an example of "the space between the teacher and the student" (Saginor, 1999), and it is where the most valuable learning takes place.

When the teacher models respectful challenging of ideas, the culture of the classroom mirrors that, with students treating each other the same way. CU#6 is the Classroom Culture indicator that focuses on student-to-student interactions. This time, supervisors are directed to observe the way students act toward each other whether the teacher is looking or not. Is there a sense of camaraderie and cooperation? Do students share their thinking and assist each other in tasks? Some teachers use specific techniques to help students develop the ability for cross-talk, debate, and honest disagreement as they grapple with possible solutions. They may be asked to address each other by name, use taglines such as "I'd like to build off what [student's name] said," or having the students address each other by name and by paraphrasing what each other has said. It is this give and take between and among the teacher and students that builds a dynamic classroom culture where discovery is always possible. A culture of careful listening and respectful challenging opens the door for learning for all.

CU#7 is the "equity box." It asks you to look at the extent to which this is truly an equal-opportunity learning environment. DCO directs the observer to note the

Example 4.9

CU#5 and CU#6

PHRASES FOR RESPECTFULLY CHALLENGING STUDENT IDEAS BY TEACHER AND STUDENTS

- That's an interesting idea. Tell me how you got there.
- Let's see how that might work in this (other) situation.
- I'm wondering if anyone has another idea.
- I hear what you're saying, but I'm not completely convinced. Help me understand.
- How would you be able to prove that to me?
- There may be another way of looking at that.
- I agree with what you've said, but there may be some more to it.
- You might want to rethink that in light of this evidence.
- Do some more thinking about that. I'll check in with you later.
- I've never considered that before. I may have to give it some more thought.

Box 4.10

Indicator CU#7	
Indicator	**Examples of Evidence**
CU#7. All students have equal access to the total educational resources of the classroom	• Students have equal access to teacher attention, materials, technology, and assigned roles • The pattern of inclusion of all students shows attention to issues of gender, race, ethnicity, special needs, and socioeconomic status • Teacher discourages dominance of individual students and encourages reticent students • Groupings maximize each student's ability to participate; group dynamics are monitored by the teacher • Teacher addresses diverse needs and abilities • Teacher recognizes exceptional participation and creates opportunities for students to exceed standards

patterns of inclusion and exclusion. You may be surprised to note a pattern of calling primarily on a single gender or addressing the higher-order-thinking questions to one group as opposed to another. Patterns are best observed over time. This indicator asks you to carefully examine who's in and who's out. This can be noted in the room arrangement, the pattern of questioning and answering, and most important, the groupings of students. Is the group size appropriate to the task, and is every member of the group included at all levels? Is the teacher monitoring the group dynamics to ensure that no student dominates and that the quieter voices get their ideas expressed and considered? In general, pairs work well to ensure that no one gets left out, but how the pairs are assigned and how they function both need to be overseen. Individual responses, such as journals or other records, should be collected and assessed. Students should be encouraged to work with different partners, and accommodations for special needs should not single out a student or exclude him or her from high expectations.

Important in classroom discussions is who is called on, how often, and in what manner. DCO asks observers to note levels of participation to discuss them with teachers after the class. Teachers have employed various techniques to ensure fair shares of "air time." The best ones ensure students who have ideas they wish to share are given the chance while those who sit and wait for others to respond are encouraged to participate. Some successful ways to accomplish this are:

- having students jot down ideas before the teacher picks a spokesperson,
- asking students to share their thoughts with a partner, then having the spokesperson share his or her partner's idea,
- alternating boy and girl respondents, and
- making a note of who has spoken to make sure to give others a chance tomorrow.

How can we guard against harmful practices when they are unintentional or when we have no awareness of them? Videotaping a class allows you to monitor specific habits, such as patterns of calling on students, how disciplinary comments are meted out, how groups are formed, and how they function when you are not with them. Or you can invite an observer in to log how many times each child speaks publicly and how much individual attention is received by each child, and to note comments you typically make that might be unintentionally offensive. Only by opening the curtain on our hidden biases can we begin to eradicate them from our practice.

Example 4.11

An Example MS-CU#

WHAT DOES INCLUDING EVERY STUDENT LOOK LIKE?

A fifth-grade class is in the process of discovering what complete, series, and parallel circuits are and how they work. The materials on their tables include batteries, wires, and bulbs. The diverse group includes students of varying academic abilities, students who speak three different languages, and students on Individualized Educational Plans (IEPs). Every student has a science journal, every student has received the same directions, and every student is performing the same investigations. Each group is made up of two pairs of students. Two students, a girl and a boy, who have just arrived from Bosnia, are together with an English as a Second Language (ESL) teacher assisting them. They are paired with a pair of English-speaking girls. The ESL teacher actively joins the discussion with the four girls, encouraging the Bosnian girls to use English to name the items that they are handling, drawing, and labeling in their journals. Two Chinese boys are paired with two English-speaking boys. The ESL teacher checks in with them occasionally, but the boys are already speaking reasonably fluent English. A boy on an IEP is paired with another boy and is accompanied by his paraprofessional, who sits quietly watching the boys work, only intervening when her student needs assistance writing in his science journal. They are paired with two other boys. It is not immediately clear to which boy the paraprofessional is attached until she begins to work with him on his journal.

In each of these cases, some of these students might have been removed from science class to have special assistance or lessons in English. Instead, their language skills are being nurtured in the context of other things that they need to learn. They are not being isolated, but integrated. They do not detract from the learning of others, and the presence of others enhances their learning.

Box 4.12

Good Classroom Culture Ideas That Go Bad (CU#7)

The idea: Students with disabilities should be included in regular classrooms.

A fourth-grade class is having literature discussions in groups of about eight. A member of one group has a significant speech impediment and is normally quiet during discussions. One day, the student finds her voice and dominates the discussion for the entire period, completely silencing all others. The teacher, pleased that she is finally speaking, allows the discussion to continue, even though there is visible discomfort observed both in the teacher and the rest of the students, who remain quiet out of respect.

HOW IT COULD HAVE GONE BETTER

The teacher might have paid more attention originally to the assigning of groups. Seven or eight students in a discussion group is too large regardless of the group make-up. A student with a speech impediment should be assigned to a small, caring group where she can make small but steady progress in self-expression, as opposed to a months-long silence with a sudden (and potentially embarrassing) explosion of talk.

The idea: Hispanic students with limited English proficiency should be assigned bilingual teachers who can move them from a dependence on Spanish while still maintaining their native tongue.

A second-grade bilingual teacher has a class of predominantly Hispanic students. She moves easily between Spanish and English, sometimes saying everything in both languages, sometimes slipping into more Spanish with less translating. There are four students in the class who remain silent during the entire literacy lesson. They appear to be African American. In checking with the teacher afterward, it is verified that these students do not have Spanish as their native language. They have been unintentionally excluded from a good portion of the lesson.

HOW IT COULD HAVE GONE BETTER

If classes are to be taught partly in another language, either only students with that language as their original language are assigned to that class or the teacher intentionally makes all learning accessible to all students. Learning Spanish can be a goal and a bonus for non-Hispanic students.

Box 4.13

Good Classroom Culture Ideas That Go Bad (CU#7)

UNINTENTIONAL YET DAMAGING SLIGHTS

- A white, female second-grade teacher in a class of Asian, Hispanic, and African American students has general class control problems, and there is constant movement and an elevated noise level. There is an African American girl who is tall for her age and has a naturally loud voice. In a half hour of literacy work in which students are working in table groups on printed worksheets from their basal reading text, the teacher calls out this girl's name preceding almost every attempt to lower the noise level of the room, whether or not she is talking. She occasionally calls out the girl's name for doing something correctly, such as putting her paper in the proper bin. I count a total of twenty-two times her name is mentioned publicly during the ninety-minute literacy block. No other students are singled out in a similar fashion.
- A white, male teacher in a racially mixed fifth-grade class gives a writing assignment. Students are mostly busy working on their drafts. Three African American boys wander around the room at different times, none of them seriously attempting the assignment. The teacher circulates around the room, assisting some students, but ignoring the "wanderers." Aside from the fact that these boys have had thirty minutes of instructional time squandered, they will be penalized later either with extra homework, lost recesses, or a zero for lack of work completion. In addition, they are being taught that the timely completion of their work is not expected of them.
- An African American, female kindergarten teacher has a class with mixed Hispanic, African American, and Asian students, with one white girl. The white girl sits in the back during "rug time" and is the only student who is never called on or made eye contact with. She is sitting with her jacket on, although the temperature of the room is normal and all the other children have hung their coats in their cubbies. When they move from rug time to their tables, the teacher finally notices that she still has her coat. She scolds her and sends her to her cubby to hang it up.

(Continued)

(Continued)

- A teacher and the majority of a fifth-grade class are Hispanic. They are studying the issue of immigration during a time when this issue has come to the forefront due to presidential and congressional discussions. The news is filled with large demonstrations by immigrants, noting the many contributions to this country of its immigrants. The teacher refers to all living in America as immigrants and has a number of tasks assigned, including doing some research, reading, and writing about immigration. There are, however, several African American students and, in this part of the country, very possibly some Native Americans in the class. These students do not have immigration in their background and are possibly offended by the idea that "we are all immigrants" when some of us arrived against our will and others were here originally and were displaced by our earliest immigrants from Europe.
- A white middle school teacher is teaching in an all-white class, which is heterogeneously grouped. There is an achievement discrepancy in the socioeconomic status of her students. Her students living in poverty, as defined by those qualifying for free and reduced-price lunch, have a significantly lower pass rate. She dismisses this with comments such as, "They never do their homework," or "Their home life gets in the way of doing their homework." She points out how hard it is to get parents to come to school for a conference and assumes that they "just don't value education." She resists suggestions to look at her instructional practices because she feels they are effective for the students who "do their work."

Box 4.14

Good Classroom Culture Ideas That Go Bad (CU#7)

ADULTS DO IT TOO!

Example 1

A professional development workshop was designed to immerse elementary teachers in the process of inquiry by combining them with graduate students in science from a local college and giving them an engineering challenge involving physics concepts such as inertia, gravity, mass, and acceleration. Groups were assigned by the workshop presenters to ensure a mix of gender and scientific expertise.

As the activity proceeded, the workshop presenters observed that in every group but one that had a male member, whether that male was an elementary teacher or a graduate-level scientist, the building of the model was being done by that male. The females, both elementary teachers and scientists, were either just watching or offering occasional advice from the sidelines. This was noted by the presenters (one male, one female) so that in further training sessions, it could be discussed as an issue and thus intentionally averted in the future. The discussion will also sensitize the teachers so that as they continue to provide inquiry opportunities to their classes, they are vigilant so as to avoid the repeat scenario.

Example 2

In a doctoral program with approximately equal numbers of males and females in a class of about thirty, two female students undertook an experiment. In a designated period of class discussion time, they logged who was speaking and for how long. The discussions in the class centered on issues of economic advantage and inequitable preferences in our schools. In a group in which freewheeling discussions were the norm and which would have prided itself on its respect for women (in fact, which might be more likely to identify racial and ethnic biases as a problem), the experimenters found a startling and significant unbalance of "air time" favoring men.

The other side of ensuring that the needs of all students are met is the exceptional student. With the emphasis on heterogeneous grouping comes various worries. I have discussed at length how some students can be left behind. What about the students whose readiness to learn is already at a heightened level? Providing for students of varying abilities poses challenges for teachers. Offering differentiation of instruction is an acquired skill, requiring training in understanding student learning styles and helping students make appropriate choices that honor their abilities and offer challenges for growth. Some of the traditional ways teachers try to encourage students who progress more quickly are:

- grouping students in class so that different groups are given tasks of differing complexity (leveled reading groups are an example of this),
- providing extra credit work for students who finish assignments early, and
- sending students ahead to the next chapter.

All of these can be used effectively but carry with them some dangers. Leveled work can create differentiated expectations along with the differentiated tasks. Rewarding students who finish their work early by giving them more work is a recipe for encouraging capable students to drag their feet and avoid completion. Extra credit work can be effective, provided that the challenges deepen understanding of the concepts in the lesson and do not fall into the category of meaningless or tangential "neat activities," or become busywork that the teacher doesn't grade. Beyond the highly successful formal approach of "differentiated instruction" (Tomlinson, 1999, 2004), there are some simple ways to challenge students without singling them out or seeming to give them extra work. The following are some examples both from literacy and math/science investigations. These examples demonstrate how students of all abilities can productively engage in a well-thought-out activity, and students who are ready can be challenged to exceed the basic expectations of the activity.

Example 4.15

MC-CU#7

WHAT DOES PROVIDING OPPORTUNITIES TO EXCEED STANDARDS IN MATH AND SCIENCE LOOK LIKE?

Example A: Extending the Problem

A fifth-grade math teacher is working with students on patterns, with the ultimate goal of having them understand algebra as a language for expressing patterns in numbers and learn how algebraic expressions work. Students will be generating a rule that applies to a given pattern, which is presented to them both numerically and graphically. The problem involves a pattern of cubes that form a pattern of arches. The students see a diagram of six arches built by cubes and are provided with a table that indicates the number of arches and the total number of cubes required to build each amount of arches. Students are also provided with wooden cubes to build the arches if they wish. They are to determine the number of cubes in ten arches. Students work individually for about five minutes. They are then directed to share their work with a partner and come up with at least one way of solving the problem.

(Continued)

Students can solve the problem by:

- using the cubes to construct ten arches and counting the cubes, then noting that each time you made another arch, it took four cubes; or
- using the given table and noting that each arch adds four cubes, then adding four times until you will have used thirty-nine cubes.

As the teacher circulates, she challenges the students who have easily solved the problem in a matter of minutes to figure out how many cubes 100 arches will need. They do not have enough cubes to build those, nor are they eager to add four 100 times. She extends the problem by asking, "What if I asked how many cubes any number of arches (n) would take?" There are three possible algebraic expressions that represent the solution: cubes = $4n + 3$, cubes = $n + 3(n + 1)$, or cubes = $7 + 4(n - 1)$. Eventually, the teacher has these students compare the expressions to see that using the distributive law, these equations become the same. While all students are working on the same problem and most will arrive at the correct answer via some valid approach, those that are ready will be engaging in algebraic processes.

Example B: Offering a Task That Can Be Completed at Different Levels of Complexity

A tenth-grade biology teacher has assigned a lab that explores the relationship between heart rates and breathing rates. In addition, it requires students to consider a problem, develop a hypothesis, and design an experiment that will test that hypothesis. Students work in small groups to read an initial study that establishes a correlation between higher breathing rates and a faster pulse. They are directed to further explore this relationship. They are provided with the lab challenge as well as a sheet for individual responses to three constructed response questions that uncover understanding about the interplay between the circulatory and respiratory systems and various conditions requiring increased need for oxygenation of blood.

Students work in self-selected pairs, with the teacher monitoring the groups to ensure full participation. Students design experiments that reflect different levels of sophistication. Some replicate the experiment as it appears in the initial study; others add, manipulate, and control for variables including differences in sex, age (some students involve a paraprofessional in the class in the study), and length of time and intensity of exercise. The teacher circulates and checks that every group has posed a testable question of appropriate difficulty. If she feels that students have either made the task too complex or too simple, she uses probing questions to challenge them to rethink their choices.

Every student, including those receiving special education support, participate and produce an experiment based on a testable question, but advanced students have had the opportunity to deepen their experience by asking a more complex question and engaging in a challenging investigation.

Example 4.16

L-CU#7

WHAT DOES PROVIDING OPPORTUNITIES TO EXCEED STANDARDS IN LITERACY LOOK LIKE? (L-CU#7)

Example: The Same Assignment Is Approached From Differing Levels of Sophistication

A fifth-grade teacher is developing reading strategies in his students. The students are in groups created on the basis of which from among four books offered each student has chosen to read. Before literature discussions for the day begin, the teacher opens the literacy block with a new approach to the traditional book report. Each day, two or three students present a book that they have picked for their independent reading. They briefly introduce the book, but the presentation focuses on the challenges that the book gave them and the strategies they used to meet those challenges. Some examples are:

- The first student, described by the teacher as a "reluctant reader," is reading a book about a girl in an Islamic country. On the first page, the student encounters the word, *chador* which she has never seen before. Instead of interrupting her reading at that moment, she uses context clues to deduce that it refers to some article of clothing and continues with her reading. However, she marks the spot with a Post-It Note and makes a note to look up the word. When she has time, she goes to the Internet and finds not only the meaning of the word, but a picture as well. She proudly shows the picture of a full-body covering that Islamic women wear in public and explains it to the class.
- Another student, identified by the teacher as one of the top readers in the class, discusses a book that has an unusual format. Instead of the usual chapter following chapter, this book has interspersed poems or letters written by the characters in between the chapters. The student reports that at first this confused him. He originally skipped the first one, thinking that it wasn't part of the story and was unnecessary to read. As he encountered more of these as the narrative went on, he realized what they were and he had to go back to re-read the ones he had skipped.

This routine allows equal participation of every student, applying the same criteria in terms of the presentation of reading strategies, but providing student-chosen and teacher-guided differentiation in the choice of book and the complexity of strategies needed and used by the students. The second student has been able to tackle a challenging reading selection, while at the same time demonstrating to all students that even the best readers come up against difficulties that require them to go back and reread.

From Annenberg/CPB Math and Science Collection. 2002. *Teaching reading: A library of practices.* (Videotape). Burlington, VT.

The public imagination has been captured by the capacity of information technologies to centralize and organize large bodies of knowledge. What has not been fully understood is that computer-based technologies can be powerful pedagogical tools—not just rich sources of information, but also extensions of human capabilities and contexts for social interactions supporting learners . . . Like a textbook or any other cultural object, technology resources . . . function in a social environment, mediated by learning conversations with peers and teachers. (National Research Council, 2000, p. 230)

Box 4.17

Indicators T-CU#8, T-CU#9, T-CU#10, T-CU#11, and T-CU#12	
Indicators	**Examples of Evidence**
T-CU#8. Students exhibit positive attitudes or leadership in using technology to support learning	• Students mentor each other and troubleshoot with technology • Students take charge of their own learning and are able to make choices about when and how to use technology to support that learning • Students have backup plans in case of a problem with the technology
T-CU#9. All students are guaranteed equity of access and opportunities for learning through a wide variety of technologies regardless of gender, economics, race, first language, special education, ability, or learning style	• Gender inequities are recognized and addressed • Technologies support learning that is socially and culturally diverse • Special provisions are made to increase access for students who do not have access to technology at home • Assistive technology is used to enable all students to achieve the learning goals • Each computer has Internet access • Network access allows use of file and print services • Phone is available for outside communication • Internet response is rapid enough for viable use
T-CU#10. Appropriate technologies are present and available in the classroom in sufficient quantity	• Students and teachers have as-needed access to technology adequate in quantity and variety (computers, calculators, microscopes, probes, video, etc.), such as: equipment and software (simulations, word processing, spreadsheets, databases, modeling), tutorials and other support materials, assistive technologies for diverse learning needs, technology for administrative tasks, and communication tools (i.e., telephone, fax)
T-CU#11. Physical layout of technology makes the resources accessible and supports learning for all students	• Equipment is easy and safe to use and in good repair • Equipment and resources are arranged so that teacher can easily monitor and guide the use of technology • Students move freely in the classroom to access technology as needed • The layout and location of technology tools contribute to their regular use
T-CU#12. Students understand ethical and appropriate uses of technology	• Teachers model ethical use of technology • Students demonstrate ethical use of technology • Ongoing discussion of ethical use is evident • Students dialogue about uses of technology in daily life and the advantages, disadvantages, and responsibilities of those uses (from the International Society for Technology in Education)

There is a significant technology portion of the Classroom Culture section of DCO. Here, the technology indicators focus on student interaction, with students taking responsibility for their own learning, and equity of access, including sufficient numbers of computers or other technological tools and a classroom layout that makes access easy and routine. While we can never control the access to technology that students have in their homes, we can ensure that school affords every opportunity for students of all economic classes to learn the same skills and achieve the same comfort level to use, discuss, and navigate the world of technology. This will guarantee them equal access to the more attractive jobs of the future, which will certainly involve a facility with information technology.

This section also asks the observer to assess the attitudes toward technology (Are students excited about technology work? Do they help each other, and are they becoming comfortable troubleshooting when things don't go as planned?) and the degree to which the class is dealing with various ethical issues such as privacy, fact versus opinion, and plagiarism. Are students and teachers involved in discourse about the ethics involved? Do they examine examples of Web-based information to analyze and fact check them? Are student research products developed with Internet resources coupled with an oral presentation that requires

Example 4.18

T-CU#8 and T-CU#10

WHAT DOES EQUITY OF ACCESS LOOK LIKE? HOW DOES A TEACHER COMPENSATE FOR FEWER THAN NEEDED COMPUTERS?

A fourth-grade teacher is teaching a lesson on graphing. After reviewing what graphs are and how they are used, she directs the students to create a graph that indicates the relative popularity of consumer goods of their own interest. The students create a chart in their journals and begin polling their classmates about their preferences in foods, clothing, hobbies, and toys. When they are done, they are expected to feed their data into a spreadsheet and create a graph. There are only two computers in the classroom, and there is no lab for the students to go to, so the teacher creates math centers where students can continue to do math work while they await their turn at the computer. The two students at the computers help each other create their spreadsheets, which is obviously a newly acquired skill. There is a sense of excitement about all the different options, making every graph distinct.

It takes a while, but when all the students have completed their graphs, they gather around the computers, which are hooked up to a TV monitor so that all the students can see. Each student presents his or her graph, and the teacher leads a class discussion about what can be learned from looking at each graph.

While this is not the ideal classroom setup, the teacher has attempted to make up for the fewer than desired numbers of computers in a few ways. First, she has managed within the class period to make sure that every student gets a turn. Next, she has provided for meaningful math projects for those who are not on the computer. Finally, she uses a large monitor so that all students may share in the processing of the learning.

From the Southwest Educational Development Laboratory (2000).

Example 4.19

T-CU#9

HOW DO SMALL, RURAL SCHOOLS ACCESS EQUAL LEARNING OPPORTUNITIES THROUGH TECHNOLOGY?

We are used to thinking about information technology as computers and nothing more. Small, rural schools, such as those in Vermont, struggle with affording sufficient numbers of computers, high-speed Internet access, and specialists who can assist and train teachers to use technology efficiently.

Through an innovation called the Interactive Learning Network (ILN) and a complex set of grants, Vermont Institutes, a professional development organization, was able to provide the technology to virtually every high school in the state to access a statewide audiovisual network that allowed schools to move ahead on several levels. The opportunities available through the ILN included:

- making advanced placement and other low-enrollment courses available to all students,
- providing professional development opportunities to teachers and administrators in remote areas who would otherwise be unable to travel to them, and
- allowing students to interact with others across the state in special events or projects.

From programs and services of Vermont Institutes.

Box 4.20

Good Classroom Culture Ideas That Go Bad (T-CU#8, T-CU#9, T-CU#10, T-CU#11, and T-CU#12)

The idea: Technology should be integrated into the curriculum.
The inclusion of technology as a matter of course in all areas of instruction:

- creates a positive attitude about technology in students,
- provides access to resources to all students, even those who do not have a computer at home, and
- makes students adept at and aware of emerging technologies.

HAS IT GONE BAD?

- Do the computers have their dust covers on, or are they positioned behind the teacher's desk or some shelves? If so, they might as well not be there.
- Are computers used primarily as a reward for finishing work early? In that case, only the quick students ever get to use them. Those who work more slowly may never get an opportunity.
- Is use of the computers restricted to canned computer software that drills isolated skills, perhaps in a game format, with no accountability for work completed or skills mastered?
- Are groups assigned to a single computer so that clusters of students gather around with only one student having his or her hands on the controls? If this happens, even in pairs, those not touching the computer are not building their skills and may even be having their confidence diminished.

answers to questions about the methods of research as well as probing questions of the content to ensure that the student has actually thought through the information and is presenting his or her own conclusions about it? Schools should have technology policies as part of their student and faculty handbooks, and principals should be encouraging and overseeing the effective and appropriate use of technology by every teacher.

APPLYING THE CLASSROOM CULTURE CRITERIA

Method 1: General Discussion Questions

Whether your administrative team or supervisory support group has decided to conduct co-observations or present observations that you have done separately, choose a period of time during the observation when you focus on the Classroom Culture criteria.

1. Take time to look around the room, and note the arrangement of the desks and note who was sitting where. Did the configuration maximize the participation of all students?

2. What accommodations were made for students of differing ability?

3. How did the teacher interact with the students? Who did most of the talking? Did the teacher monitor the activity of student groups to ensure participation of all?

4. How did the students interact with each other? Did every student have an audience for his or her ideas? Were groups inclusive or exclusive? Was each student placed in a group that maximized participation?

5. Was the climate orderly but comfortable? Was there enthusiasm evident from both teacher and students? Was current student work displayed?

6. What was the role of technology in the lesson? Was there equal access and sufficient technology available?

Method 2: Focused Discussion Questions

With your administrative team or other appropriate group of peers, discuss the examples in Chapter 3 as well as the classrooms you have visited and consider the following:

1. (CU#1) Discuss the merits and effectiveness of various behavior management systems you have seen.

2. (CU#4) How is student work displayed and used in class? Is it mere decoration or is it indicative of active learning?

3. (CU#5, CU#6) Did the classroom feel respectful? Did the teacher model respectful interactions? Did the students seem comfortable in the class? Did

you see any evidence of students feeling intimidated or reticent about participating? If so, how was this dealt with?

4. (CU#7) Explore the idea of equity of access. How were students grouped? What patterns of inclusion were noted? Are there some habits that teachers might be unaware of that affected learning of one or more students?

Method 3: Scoring Culture

Using the scoring sheets from Chapter 7, analyze the examples in this chapter and come to consensus with your study group about what score you would give each lesson for selected indicators. Try applying the scoring criteria to examples presented in your group. Note the areas of agreement and disagreement, and explore what standards of equity are desirable in your setting.

CONCLUDING THOUGHTS ON EQUITY OF ACCESS

The environment in which students learn has been long understood as a significant factor in their learning. The Danielson (1986) Domain of Classroom Environment includes caring, respect, safety, peer interaction, pride, curiosity, and orderly routines for monitoring and dealing with student behavior. The outstanding differences offered by DCO are the issues of equity and technology. Achievement gaps exposed by national testing demand that we pay attention to the inequities of opportunity extended to students of underrepresented groups, whether they be based on race, ethnicity, language, or economic status. Technology, with its issues of equal access along with vigorous and appropriate use, has global implications in addition to practical, classroom-based ones. It is the hope that the Classroom Culture section of DCO builds positively on what has come before, enhancing the body of work by addressing more current concerns. While the general importance of the existing norms is reconfirmed in DCO, it is the hope that the bullets in the Examples section produce a more vivid picture of the specifics in classroom culture that will help ensure that each general indicator is operating to the fullest extent in our schools.

Chapter 5

Assessing Assessment

Much has been said and written about assessment and how good data impact student learning (Love, 2002; Reeves, 2006). Data come from many sources. The No Child Left Behind Act guarantees yearly data from mandatory, large-scale testing. To avoid momentous decisions that rest on a single test score, many districts choose additional assessments that may be norm-referenced, comparative data or criterion-referenced, standards-based data. These assessments, which provide districtwide data, are an important part of decisions about programs for students, professional development for teachers, and other work aimed at improving student performance. Used thoughtfully, large-scale assessments can point the way to changes that make a significant impact, but they are certainly not the whole picture.

The formative assessment that is classroom based, gives ongoing information about students' developing understanding, and guides teachers' instructional choices has also been much heralded (Ainsworth & Viegut, 2006; Black, Harrison, Lee, Marshall, & Wiliam, 2003). This has now become a routine element and a lovely new buzzword that has become part of the veneer of best practices. If a principal can contribute only one improvement to instructional practice, research suggests that effective classroom formative assessment may have the single most powerful impact, being a key element that has been consistently linked to higher student achievement. But how does a classroom observer know when good assessment is happening? Furthermore, if it isn't, how do you recognize and challenge poor assessment practices? Diagnostic Classroom Observation (DCO) offers some guidelines for assessing the assessment used by teachers daily and weekly in their classrooms.

Assessment means different things to different people. For the purposes of this discussion, let me make it clear what I mean by "assessment." Assessment is a task that distinguishes between those who have an identified skill, piece of knowledge, or conceptual understanding and those who do not. A *valid* assessment is one in which *all* students who have that skill or knowledge can complete the task and *only* those students having that skill or knowledge can complete the task. In addition, *all* students who do have that skill or knowledge *cannot* get a question wrong due to other interfering factors. In other words, trick questions may be popular with some teachers, but they do not make for valid testing information. To build a valid assessment, you must have a clear idea of what you are assessing or looking for and identify the "critical evidence" of that skill or conceptual understanding (evidence that convinces you that the student has the targeted skill). The challenge is to create a task that *cannot* be performed or completed without the particular knowledge or skill being assessed.

True formative assessment is an intentional strategy devised by teachers to monitor and track the ongoing progress of each student in the acquisition of an identified skill, piece of knowledge, or conceptual understanding *and* that is used to inform instruction. Formative assessment is used in classrooms while teaching a unit to track the developing understanding of students. Good formative assessments uncover students' misconceptions, not just their ability to follow procedures. Many teacher-given tests and quizzes are used for grading purposes. They can be the cause of satisfaction, relief, or hand-wringing as teachers consider their results. Teachers may call these formative assessments, but unless they are used to adapt instruction and impact student understanding, they are not formative.

Standards-based assessment adds the emphasis to focus on specific concepts. The constructed response format with a good scoring guide allows you to diagnose exactly where the understandings have gone awry and track the data on your students. Here the key is that the assessment is focused specifically on a specific piece of knowledge or understanding as articulated in a state or national standard.

Summative assessment, the kind that you are more likely to find happening on a regular basis in schools, either comes at the end of a unit as a final test or project or along the way in the form of a quiz. The key difference is that it is used more as a grade and less as a method of diagnosing students' misconceptions for the purpose of correcting them before moving the students on. To sum up the differences between the three: "Formative assessment is when the chef tastes the soup; summative assessment is when the customer tastes the soup" (Hopkins, as cited in Budge, 2005; Black & Wiliam, 1998). "Summative assessment is when the customer tastes the soup. Standards-based assessment is when you follow the recipe (the standards) to make the soup" (Saginor, 2006a). This chapter will give multiple examples varying in subject matter and grade level of standards-based assessments with guidelines on how to develop and score them.

Box 5.1

Indicators MS-CO#3 and L-CO#3	
Indicator	**Examples of Evidence**
MS-CO#3. Teacher collects and assesses evidence of student progress to enhance teaching and learning	• Assessment is systematic and ongoing so that teacher can track student progress and adjust instruction • Students' misconceptions are identified so that they can adjust their thinking • Agreed-on standards are used to judge the quality of student products and performances • Assessments are varied (journals, performance tasks, presentations, tests) and target concepts *and* skills • Students self-assess by using rubrics or reviewing past work to see their progress • Assessments clearly indicate conceptual closure

Indicator	Examples of Evidence
L-CO#3. Teacher collects and assesses evidence of student progress to enhance teaching and learning	• Assessment is systematic and ongoing so that teacher can track student progress and adapt instruction • Clear criteria are used to judge student work • Students' misconceptions are identified through formative assessment so that they can adjust their thinking • Assessments clearly target concepts *and* skills • Assessments are varied in the kind of tasks required • Teacher gives oral and written feedback • Assessments test spelling and vocabulary with an emphasis on context • Teacher guides students to focus on criteria or rubrics to edit writing for final copy • There is evidence that teacher conducts both informal and scheduled reading and writing conferences that are focused and positive • Assessments clearly indicate conceptual closure

The assessment boxes of DCO try to help you distinguish first if what you are seeing qualifies as assessment. Much of what passes as assessment in the minds of teachers does not actually assess anything of real value (more about that in the "good ideas gone wrong" department!). Let's take a close look at the bulleted examples of evidence that help define exactly what elements need to be present for a quality assessment approach that enhances instruction and solidifies learning.

THE BULLETS: CHARACTERISTICS OF GOOD ASSESSMENT

Systematic

To avoid the mere "assessment by wandering around," one must be systematic about assessing. Assessment means more than checking to make sure students are on task, understand their assignment, and are not stuck. These must be done as well and can certainly be achieved simultaneously with actual assessment. However, while circulating around the room is a way in which some kinds of assessment can take place, a few elements are necessary to qualify this activity as assessment. First, the teacher must have a clear sense of what he or she is looking for. Next, the teacher must have a method of tracking where students are in relation to the skill or knowledge being assessed. There are many convenient strategies for doing this. One suggested way of looking at student progress during a task is to apply this simple rubric and give each student a score for the work being evaluated. A clipboard and a simple notation as to what the task, standard, or skill or understanding in question are all that is necessary. Students should be familiar with this rubric and may be asked at times to score themselves along with a reflection as to the rationale for their score.

Box 5.2

Systematic Assessment Rubric				
1	**2**	**3**	**4**	**5**
Unable to do task	Has some rudimentary elements of understanding and can do parts of task with much teacher direction	Can do task with some teacher prompting and direction	Can do task independently and consistently	Does task independently and consistently *and* makes extensions or connections

Some teachers like to have this information on a separate page in their grade book labeled "formative assessments," "class participation," or "classwork." These scores, when looked at over the span of a marking period, can give much information (and documentation for parents and students) about individual student progress. They can also inform the teacher as to the effectiveness of instruction. If too many students are unable to independently complete tasks, there needs to be some recalculation on the part of the teacher. Is the task too complex? Have there been enough activities to develop the needed understanding or skill? Do the activities need to be rethought altogether? If this becomes part of your supervisory practice, it opens the possibility for these questions to be considered collaboratively in a post-conference setting.

Another simple method uses "exit notes" that students hand to teachers on the way out of the class either answering a simple but central question about the day's work or indicating what they learned today and what questions they still have. Also helpful in math classes or in cases in which short answers are required is the use of erasable white boards on which students write answers to questions and hold them up. Teachers can note who is having difficulty and can easily call on a student with the right answer. This alternative to the typical question-and-answer format requires that everyone do the thinking, not just the students with their hands raised. Also, it avoids the embarrassment of calling on a student who will give the wrong answer while at the same time allowing the teacher to keep track of who those students are and what their misconceptions might be. You might even discover a teachable moment when a wrong answer that surprises you directs you to a line of clarification that you had not thought of.

A common classroom practice is the "warm-up," or the quick exercise at the beginning of a class to get the students working right away. These may be quick, skill-based tasks such as a few arithmetic examples or a sentence or two from Daily Oral Language (Byers, 2001). These are handy lesson-opening devices, provide reinforcement for basic skills, and help the teacher track who is still struggling with fundamentals. They are not, however, to be confused with a well-rounded formative assessment approach. Equally important to checking and rechecking basic skills is the attention to underlying concepts. It is this part of student learning that frequently goes unassessed and may be at the root of student failures in the long run. Ability to perform basic skills tasks, while important, does not guarantee enduring understanding. Further on in this chapter, I will discuss how to use the Rigor/Relevance Framework (Daggett, 1995) to ensure that formative assessment goes deeper than the basic skills quiz or warm-up.

Ongoing

As you can see, there are varied ways of turning normal classroom activities into systematic formative assessment. The important thing to take away from this is that these strategies should be part of daily routines in every teacher's class. The data that you gather as you look in a systematic way at learning during the time it is actually taking place give you great power to affect the quality of the final product *before it disappoints you*. Frequently, when conducting observations, we will see no evidence of assessment at all. That may be because we tend not to observe when teachers are giving tests or quizzes. However, as you can see, assessment encompasses more than simple testing. When it is part of the instructional repertoire, there is no need for teachers to feel that they are being pressured to constantly assess and thereby have less time to teach.

Help Students Adjust Their Thinking

When a test has been given, graded, and gone over, it is done and frequently tossed away by students (unless there is an expectation to maintain a portfolio, notebook, or journal). Going over a test is rarely helpful in getting students to readjust their thinking. Some students will listen carefully to discover their mistakes so they will not repeat them, but students who have done well already know it, and students who did poorly can be demoralized and may tune out the explanations. Formative assessment techniques that have been described previously are less threatening than a test or quiz returned with a grade assigned. Feedback given in less formal ways has a real chance of helping students reconsider their trains of thought and make adjustments, and it has the advantage of being given at the time that ideas about the topic are being formed. There are multiple possibilities for reviewing assessments meant to instruct more than grade. Students can work in pairs to compare answers and attempt to come to consensus on solutions, which they then present along with their rationale to the class. Or they can peer-edit written pieces either before or after the teacher has reviewed them. The goal of going over student work, whether a quiz, test, or other product, is to have students reconsider their work and learn from the experience.

Help Teachers Adapt Their Instruction

How many times have teachers given tests or quizzes at the end of a week or a unit, only to be devastated by the number of low grades received? Do they reteach the unit, or do they move on? What should they do differently next year? What about this year? They have students in their class who didn't get what was so carefully planned for them. Tests can tell what the students know. Good tests can even tell what specific misconceptions they have, but the information comes too late to make a difference. Ongoing and systematic formative assessment gives teachers the information they need when they need it so they can rethink their plans if things seem to be going awry. They can stick with the students who are struggling and challenge those who are moving ahead. In the end, everyone learns more.

Clear Criteria are Used

Rubrics have become a staple of classroom assessment. Some are overly complex, while others include levels of achievement that are tangential to the core understandings of the standard. Grades are more traditional, but still account for much of the evaluation of students that takes place in our schools. Some feel that grades are more precise and rubrics too subjective. Others like rubrics because they are descriptive and see grades as too arbitrary. What is missing in all this is the essential question, "What is it you are trying to assess?" Without honing in on what piece of knowledge or understanding you are trying to evaluate, any form of assessment can lack trustworthiness. Without a clear understanding of what you are looking for, students are left uncertain and are unable to assess their own progress.

The standards movement has done much to help by defining the target knowledge and describing what it looks like when a student has achieved it. Still, there is a sloppiness in teacher-made tests that undermines the resulting data. In the last section, I will present an exercise you can use to explore how standards can focus assessments squarely on the knowledge and skills you desire. A clear articulation of exactly what you are looking for and a public and consistently applied set of criteria will not only help you arrive at a fair and helpful grade, but help students know what they have to do to get where they need to go.

Demonstrate Conceptual Closure at the End Point of a Unit

When your target learning is clearly articulated, what the student should know and be able to do is defined. This is when summative assessment becomes important. Accuracy demands that you ensure that the assessment actually measures the desired skill and that it fulfills the definition of validity (*all* students who have that skill or knowledge can complete the task and *only* those students having that skill or knowledge can complete the task). No one sets out to create an invalid test, yet many classroom tests do not test what they set out to. There are many reasons for this. To construct valid standards-based assessments, take some time to consider the task you have developed and ask yourself the following questions:

- Does it correspond to an appropriate standard? Does it target a specific concept? Does it look for concept development in students, or just correct answers?
- Does the task require that the skill you are looking for must be used? (Can students who don't get the concept complete the task by using some other skill? Can students who do get the concept get the task wrong due to unintended distractions in the question?)
- Does it give guidelines for what a good "got it" response would look like so that you are consistent in what you are looking for and students are clear as to what their work needs to include?

CHOOSING THE RIGHT ASSESSMENT FOR WHAT YOU WANT TO KNOW

Assessments come in multiple forms, all of them serving a particular purpose. Before assessing, it is important to know what you want to know about student understanding. The first step is defining for yourself and your students exactly what that is. Using the Rigor/Relevance Framework (Daggett, 1995) can help ensure the use of multiple assessment measures. Throughout a course, one should take care to assess in all four quadrants. What does this look like?

Quadrant A: Acquisition

- Student learns an algorithm in math and does ten problems using that algorithm.
- Student learns the process of photosynthesis and takes a quiz on the steps involved.
- Student learns the facts about the Civil War and answers questions about the events, major personalities involved, and the results.
- Student learns musical notation to read or write specific notes on a piece of sheet music.

Quadrant A is best tested by selected response items (fill-in, multiple-choice, matching).

Quadrant B: Application

- Student uses the algorithm in various types of examples and in solving problems that use that algorithm.
- Student fills out a flowchart demonstrating the cycle of photosynthesis and sets up an ecosystem on paper that allows the process to successfully take place.
- Student writes an essay about the causes of the Civil War that includes making connections to the novel *Uncle Tom's Cabin.*
- Student plays a tune or sings a song by reading music that he or she has never seen before.

Quadrant B is best tested by essay-style items and simple performance tasks.

Quadrant C: Assimilation

- Student takes the algorithm in math and does complex word problems in which the algorithm can be useful.
- Student learns the process of photosynthesis and describes how the process would be disrupted if one of the steps were to be prevented (i.e., lack of light, lack of oxygen).
- Student is asked to liken our Civil War to current events in answering the question, "Is there a civil war happening now in Iraq?"
- Student reads complex pieces of music.

Quadrant C is best tested by constructed response items.

Quadrant D: Adaptation

- Student engages in an inquiry in which an algorithm for solving certain problems is generated.
- Student designs and carries out an experiment that answers a testable question involving photosynthesis.
- Student constructs a plausible scenario that could have avoided a civil war while still solving the problem of slavery in our country.
- Student writes an original piece of music and plays it.

Quadrant D is best tested by performance tasks or combinations of constructed response and performance tasks.

The examples in Box 5.3 demonstrate how to decide which form of assessment to use based on what you want to know about student understanding. They illustrate how the different quadrants are accessed by reaching into the four quadrants and giving students the opportunity to engage on all four levels of abstraction and application. The examples use two essential understandings: knowledge of photosynthesis and understanding of the Civil War. These examples can be adapted for different grade levels and used to extrapolate to other content areas.

Box 5.3

Examples of Assessments Across the Rigor/Relevance Framework (Daggett, 1995, p. 16)

SELECTED RESPONSE (MULTIPLE-CHOICE, FILL-IN, MATCHING, TRUE/FALSE)

1. tests recall, association, and connection of facts

2. usually uses points to indicate level of success

3. is primarily Quadrant A

What Do Selected Response Questions Tell You About Student Understanding?

- Can students name the processes involved in photosynthesis?
- Can students identify three main causes of the Civil War from a given set of possible responses?

SYSTEMATIC OBSERVATION (INFORMAL FORMATIVE ASSESSMENT, ORAL QUESTIONING, PROBING, OBSERVING, AND LISTENING TO STUDENTS):

1. assesses process, monitors conceptual understanding

2. uses checklists, narrative notes, recorded observations

3. depending on the task, can be in any and all quadrants

What Does Systematic Observation Tell You About Student Understanding?

- Are students building their understanding of photosynthesis through classroom work and activities?
- Can students discuss the issues involved in the Civil War as they work on a project involving an analysis of the social system of the United States at that time?

CONSTRUCTED RESPONSE (ESSAYS, EXPLANATIONS, DIAGRAMS, TABLES, GRAPHS, MODELS)

1. tests conceptual understanding as well as appreciation for process

2. uses "key elements" to identify level of success

3. takes knowledge from Quadrant A and can reach into both B and C

What Do Constructed Response Items Tell You About Student Understanding?

- Can students explain photosynthesis in the context of the interdependence of living organisms? Can students demonstrate understanding of photosynthesis via diagrams or models?
- Can students explain the issues central to the Civil War from the point of view of a southern plantation owner? A runaway slave? An abolitionist?

PERFORMANCE ASSESSMENT (TASKS, PROJECTS, SIMULATIONS, REPORTS, PRESENTATIONS)

1. tests conceptual understanding, connections, process

2. uses rubrics to communicate level of success

3. can be just Quadrants B and D, but when done with a carefully constructed rubric, can reach all four quadrants (see the following examples)

What Does Performance Assessment Tell You About Student Understanding?

- Can students apply their understanding of the process of photosynthesis by setting up a controlled environment where living organisms support and sustain themselves and each other?
- Can students apply their understanding of the Civil War by creating a diary of the time from the point of view of someone impacted by the war? Can students debate the issues from the point of the North and the South?
- Demonstrate conceptual closure at the end point of a unit

CREATING VALID CONSTRUCTED RESPONSE ITEMS

Because constructed response items are a highly effective way to probe student understanding while you are still in the process of teaching, and because a good constructed response is not so easy to create, it is worth taking a closer look at how to build a valid and useful constructed response. Wonderful sources of constructed response items in science and mathematics are *Uncovering Students' Ideas In Science: 25 Formative Assessment Probes* (Keeley, 2004) and *Uncovering Student Thinking in Mathematics: 25 Formative Assessment Probes* (Rose, Minton, & Arline, 2006). Along with the assessments, you will find guidance in the analysis of student responses to better understand and be able to correct common student misconceptions.

There are many ways to build good assessments. Here is one step-by-step method that is useful in developing your test creation skills.

1. Select a standard that is *essential* for the understanding of your content area.

   Example: Students demonstrate their understanding of the properties of a gas by using real-world examples (tires, balloons, soda) to predict and explain the effect that a change in one variable (pressure, temperature, or volume) will have on the others.

2. Create a multistep question that allows access to most students and builds on the concept, allowing students to demonstrate their depth of understanding.

   Example (used with permission of the Vermont Institutes for Science, Math, and Technology):

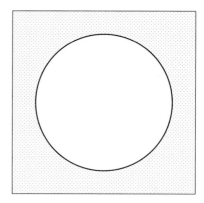

A. Hot air balloons are called "lighter than air." Is the hot air inside the balloon lighter in weight than an equal amount (volume) of air outside? Why or why not?

B. Students have been playing with a fully inflated beach ball and then leave it outdoors overnight. In the morning, the ball is soft. Assuming that no air leaked out, what happened?

C. Here is a hot air balloon and a simulation of the air molecules outside of the balloon. Place the dots in the balloon that represent the air molecules inside of the balloon when it is rising.

3. Develop a scoring guide that identifies the key elements of a correct answer, assigns points to those elements, and sets a cut-point for how many key elements or points are needed to indicate adequate conceptual understanding.

Key elements (any answer indicating the following understanding; need five points to pass):

A. 1 point: No
   1 point: Heating does not affect the weight or amount of air molecules
   1 point: Heating affects the activity and distance between molecules

B. 1 point: While the warmer air molecules moved more quickly and were more spread out, they exerted more pressure on the inside of the ball.
   1 point: The air inside the ball cooled. Cooler air molecules move less quickly and are closer together, exerting less pressure on the ball.

C. 2 points: Dots inside the balloon are evenly spread, but more dispersed than the ones in the box.

How can you tell if you have developed a valid assessment? The following are examples of assessments done right and some with good intentions that have gone wrong. These examples come from varied content areas and grade levels. All of them come from the real world of classrooms.

Box 5.4A

Example 1: Carrying out a Science Performance Assessment

STANDARDS

- Develop a testable question appropriate to the scientific domain being investigated.
- Write a plan related to the question and prediction that includes a procedure listing significant steps sequentially and that describes which variable will be manipulated or changed and which variables will remain the same ("fair test").

Activity: Students are investigating forces and motion by rolling vehicles down a ramp.

Task: Choose a variable to investigate, formulate a hypothesis (testable question), and design and carry out an experiment that will test that question.

Doing the assessment: Teacher circulates around the room with a clipboard and visits each group, asking students what variable they are investigating and what their hypothesis is.

1. Teacher notes if:
   - an appropriate variable has been chosen
   - the hypothesis proposed is a testable question

2. If those two conditions are met, teacher moves on to next group. If not, teacher probes thinking, asks questions, or poses a problem that pushes students through their misunderstanding to a better plan. In either case, teacher records results.

3. If, after stopping at a few groups, teacher discovers that most groups are struggling with this task, class is called back together, and together they review what a testable question is and how to design a fair test for that question.

What Do You Have After Having Conducted This Process?

- a record of who was able to do the task correctly at the outset,
- a record of who was struggling and the specific issues that they were struggling with,
- a plan that possibly addresses problems before students hands in a "failing" lab report, and
- a higher level of student success.

What Have You Lost Conducting This Process?

- Time? No, because you were having the students doing the task anyway.
- Ability to "sort" students by ability? No, because you have a record of what students were doing well without additional instruction.
- Ability to differentiate instruction? No, because those who were not struggling can move ahead while you conduct the additional mini-lesson on testable questions and fair tests.

How Does This Differ From a Final Lab Report as an Assessment?

- It centers on a physics concept, but requires each student to grapple with the variables that might be coming into play.
- Each group's report will be different, as they will have chosen different variables and created their own fair test.
- Students are more likely to own what they have learned because of the choices they have had to make and the thinking that those choices required.

Box 5.4B

Example 2: A Math Constructed Response

Example #2: A math "constructed response." (Grade level can vary from 5 all the way to beginning algebra depending on focus of lesson)

Standard: *Identify and extend to specific cases a variety of patterns (linear and nonlinear) represented in models, tables, or sequences; and writes a rule in words or symbols to find the next case.*

<u>**Task:**</u>

If it takes 7 blocks to build one arch, how many will it take to build 10 arches? 100 arches? *n* arches?

Arches	Blocks
1	7
2	11
3	15
10	?

Write a rule that expresses how you would figure this out for *n* arches. Demonstrate and explain your solution.

<u>Algebraic solution:</u> $4n+3$
<u>Numeric solution:</u> 10 arches = 43 blocks; 100 arches = 403 blocks

<u>Graphic solution:</u>

<u>Explanation:</u> After the first arch, each additional arch takes 4 more blocks. To get the total blocks, multiply 4 times the number of arches you want and add the three at the end that were part of the original 7.

What is the difference between being asked to solve a problem and solve and demonstrate or explain how you did it?

Students are more likely to understand what they are doing when they are in the habit of having to explain their thinking. There are some possible correct variations in the above answer, including algebraic equations that look at *first glance* somewhat different from the one given. They ultimately simplify to the same answer but they demonstrate a different thinking process that leads to the same correct answers. Consider one possible alternate set of answers:

<u>Algebraic solution:</u> $n + 3(n+1)$

<u>Explanation:</u> I let *n* equal the number of arches which was the same as the number of single blocks on top of the columns. Each column had three blocks, but there was one more column than arches, otherwise the last arch would have fallen down.

<u>**Scoring guide**</u>

Key elements: 1 point for algebraic equation that works
                        1 point for correct numerical answer
                        1 point for appropriate graphic representation
                        2 points for sound reasoning that supports algebraic solution

(4 points needed to pass)

Box 5.5

Example 3: Analyzing Literary Text

An extended constructed response is applicable to any grade level depending on the text read and level of guidance provided by teacher.

Standard: Analyze and interpret elements of literary texts by describing characters' physical characteristics, personality traits, or interactions, or by providing examples of thoughts, words, or actions that reveal characters' personality traits, their changes over time, or possible motives.

Task:

1. Using a graphic organizer, describe the main character's:
   o physical characteristics (give at least three)
   o personality traits (give at least two)
   o possible motives for actions (give at least one)

2. Identify excerpts from the text that support each of your statements.

3. Make a prediction based on one of the characteristics, traits, or motives that you have selected, and describe why you think it will happen.

4. Using notes from your graphic organizer, write an essay about your impressions of the character and what you think will happen to that character at the end of the story.

This task demonstrates the combining of a formative assessment, such as the use of a graphic organizer, and a constructed response, which can be formative during the drafting and editing phases and summative in final draft.

Scoring Guide:

Key Elements

Part 1

3 points	Three distinct physical characteristics named (extra points for additional characteristics)
2 points	Two adjectives appropriately describing character (extra points for additional adjectives)
1 point	One reasonable motive (extra point per motive)

Part 2

1 point	Per excerpt that correctly correlates to each statement

Part 3

2 points	Reasonable prediction with rationale

Part 4

10 points	Use "response to writing" rubric to determine points (elements of language mechanics, organization, and relevance of observations)

Box 5.6

Assessments That Miss the Mark

ASSESSING THE WRONG SKILL

An eighth-grade math teacher is teaching a unit on angles. He wants the students to understand that adjacent angles on a straight line, called supplementary angles, add up to 180 degrees. Knowing this will help them solve problems involving congruence and similarity later in the unit. He gives a quiz with twenty examples in it. At the top of the quiz, he provides the term *supplementary* along with the definition. Each item asks the students to find the supplement of a given angle. Many students pass the test; a handful of students fail it. The teacher is relatively pleased.

If you look at what the students needed to really know to pass the quiz, you find that all who could read the definition and accurately compute angles that add up to 180 degrees passed. The students who failed made arithmetic errors or forgot the formula and neglected to read the definition at the top of the page. The teacher has assessed the following of directions and simple addition and subtraction.

STUDENTS WHO HAVEN'T MASTERED ANY SKILLS DO WELL ON THE ASSESSMENT

A third-grade teacher is doing a unit on habitats of mammals. As part of state standards, students are expected to demonstrate their understanding of equilibrium in an ecosystem by explaining how one organism depends on another to survive, by experimenting with a closed ecosystem, and by describing how an environmental change affects the system.

As an instructional activity, each student is assigned a mammal about which they must conduct some research and prepare a poster to present to the class. The rubric for the presentation notes the following criteria:

- organization and neatness
- appropriate illustrations
- correct spelling
- accurate information
- oral presentation with good eye contact and voice

Note that it would be possible for a student to do a lovely and accurate presentation on bears, where they live, what they eat, and how they care for their young without understanding the bigger ideas about why they live where they do and what would happen if their food source was depleted, not just to the bears but to other species with which they interact.

STUDENTS WHO HAVE THE SKILL DO NOT PASS FOR THE WRONG REASONS

A tenth-grade social studies teacher is giving a unit test on immigration to America in the late nineteenth and early twentieth centuries. The students have had many discussions, done family trees of students in the class, learned about Ellis Island by exploring its site on the Internet, and read the chapter in their book. The test contains many multiple-choice questions, one matching question, several fill-ins, and one essay.

One of the more successful students in the class did more poorly than expected. On examination of his paper, the teacher discovers that he lost many points on the matching question because he chose the first response incorrectly. That resulted in several forced errors. On a few of the multiple-choice questions, the student fell into some of the traps set by the "trick questions" that the teacher was so proud of having written. On a few of the fill-ins, the teacher noted that the questions might have been too open ended, thereby inviting off-target answers. The essay question was the only one that the student scored well on, indicating overall understanding of the issues involved in that period of our history.

"ASSESSMENT BY WANDERING AROUND" (THIS IS MUCH MORE PREVALENT THAN WE WOULD LIKE TO THINK!)

A sixth-grade class is exploring the equivalence of different fractions. They are playing a game in pairs designed to have them convert halves to fourths and eighths, thirds to sixths, and fifths to tenths. As they draw fraction cards and make their moves with chips, the teacher circulates. During the class period, the teacher can be seen looking over the shoulders of some students, just watching, correcting negative behavior, answering questions about the procedure (e.g., "Do you lose a turn if you don't have a move that will work?"), and questioning some students who have made an error until they correct it. They play until the lunch bell rings.

The teacher reports that she was informally assessing students throughout the period. Although every student has participated in the game, there is no "paper trail" as to the correctness of their moves. The teacher did not make notes about who was having difficulty with which fractions or who was able to make a more sophisticated move, although she might remember some of this information anecdotally. The students did not track their moves on paper, so there was nothing to collect. There was no debriefing at the end of the lesson, so that students could report their successful strategies and their challenges or listen to others' experiences. There was no closure about what was learned about fractions. The teacher moves on the next day to mixed numbers without having any substantive record about who understood what about simple fractions. She will give a big fractions test at the end of the unit and may find that her results are not what she would have hoped.

LEARNING TO ASSESS ASSESSMENT

What does all this mean for instruction? We know that what gets assessed gets taught and what gets assessed well gets taught well. As the teachers in your school get better at focusing their assessments squarely on what they want students to know and be able to do, they will find more and more students fulfilling those expectations. Therefore, it is well worth your time to integrate supervision of assessment into your supervisory practice. The following are several ways for you and your supervisory or administrative team to engage in some of the key concepts surrounding effective assessment practice.

Method 1: Matching Assessments With Instructional Strategies

Lesson design should be geared to the learning of identified outcomes, and assessments should target those outcomes in such a way as to reflect the resulting learning. This concept has been expressed as "backward design" (Wiggins & McTighe, 1998).

While we don't like to "teach to the test," we should be teaching to the desired outcomes or standards. In a bit of circular reasoning, if the assessment correctly embodies
those standards, then teaching to the test is no longer a liability but an asset. Boxes 5.7
and 5.8 illustrate differing choices of assessment depending on what it is you want to
test. With your supervisory team, consider the standards and assessments in Boxes 5.7
and 5.8. Discuss each example in light of which quadrants from the Rigor/Relevance
Framework (Daggett, 1995) you think it comes from. Which lessons and assessments
are most likely to guarantee the targeted understanding and why?

Box 5.7

Linking Lesson Design to Assessment: A Science Example

Intended Science Standard: Students will describe and show examples of the interdependence of
all systems that support life.

Instructional Strategy	Assessment
Activities-based: Students collect specimens from the woodlands near the school and make a terrarium.	• Students present their terrariums to the class, telling how and where they collected their specimens.
Content-based: Students study the woodland habitat near the school to discover the plants and animals that live there.	• Students write an essay on the woodland habitat, naming the plants and animals that live there and telling what each one needs from the ecosystem to survive.
Standards-based: Students do all of the above and, in addition, design experiments to see what would happen if some element in the ecosystem were to change.	• Students design an investigation of a woodland habitat that answers the question, "Who lives here and why?" They include an inventory and description of the species found and explain what each species contributes or extracts from that habitat. They choose one aspect of the ecosystem to suddenly change and observe and describe what happened to the ecosystem as a whole. • As a constructed response, for a given habitat, students explain what would happen if one specified aspect of the ecosystem were to suddenly change, and apply that concept to the extinction of a species.

Box 5.8

Linking Lesson Design to Assessment: A Social Studies Example

Intended Social Studies Standard: Students show understanding of various forms of government by
describing the basic principles of American democracy.

Instructional Strategy	Assessment
Activities-based: Students hold class elections, create campaigns, and practice concepts of free speech and majority rule, creating class rules that guarantee equal access and protection.	• Students conduct a campaign, elect officers, and create classroom rules.

Instructional Strategy	Assessment
Content-based: Students study the Bill of Rights and report on the protections that they guarantee.	• Students write an essay on the Bill of Rights, discussing the meaning of each article and the protections that each guarantee.
Standards-based: Students do all of the above and choose one of the basic rights guaranteed in the Bill of Rights to imagine what life would be like if we did not have that right.	• Students create an imaginary society that does not have protected rights of citizens and describe the life of its citizens. (I think George Orwell did that.) • Given a scenario in which the freedom of the press is no longer a protected right, students explain three examples of what you might expect to see happening in our country as a result.

Method 2: Co-observations

Conduct some co-observations with your peers, or share experiences from your individual observations. A walk-through will not be sufficient for this discussion. It is hard enough to collect observation data on teachers engaging in real assessment as it is; the chances that a walk-through will catch moments of assessment are slim. Consider the following:

1. Are you encountering actual examples of assessment as you conduct your observations?

2. What kinds of activities are the students engaging in that could be classified as assessment? Are they varied enough to span the four quadrants (Daggett, 1995)?

3. Discuss the specific assessments given during a class that you have observed.
   A. What exactly did the student need to know to correctly respond?
   B. Could the student get a good grade on the assessment without really mastering the target skill or understanding?
   C. Were there clear rubrics or scoring guides that the teacher established and students understood? Do the scoring guides give points for correct articulation of concepts, or are the points awarded only for presentation skills (neatness, clarity, good posters, etc.)?

4. What concerns about classroom assessment have been raised by your observations?

CONCLUDING THOUGHTS

You may enter a class to observe and be told by the teacher that he or she is not teaching today; the class is testing. Alternatively, in a postconference, when you ask a teacher about what forms of assessment he used, he may answer that he was teaching that day, not assessing. While there is obviously a need for assessment that comes after and stands separate from instruction, we must encourage the lines to blur more. A good assessment is a teaching tool, and continuous assessment is critical as students explore and formulate new ideas. The better we become at assessing, the better we become at teaching. For those of us responsible for the professional growth of our teachers, the better we become at assessing assessment, the more successful the teachers in our schools will be.

Chapter 6

Putting It All Together

Taken in its entirety, Diagnostic Classroom Observation sets a very high performance standard for teachers. No teacher is perfect, and any given single lesson is unlikely to be exemplary in every aspect. The problem is that the complete absence of any of these indicators can cause a failure to produce satisfactory student learning, particularly if the absence is endemic to a teacher's practice. This explains why a supervisor may leave a classroom observation with the suspicion that something was not right, but not being able to articulate exactly what it was. Diagnostic Classroom Observation defines the technology of good instruction and serves to identify all the necessary components, allowing an observer to pinpoint the source of the difficulty. Just as in good gardening, it all must come together for beautiful flowers to grow. The content is the seed, which must be sound to produce a healthy plant. Implementation is the skillful planting of the seed, setting it at the right depth with the just the right amount of water, sun, and soil. Culture is the fertile ground, which, when not properly prepared, cannot receive even the most carefully planted and robust seed.

This means that all teachers need to become accomplished in managing implementation, mastering the content, and generating a positive classroom culture. It may sound harsh, but research has firmly established how critical a highly qualified teacher is to student success (Darling-Hammond, 2000a, 2000b). The Education Commission of the States (2006) asserts that

> a growing body of evidence . . . confirms that, outside of home and family circumstances, teaching quality is the single most influential determinant of student academic success. In fact, studies show that, regardless of socioeconomic factors, students who have the most effective teachers make the greatest educational progress.

Our laws now require that teachers demonstrate that they are highly qualified. They do so by attaining the proper certifications. Diagnostic Classroom Observation provides a means for them to continue to grow in the classroom so that "highly qualified" becomes a reality, not just a notation on paper. It is not meant to set a bar too high to clear, nor is it to be used to criticize professionals for gaps in performance for the sake of finding fault. It is an honest attempt to analyze and diagnose those actions that bring us closer to the goals we seek and ferret out those that impede our progress. Chapter 7 will deal in depth with creating a partnership between teacher and supervisor with the common goal of producing the best learning for their students. Specific techniques for collaborative inquiry will help shift the balance from critical feedback to strategy sessions for maximum student impact. The following are three examples of why all of the areas must be functioning well to produce the results we need. A caveat: These are only examples. Although they are drawn from live classrooms, the vignettes do not pretend to capture the complexity of the teaching moments they describe. They do not make light of the highly professional effort involved in planning and pulling off any teaching and learning event. They only serve to point out the ways each of the criteria forms one leg of a tripod, which wobbles unless all three legs are equally stable.

EXAMPLES: WHY "PRETTY GOOD" IS NOT GOOD ENOUGH

Box 6.1

Example 1: Implementation + Content – Culture = Spotty Learning

WHAT HAPPENED?

A fifth-grade science class is about to take the batteries and bulbs challenge. The teacher has gathered the students on the rug to set the stage for the importance of understanding how electricity works with a K-W-L exercise on what they already know about electricity. She has kits awaiting each group of four or five students that will eventually help them accurately determine how to form simple, series, and parallel circuits. They seem to understand their task, answer her preliminary questions well, and go off to begin the task. Immediately, in almost every group, two students take charge and start handling the materials. The others stand around and watch. In one group, two confident girls are lighting bulbs with excitement and writing down answers for the group. Two others, a boy and girl, quietly sit and watch, saying nothing. Fifteen minutes into the activity, an English as a Second Language (ESL) teacher enters the room and sits with those students. It seems they are both newly arrived from Bosnia and had no language with which to insert themselves into the activity. They come alive as the ESL teacher hands them the materials, but in five minutes, the time is up and they have to put the kits away. In another group, two boys have drifted away from the table where two other boys are squabbling about how to proceed. They join up with some other excluded students and begin wandering and involving themselves in extraneous activities, such as washing their hands, going for a drink, looking in their backpacks, and so forth. The teacher works with one

---

(Continued)

(Continued)

group at a time, getting them to attend to the task for as long as she is with them. But she raises her head at increasingly smaller intervals to quiet the class down and sharply scolds several students. By the end of the period, at least three students have had to "change their color" by moving their clothespin from green to yellow or yellow to orange. No one has lost a recess, and only about half the students have actually completed the activity.

HOW CLASSROOM CULTURE ISSUES CAN COMPROMISE STUDENT LEARNING

The initial implementation is strong. Students are engaged in a good discussion using the K-W-L format. Sound content is evident in the preparation of good materials and creation of a task that, if done in earnest, will uncover the patterns of the various circuits.

What are some culture issues that have caused a problem?

- CU#1, CU#2, and CU#3
  The engagement of all students reduces greatly the need for discipline. Establishing a culture of inclusion and the sense of a learning community where the contribution of each student is expected and noticed is complex. However, when needed, behavior routines should be respectfully implemented and have a predictable consequence.

- CU#5 and CU#7
  The grouping did not maximize the participation of all students. Four or five students are too many for this activity. If materials are scarce, pairs of students—each accountable for completing the task—can share. The required contribution of all students is one way to demonstrate real respect for student ideas.

- CU#7
  If there are students with special needs, such as non-native language, learning challenges, or social issues, a plan should be in place at the outset to accommodate for them before they are lost to the activity.

Box 6.2

Example 2: Implementation + culture – content = the "neat activity syndrome"

WHAT HAPPENED?

A fourth-grade teacher is working with students on multiplication. They have learned their multiplication facts and are about to do an investigation into how patterns of numbers behave when they are either added to themselves or multiplied by themselves. The teacher introduces the task in which groups of students will use graph paper to chart two rows of three squares next to three rows of three squares all the way to two rows of ten squares and ten rows of ten squares. They are asked to compare the "products and sums" to see what patterns they notice.

In voice-overs on the tape of this lesson, the teacher acknowledges the importance of having the students communicate their math thinking to each other and to her. She is aware of the power of dialogue in teaching and learning, and the students are adept at getting into a group task and carefully listening to each other. Every student appears involved and the discourse demonstrates honest attempts to come to some important mathematical conclusions.

Some students note that the numbers multiplied by themselves produce squares (an important concept that we sometimes forget – ten squared means a *square* of ten by ten) and all the numbers added to themselves were even numbers (by definition, of course, because they are 'doubles'). Some even note the interesting pattern of progression as squared numbers increase by one. They present their patterns at the close of the class, but are not asked to explain their thinking. All patterns presented are welcomed with equal interest by the teacher, even though some demonstrate fuzzy thinking at best. The activity ends with a journal write in which students are asked to write about why they like looking for patterns.

From the Annenberg/CPB collection, 1996.

HOW CONTENT ISSUES CAN THWART DEVELOPMENT OF CONCEPTUAL UNDERSTANDING

Making a space for students to do an investigation and work in groups, then to reconvene to articulate and process their findings are good implementation strategies. A classroom culture in which students collaborate and build off each other's ideas and that includes everyone in the activity demonstrates respect for individual's ideas and habits of shared learning.

What are the content issues that have caused a problem?

- CO#2, #7
  The teacher has not nailed down what math concepts she is trying to teach. She has called the activity, "Products and Sums," but the patterns they are working with are 'doubles and squares.' It would be incorrect for students to come away thinking that sums are always even and always form a rectangle. Worse would be the misconception that products are always squares. The model used will leave them with that image, although 'squares' are very special products that have their own patterns of behavior. In the meantime, the opportunity to teach that numbers multiplied by themselves always form a square—key mathematical concept—has been lost.

- CO#3
  There will be no assessment of understanding of important math concepts, since none have been identified as noteworthy. The journal-write will only reflect student interest level—not unimportant, but not sufficient for learning of concepts.

From the Annenberg/CPB collection. (1996).

Box 6.3

Example 3: Content + Culture – Implementation = No Construction of Knowledge

WHAT HAPPENED?

A fourth-grade teacher is using a portfolio task in which students have to solve a problem involving the concept of perimeter and articulate their process and their conclusions. The teacher has led the way in her school for incorporating cooperative learning into everyday practice. Her students are used to community tasks and are sitting in groups of four, called teams. One special-education student sits with her team with a paraprofessional assigned to support her in her classroom.

(Continued)

(Continued)

The teacher introduces the task and hands out packets to each team's leader. Although they are sitting in groups, there is a packet for each student with a series of copied papers. They are to compare the perimeter of differently shaped spaces. Their understanding of the sides of various polygons is the key. The packets provide everything they need, even the charts for plotting their data and spaces to write about how they solved the problem and why it worked. She gives them about three minutes to look through the task and discuss it with their peers. Before much discussion takes place, she calls their attention to the board and walks them through the problem, demonstrating the algorithms for rectangles, squares, and trapezoids, and having them fill out the data charts together.

HOW IMPLEMENTATION ISSUES ECLIPSE STUDENT LEARNING

The teacher had established the collaborative culture of the classroom and the students had developed team habits, including taking assigned roles and sharing responsibility. The content of the math problem was appropriate to the grade and was designed to develop the skill of organizing data, preparing and using arrays, and analyzing data.

What are the implementation issues that have caused a problem?

- IM#1
  The teacher has overly controlled the mathematics that could be brought to bear on the problem by supplying the algorithm, the data display, and the conclusions to be drawn. This is a potential sign that she is either unsure of the mathematical possibilities or is not comfortable helping to untangle the mistakes that students might make. Or it may just be a sense that the most efficient way of solving the problem is the only one worth discussion. Other ways might just take them down unproductive roads. Or it might be that she is unsure of the students' ability to come up with the right answers. Regardless of the reason, efficiency is not the issue for portfolio problems; without the process, it's just an exercise.

- IM#2, IM#3, IM#4, and IM#6
  By truncating the student-to-student conversations, the teacher has missed the opportunity to truly engage the students, to probe and challenge their thinking, and to allow them to construct their own knowledge. The papers that the students turned in were all identical, even the explanations of reasoning. Not only will this make assessment meaningless, it deprives the teacher of the ability to discover students' misconceptions.

- IM#5
  The amount of time for discussion is insufficient for students to process the problem. The solution, and the only way of reaching the solution, comes to them quickly. The period ends when the team leader collects the papers and turns them in. There is no closure other than the teacher's completion of her explanation.

PUTTING IT TOGETHER FOR YOURSELVES

Method 1: Scoring the Examples in Chapter 6

Using the scoring sheets as described in Chapter 7 and found in Appendix F, analyze the examples in this chapter and come to consensus with your study group about your scores. In this chapter, you will be attempting to score the lessons on at least three indicators, one from each of the sections of criteria. Note areas of interplay and overlap of the criteria. Which areas generate the highest levels of agreement or disagreement? Can you think of teachers of whom you are reminded when you read these examples?

Method 2: Focused Questions

With your administrative team or other appropriate group of peers, consider the following:

1. (CU#1, CU#2, CU#3) Have you observed teachers whose major challenge seemed to be in establishing a positive classroom climate, perhaps struggling with student misbehaviors even though the lesson planned is otherwise sound?

2. (CO#1, CO#3) Share some examples of teachers who have clearly identified certain skills or standards in their preconferences or lesson plans, but who depend on catchy activities that may not produce the intended learning and who fail to sharpen their assessments to uncover that reality.

3. (IM#3) What happens when a teacher with strong content knowledge fails to engage students in meaningful activities? Share some ideas about how to get a "content-bound" teacher to let go a bit and try turning the learning over to the students.

4. (Composite version) Do you have any good examples of content-area teachers who have used the teaching of reading and writing to deepen learning of their subject areas?

Method 3: Observing Classrooms in a More Extended Visit

After having practiced short observations using one section at a time of the version of the tool that you are learning to use, try an observation of longer duration using the "cheat sheets" found in Appendix G, and discuss your co-observations or your presentations with your supervisory study group. Walk-throughs will not be sufficient to be able to accomplish the in-depth look that the entire tool requires. This time, focus your discussion on the observation process as you consider the following discussion questions.

DISCUSSION QUESTIONS

1. Did you find that observing the classroom instruction changed at all for you as a result of your reading? Were you looking for different things? Did you notice things you hadn't in the past?

2. How did you take notes while you were observing? Were the cheat sheets helpful in keeping you focused and reminding you what to look for?

3. Did you circulate during instruction? Did you engage in conversations with groups or individual students? What did those conversations reveal about student understanding?

4. What were the indicators and evidence that you as a supervisory group found most frequently lacking in the classrooms observed?

5. What were the indicators that you as a group found most skillfully implemented by the teachers you observed?

CONCLUDING THOUGHTS

This system has been called Diagnostic Classroom Observation for a reason. Because there are so many elements of good teaching, it can be overwhelming to visit a classroom and put your finger on what is going right and where the teacher needs to grow. The usefulness of this tool as a diagnostic instrument crystallized during the reliability phase of one of the national research studies in which it was employed. After having trained approximately thirty field researchers in its use, I had the opportunity to co-observe at least once with each of them. The purpose of the co-observations was maintaining interrater reliability and preventing experimenter "drift," which can occur over time. The co-observations kept each experimenter grounded in the indicators and evidence, mitigating the tendency through increasing familiarity with the contents of the system to move away from the scoring protocols and rely more on instinct. (This is a reason why occasional co-observations over time may be useful in your setting as well.)

During these co-observations, we were able, in our debriefing sessions, to pinpoint what was going right and where things were going awry. I was able to say to one observer in a classroom where large workgroups caused several students to languish while others completed the task, "Do you see why we favor pairs of students as opposed to larger groups?" Or in a classroom where a teacher used probing questions posed to each student as she circulated to spur enthusiasm and confidence as they approached a writing assignment that had some of them stumped at the outset, we were able to see how a circulating teacher could be more than a mere monitor. We saw classrooms where the lesson was interesting but excluded certain students by either physically isolating them or marginalizing them in subtle ways—things that may well have been overlooked in past observations. And we saw multiple examples of the neat activity syndrome, where busy students, sometimes mixed in with aimlessly wandering students, were completing tasks that would never be processed by the students or assessed by the teachers. Most distressing of all was how few accomplished uses of reading block time we saw. We saw all varieties of wasted time, meaningless activities, reading centers leading nowhere, and huge inequities in the quality of instruction offered to minority students. We also saw many exciting and reassuring occasions of well-honed lessons delivered in a climate of respect and mutual responsibility, which offered rich examples for many of the indicators. We were able to say, "Did you see how he made the activity available to every student?" or "Look how she got the students to articulate exactly what they had learned." It was so much more satisfying than saying, "That was a great lesson."

In the next chapter, we will explore how to use the information gathered by this in-depth method of observation to improve instruction, in classrooms where instruction is already rather accomplished as well as in those where there are many challenges. We will take a fresh look at old routines, including the preconferences and postconferences, so that they hold more promise for helping teachers reflect on their practice with a real willingness to grow. Approaches and tools will assist you in using this system, in its entirety or just its elements that most appeal to you, to enhance your supervisory practice.

Chapter 7

Using Diagnostic Classroom Observation to Improve Instruction in Your School

SECTION 1: LEARNING TO USE DCO

My experiences as a professional developer taught me that many wonderful ideas presented to educators at all manner of workshops, institutes, and courses had a tendency to die as the newly indoctrinated left the training, heading back to the routines and cultures of their home schools. I knew that fact well, even as I worked with a cadre of teacher leaders to craft an engaging and compelling two-day session to teach the earlier iterations of DCO. On occasion, colleagues months and years later would thank me for fundamentally changing the way they looked at instruction when they performed observations. But more frequently, I would meet with sheepish former participants who hadn't been able to implement the system. At first, I was puzzled. I had designed the sessions carefully using the "twelve principles for effective adult learning" (Vella, 2002), and the training sessions themselves had been successful. Most participants left with a good understanding of how to use the tool and had expressed enthusiasm about incorporating it into their practice. The sessions had all adhered pedagogically to the indicators of the tool itself and were debriefed so that participants would get a metacognitive sense of what we were doing at each step and why.

So, what was going wrong? My answer could be found in the Rigor/Relevance Framework (Daggett, 1995), which, ironically, had been part of the training sessions from the beginning to demonstrate why this new brand of teaching was so critical to student learning. The missing piece of our training was the *application*. A two-day, off-site workshop did not provide the participants the opportunity to see the process work in their own settings and then come back together to debrief about the experience. We had only included a cursory discussion of how to cope with the data from an observation with a teacher once it had been gathered.

During an opportunity I had to co-teach a course in *Lenses on Learning* (Grant et al., 2002) some time prior to its actual publication, I saw the critical need for application over time. Necessary too was the opportunity to engage with the concepts, go back to your school to try them out, and return several times to debrief and problem solve. Even this instruction over time had an uncertain impact on actual observation and supervision practice. I found that the maximum benefit would come only if I taught the course to groups of administrators or supervisors and mentors who were part of a school or district team. Random groups of school leaders who sign up for training do not have the luxury of discussing successes and challenges while they are occurring. This professional development initiative had to be in the context of a schoolwide or districtwide initiative and provide opportunities for those using the system to connect and continually process with each other. In addition, the impact was most powerful when it included a parallel plan for training teachers. My most successful ventures were those that included a superintendent or curriculum director, all the principals in the district, and any teacher leaders who would be responsible for mentoring their colleagues.

DCO in Your Setting

We have asked teachers to work collaboratively. Now the question arises, in the face of the lessons learned just described, how does one go about the deprivatization of supervisory practice and learn this system from this book? While a facilitator is always recommended, the key to mastering this approach is simple: Do not attempt this alone. This is work to be done with colleagues, following the guidelines for practice offered in Chapter 7 and sharing the results with your team. As we ask children to deprivatize their learning by working collaboratively, as we ask teachers to deprivatize their instructional practice by becoming members of teams, Critical Friends groups (National School Reform Faculty, 2000), or lesson study groups, so now I ask you to deprivatize your supervisory practice by fearlessly sharing it with your peers. Here are the steps that I suggest for doing this:

1. Do a book study with your group. Become familiar with the elements of DCO by reading this book, examining the examples of the indicators, and sharing stories from your own experiences with which these vignettes resonate. Notice the extent to which you all appear to be in agreement about the examples shared. Do not be afraid to challenge each other if there are discrepancies. It is only by coming to consensus in a district that a consistent approach to instruction can take place. We have allowed teachers to make the most important instructional decisions one by one for many years. It sounded democratic, but it has proven to not serve our students well. Inconsistencies in practice

have hurt our children as they bounce from year to year, teacher to teacher, and have vastly different pedagogical philosophies shape their learning. The same must not be allowed to continue from a supervisory level as well.

2. Come to common agreements. There has been a misunderstanding in the teaching field about how to attain consistency across classrooms, schools, and districts. Coming to common agreements about good pedagogical practice and providing equity of access to high-quality materials and technology is one thing. Lock-step adherence to an instructional program is not the same thing and does nothing, in my view, besides limiting gifted teachers in their attempts to produce better learning outcomes in students. While some instructional programs themselves do produce better results than others, any program in the hands of mediocre teachers will fail their students. It is more important to come to common agreements among teachers and administrators as to what good instruction looks like, and then to monitor instruction along with student results. DCO can help you to accomplish that.

One way that I recommend is to co-observe classes and compare notes afterward. The best way to fine tune your antennae for DCO indicators is in live classroom observations. If you cannot find teachers comfortable enough to allow themselves to be used for their principal's professional development, a second choice is to view any of the many videotapes available on the market. While many of these tapes were expressly made to exemplify quality teaching, none of them demonstrate all the indicators, and several of them inadvertently expose missing components. There is plenty of room for discussion, disagreement, and dialogue necessary to come to consensus. In the next section, I will provide a handy tool to assist you in this process.

Coming to common agreements is easier than it was just a few years ago, now that all the research is leading us in the same direction. It is no longer a matter of opinion as to whether student engagement, inquiry, strong conceptual connections, use of literacy as a learning tool, and so forth positively impact student learning. I used to be met at workshops by the skeptical teacher who demanded that I show him or her the research that supported my point of view. My answer used to be pat. I would simply respond, "*You* show *me* the research that supports your contention." It usually ended the argument, but didn't necessarily convince anyone. At this point in time, it has become so obvious in the best practice research that it has become politically incorrect to protest, but it is still as difficult to go beyond politically correct agreements to accomplish real changes that break through the veneer of best practice.

The best way to come to common agreements for teachers is to collaboratively develop assessments that they all feel students should be able to complete correctly, then come together to analyze student results. Very quickly, they will begin to trade stories about how they achieved or failed to achieve their learning objectives. No teacher wants his or her students to fail, but we have allowed them to do just that by not demanding that they produce success. Teachers who fail their students don't do it for lack of commitment or desire; they do so because they do not know what else to do.

Now enter the supervisor, be it a principal, mentor, or other evaluator. If teachers are going to come to common agreements, so must those who support them and hold them accountable. DCO can be a guide to agreeing what to look for and require in instruction. It can also lead to the development of common approaches when teachers fall below those requirements. This chapter has some clear guidelines for the methods available to principals: the preconference, the observation, and the postconference. These are the pieces of the work that your administrative team must begin to share to help each other through the uncomfortable task of holding another adult to task without belittling or threatening him or her. Together you can make decisions about professional development for your faculties and provide teachers with the practical skills and knowledge to improve their practice. Supervising teachers was the best and the worst part of my job as principal. When it went well, it was a joy to engage in animated discussions about lessons observed and what would or could be happening next. Sitting face to face with a teacher whom I would ultimately be recommending for contract nonrenewal was a nightmare for both of us. This is a task that benefits greatly from the support of others engaged in the same activity. The support will help you discover as many avenues as possible to avoid having to take that uncomfortable step and encourage you to move forward with that process when necessary.

The DCO Score Sheets

What They Are

The score sheets, which can be found in Appendix F, were developed for two purposes:

1. to be used in training for discussion purposes and to serve as a measure around which to build consensus, and

2. to run a program audit or to determine current levels of expertise in a school or district for the purposes of making decisions about professional development.

They have also been used to provide classroom performance data in national research studies. They are simple, five-point scales that are aligned with each of the criteria of all versions of the DCO instrument. They measure the degree of presence or absence of each indicator with the following scores:

1. No evidence

2. Little evidence

3. Moderate evidence

4. Consistent evidence

5. Extensive evidence

The decisions about scoring are done by using the bulleted Examples of Evidence column next to each indicator. The observer is asked to use specific evidence from the classroom to justify the score given. The guidelines for making these decisions are just that: guidelines. Ultimately, the judgment of the observer is called on. Practice in observing and comparing scores is the best way to hone your eye so that the most correct score can be reached. What follows are some guidelines to help you with your scores.

"No evidence" sounds pretty explicit, and usually it is. If you can find no examples of evidence of an indicator in a classroom, the teacher receives a score of 1. There is one more circumstance that warrants a 1: I have called it the "pathetic attempt," the wild stab at something that a teacher has been told to do, but is so ineffectual as to have virtually no impact on students.

Box 7.1A

Indicator CU#1	
Indicator	**Examples of Evidence**
CU#1. Classroom management maximizes learning opportunities	• Teacher maintains a level of order conducive to learning (students are attending to the teacher and the activity) • There is an atmosphere of freedom and flexibility within that order • Classroom norms emphasize personal and collective responsibility to create a learning community • Directions to students are clear to avoid confusion and constant questions that interrupt the flow of the activity • During group times, students not working with teacher are engaged in relevant and important work

Example 7.1B

CU#1

A SCORE OF 1 FOR CU#1—CLASSROOM MANAGEMENT MAXIMIZES LEARNING OPPORTUNITIES

A second-grade teacher is struggling with the behavior in her class, particularly in getting the students' attention when they are working in groups or getting unruly. Her mentor has suggested that she establish some sort of signal for quiet that will get their attention and become the routine for paying attention. She has chosen a small, Native American drum, a unique and appealing item that makes a gentle but clearly audible sound.

The students are involved in a group assignment. There is some working going on, some aimless wandering about, and much off-task and loud behavior. The teacher announces, "OK, it's getting noisy. Here comes my signal." At this point, she begins drumming. The students continue on, paying attention neither to her announcement nor to her drum signal. She continues, "Oh, I'm very disappointed. You didn't hear my signal. Here it comes again." And she repeats her drumming. It takes her several times to get them to stop and pay attention.

This process is repeated multiple times throughout the period. Clearly, the drumming has become meaningless background noise to the students. Although a very few students do complete their work, as a class, they have accepted no responsibility for attending to their assignment. This is not a community of learners, but a disorganized group accomplishing random tasks. The teacher has abdicated her authority, and although she is attempting to use a recommended technique, it can be called a pathetic attempt because it has had no impact whatever on the students.

"Limited evidence" means that the attempt has been made, but it is either very inconsistent or of minimal impact. A few of the bulleted examples of evidence may be weakly or fleetingly present, but most are missing. I call this the "vague attempt."

Box 7.2A

Indicator L-IM#2	
Indicator	**Examples of Evidence**
L-IM#2. Teacher's instructional choices are effective in engaging students in literacy activities	• Assignments are varied in nature and difficulty so that all students are engaged in the activity • Lesson construction has been purposefully planned for active engagement of all students • During read-alouds, teacher reads with animation and stops to ask questions, involve students, and describe new or relevant vocabulary without interrupting the flow of the story • Students have text or reading response journals to follow along with during read-alouds • Books used are appropriate, and the students are engaged in reading or listening

Example 7.2B

L-IM#2

A SCORE OF 2 ON L-IM#2: TEACHER'S INSTRUCTIONAL CHOICES ARE EFFECTIVE IN ENGAGING STUDENTS IN LITERACY ACTIVITIES

A fifth-grade teacher is doing a read-aloud to engage her students in a social studies unit on medieval Europe. She has chosen a book that tells a folktale that takes place in the Black Forest. The illustrations are vivid and evoke a sense of color and form indicative of the era. The students are sitting quietly and watching the teacher. It is unclear to what extent they are actually listening to the selection.

As the teacher begins to get into the story, two things become evident. First, the reading level of this book is well below the fifth-grade level. It is more appropriate for a kindergarten or first-grade class. The vocabulary is very simple, and the tone is that of a fairy tale. The story itself is reminiscent of a Brothers' Grimm tale and is about two sisters separately going through the forest and encountering an ugly but magical being who turns out to be a prince. The teacher stops occasionally to show the pictures, but not to discuss the story (although there is not much to discuss regarding the plot or any cultural significance). The students begin to drift, and they are observed leafing through other books or staring at the ceiling.

The teacher made a good choice to read a book that related to a unit that they would be working on and set a tone that gave a flavor of the period, but the low reading level soon lost the interest of most of the students. While fairy tales can be representative of what was popular during the Middle Ages, no explicit connections were made.

"Moderate evidence" is seen when some of the elements of the indicator are clearly present and others are clearly missing. There may be a good attempt at a strategy that falls short of its goal for any number of reasons. The lesson may have a strong start and weak finish, or the reverse. It is what I call a "mixed bag."

Box 7.3A

Indicator MS-IM#2	
Indicator	**Examples of Evidence**
MS-IM#2. Periods of teacher-student interaction are probing and substantive	• Questions expose and draw on students' prior knowledge • Teacher probes with challenging activities *and* questions • Questions and dialogue emphasize higher order thinking (students compare, contrast, classify, use analogies and metaphors) • Students are encouraged to develop a metacognitive sense of their learning

Example 7.3B

MS-IM #2

A SCORE OF 3 ON MS-IM#2: PERIODS OF TEACHER-STUDENT INTERACTION ARE PROBING AND SUBSTANTIVE

A kindergarten teacher is teaching her students about shapes, their proper geometrical names, their properties, and their relationship to each other. She tells them that she has a challenge for them. She has a paper bag with something inside it, and they are to describe it (not tell what it is, but tell some things about it). Inside the bag are blocks in the shape of various polygons. Students take turns feeling inside the bag. They immediately name the pieces as squares, triangles, and so forth. She prompts them to back away from the names, but to describe the pieces. How many sides does it have? How many angles? Few of the students are able to use those cues. The next challenge is to work with a partner and a complete set of pattern blocks to see how many different ways you can construct or cover up a hexagon with the various other pieces, and how you will know when you have gotten all the ways.

The students work well together, and each group is able to discover all the patterns that make the hexagon. There is some going back and forth of referring to the pieces by their geometrical names or other methods of naming them, such as trapezoid or "the red piece." The teacher works briefly with each group and questions if they have found all the combinations, encouraging them to keep working if they have not. When they come back together, they share their solutions, have all found nine combinations, and are able to describe a way that they organized their work so they could be sure they'd gotten all the possibilities.

This lesson has a weak start with confusing directions, failing to do a probe of prior knowledge, and neglecting to establish the math vocabulary that was supposed to be one of the goals. But the second part of the lesson probes the students with a challenging activity as they, in pairs, actively explore the pieces and how they relate to each other. The teacher stimulates their thinking without giving them answers and redirects them without actually correcting a mistake. They discover that a parallelogram can break into two triangles, that a hexagon has six sides and one side each of six triangles can fit inside it, and that fitting squares inside hexagons are problematic because of the angles. They also discover ways to organize an investigation so that the "data" make sense.

From the Annenberg/CPB Math and Science Collection (1995).

"Consistent evidence" is what we all hope for when we observe a class. It means that the indicator is strong, the bulleted examples are well in evidence, and the lesson is generally successful. A score of 4 is most readily given when it is clear that the positive elements observed are regular occurrences in the classroom and not prepared specially for the observation. It is hard to get children to "fake it" for an entire period. A DCO observer listens to and talks with students to get a sense of their understanding and their comfort with the routine. (I liken the special lesson planned for the principal to the ratings "sweeps weeks" on television when regular programming is abandoned for the sensational and spectacular.)

Box 7.4A

Indicator MS-CO#3	
Indicator	**Examples of Evidence**
MS-CO#3. Teacher collects and assesses evidence of student progress to enhance teaching and learning	• Assessment is systematic and ongoing so that teacher can track student progress and adjust instruction • Students' misconceptions are identified so that they can adjust their thinking • Agreed-on standards are used to judge the quality of student products and performances • Assessments are varied (journals, performance tasks, presentations, tests) and target concepts and skills • Students self-assess by using rubrics or reviewing past work to see their progress • Assessments clearly indicate conceptual closure

Example 7.4B

MS-CO#3

A SCORE OF 4 ON MS-CO#3: TEACHER COLLECTS AND ASSESSES EVIDENCE OF STUDENT PROGRESS TO ENHANCE TEACHING AND LEARNING

A tenth-grade math teacher begins his integrated math class each day with a short assessment. On a small slip of paper, a straightforward example of whatever concepts they have been working on appears with two directions. First, students are to solve the problem and show their work. Then they are asked a conceptual question that asks them to explain why the process they used worked. He collects the slips each day and has a record not only of who was able to correctly solve the problem, but also has a clear picture of student thinking. He knows who has really "gotten it" and where the misconceptions are.

There are a few different things the teacher may do with these warm-ups:

• He may decide to ask the students to solve the example with a partner. As the students work on the problem, he will circulate, listen to their discourse, and apply the discourse rubric. This will give him another piece of data about their math understanding.
• He may have the students work on the problem and present their solutions and justifications to the class. This makes for a rich classroom discussion, filled with mathematical ideas and arguments in which everyone participates.

This is unlike the exercise of correcting homework in class in a few ways. Everyone has done the problem because they do it in class. No one has gotten stuck, because a partner or the teacher is there to get you unstuck.

This assessment is collected every day. The students are used to the routine and get to work on it right away. It takes about fifteen minutes to do (fifteen more if they decide to discuss it in class) and lays the groundwork for the next lesson, which is about to begin.

"Extensive evidence" is seen when not only are the bulleted examples mostly all present and strong, but there are particularly exemplary events either directed by the teacher or produced by the students as a result of the activity. Please be careful that you are not being blown away by the neat activity syndrome. Assure yourself that the activity actually fulfills the "spirit of the box" and truly advances the student knowledge and abilities described by the indicator.

Box 7.5A

Indicator L-CO#5	
Indicator	**Examples of Evidence**
L-CO#5. Connections are made between reading, writing, and other subjects and have applications to the real world	• Teacher makes connections between writing assignments and reading selections • Students have opportunities to write about what they are reading • Teacher connects reading and writing to other texts and content areas • Teacher asks students to make these connections • Student activities and discussions further lead to having them make connections • Teacher uses reading and writing assignments to point out vocabulary, syntax, and usage • Reading and writing skills are taught in a context and have relevance to students

Example 7.5B

L-CO#5

A SCORE OF 5 ON L-CO#5: CONNECTIONS ARE MADE BETWEEN READING, WRITING, AND OTHER SUBJECTS AND HAVE APPLICATIONS TO THE REAL WORLD

A fourth-grade teacher is working with students on Charles Dickens's *The Prince and the Pauper*. They are reading the book as a combination read-aloud and independent or guided reading of selected sections of the text. This allows all students, regardless of reading level, access to the direct text. They have also seen the movie. They discuss what it was like for each of the characters to find themselves in such different life circumstances from the ones to which they were accustomed.

After they have seen the movie, the teacher issues the class a challenge. What if you could look identical to anyone on earth, living or dead, real or fictitious—so identical that you could switch places and no one would know? Who would it be?

First, the class brainstorms a list of possible people that they might like to spend a day being. The list includes famous actors, sports figures, and historical and fictional characters. Each student selects someone and begins writing his or her story by making a plan. The plan must answer the following questions: How might you happen to run into that person? Under what conditions would you or the person suggest the change? What would happen, and how would you get your own life back?

The class spends a good part of a month on the project from beginning to end. They select characters as diverse as George Washington, Roger Clemens, Harry Houdini, and Julia Roberts. One boy selects both Smothers Brothers, and a girl chooses to be a chipmunk. Students do several drafts, conferencing weekly with the teacher and sometimes with a peer. The culmination of the project happens during a parents' Open House. The students dress up like the character that they have chosen and read their stories to the parents and the rest of the class.

How to Use the Score Sheets

The score sheets have certain uses to which they should be limited. I will discuss in the following section what they are *not* to be used for. Their primary use in a school setting is in the training of personnel. Whether you are working with administrators or teachers, the score sheets serve as a basis for the coming to agreement that I discussed in the previous section. After watching a tape or visiting a classroom, each participant should score the lesson individually. The score sheets provide a space for not only the number score, but also for recording the specific evidence you observed that caused you to give the score. The group then comes together, shares their scores, and engages in a detailed dialogue to come to consensus on a number. During the dialogue, people may argue and defend their points of view, or they may change their minds after hearing evidence that they hadn't previously considered. The group that attempts this together should be small enough to make sure that every person has a voice and that the trust is sufficient so that everyone can freely express their thoughts, while still being free to respectfully challenge each other. This is a time to be analytical and precise, neither to coddle less than rigorous views nor to simply find fault. Remember, the purpose is to sharpen each other's skills—not for the purpose of criticism, but for the purpose of accuracy. Preserving a safe atmosphere for trying out these new ideas may be a reason to have administrators learn separately from their teachers. Ideas for teacher use of the DCO instrument are covered later in this chapter.

Once there is general agreement on the standards for the scores, the score sheets can be used to gather data. You may want to discover the area of greatest need for precious professional development funds. You may be surprised to find that teachers lack an in-depth understanding of the math concepts they are being asked to teach, or it may turn out that you have schoolwide climate issues that should be addressed before attempting another literacy workshop. You can use the data to make decisions about materials to purchase or technology initiatives to pursue. In any case, when asked by your board or your faculty why you have chosen a particular course, your aggregated classroom data can support your choice. You can also use the data again to determine the impact of a professional development initiative. By documenting the impact, you can improve your future decisions by avoiding initiatives that are not effective.

The score sheets have also been used for research. In national studies funded by the U.S. Department of Education, this instrument has been used to provide the data for classroom performance. You may want to collect data for an action research project in your district. Before you use any data, be sure that they have been tempered by a reliability process. Like any calibration, you will need other professionals to engage with you in a standard-setting process similar to the process described in the "coming to agreement" section.

To establish the reliability for the aforementioned national studies, we established a "Gold Standard Panel" that consisted of three key professionals who each scored a test tape or live classroom independently and achieved a level of agreement that had been predetermined. The standard that we used was an agreement of not more than a 0.5 deviation of scores in each of the three criteria (Implementation, Content, and Classroom Culture). This is a stringent standard, and it takes a significant training effort to reach that level of interrater reliability. In a school setting for action research, you may wish to set a more flexible standard. You can settle on adjacent agreement with no more than one point difference on any given indicator. Regardless of the standard chosen, there needs to be a general agreement so that your results are meaningful for you and produce the level of improvement that you are looking for.

How Not *to Use the Score Sheets*

Now come the caveats. I have heard that Madelyn Hunter (n.d.), the lesson design guru from my earliest years of educational administration, was deeply chagrined that her work had been used as part of a system of evaluation that had turned punitive in some cases. DCO is not meant to hold a hammer over the heads of teachers. Instead, it holds up a mirror. I discuss in detail how to use DCO with teachers as a part of a supervisory relationship that takes a collaborative, problem-solving approach to instructional improvement and as a tool for self-assessment and peer coaching. The score sheets, in particular, are *NOT* to be used as a "teacher report card." **I can*NOT* entreat you enough** to leave the score sheets to the uses for which they were developed: that of coming to common agreements in a training or group-study format, gauging program improvement in a school or district following a professional development initiative, and aggregating results in a research study. Despite good intentions, presenting a teacher with a score sheet as part of a response to a classroom observation has two hazards:

1. In the last analysis, a final score—no matter how grounded you feel it is in the criteria—is a qualitative judgment masquerading as a quantitative measure. It is why in research we have used the Gold Standard Panel method of establishing reliability. Three well-trained eyes are better than one.

2. Regardless of how gently you deliver the results, no matter how substantive your write-up or postconference is, and in spite of the keen insights you may share with your teacher, there is a very real danger that the teacher will walk away with one single message: "He or she gave me a 3."

A high score will leave the teacher feeling relieved, and his or her practice will remain untouched. A low score will make the teacher feel hurt, angry, or defensive, and his or her practice will remain untouched. In either case, the purpose of DCO—to present the highest standard of practice and set every teacher on a quest to approach that standard—is defeated.

There is one exception to this rule: Once a teacher has *already* been placed on an improvement plan and rehiring has been brought into question, the scoring system can be helpful in documenting the extent of improvement or lack thereof. It provides the teacher with a clear picture of what needs to change and tracks the principal's view of whether those changes are being seen. I prefer to set the discussion of contract nonrenewal aside. The spirit of DCO is to focus on the highest standards of practice and the process of professional growth.

The DCO system offers a practical approach to digging beneath the surface of teaching practice for the purpose of elevating the professional discussions about instruction in your school. Its uses have been described, and its limitations clearly identified. Section 2 gives guidance and specific tools that will make DCO useful and successful in your school setting. As with the rest of this book, it is aimed primarily at the building principal, but speaks as well to any whose responsibility it is to address instructional improvement.

SECTION 2: ADDING DCO TO YOUR SUPERVISORY PRACTICE

DCO was originally created to fill a void that was becoming apparent as more and more teachers were receiving professional development in math, science, and technology in our state. While school leaders were becoming well versed in the research that supports the four assumptions of DCO, it became clear to me that making the changes in actual instruction was happening at a maddeningly slow rate. Why was this? As a principal, I attended many workshops whose goals were to train teachers in skills such as creating inquiry in math and science and using assessment to inform instruction. I went with teams of teachers from my school, sometimes spending several days overnight with them in extended institutes. As I looked around the room, I became aware that I was frequently either the only principal there, or one of a very few. I couldn't imagine sending teachers to learn new research and methods without being curious enough to know about them myself. How could I properly support them in their efforts to adjust their methods? How could I supervise their instruction if I were not as knowledgeable as they? I know that time is precious and that administrators are burdened with many pressing tasks and overwhelming pressures, but instructional leadership is one of them and, in the last analysis, it is the most important. I watched the teams of teachers that were there without their building administrators. Their reactions ranged from excitement to trepidation. How would they be able to really share what they had learned with their colleagues? Did schedule or resource changes need to be made to accommodate the new approaches? Would their principals understand and support them? Our team always left not only with new tools under our belts, but specific plans about how to implement our new learning.

In subsequent years as the director of leadership initiatives in a state-level organization funded by the National Science Foundation, I was responsible for training math and science teacher leaders in methods of inquiry and connecting their teaching to national standards. These teacher leaders ran workshops in their own schools and others across the state with the goal of transforming math, science, and technology instruction. A frightening reality began to emerge from this work. With all the new emphasis on teacher leadership and the proliferating literature extolling this new and valuable resource for rejuvenating schools (Gabriel, 2005; Lambert, 1998), the pitfalls seemed to overwhelm the promises. The essential ingredient whose presence or absence seemed to make or break the success of teacher leadership (a complex dynamic in a school to begin with) boiled down simply to this: the levels of *understanding* and *support* of the building principal. I cannot overstate this simple finding: *Training teachers without providing a parallel, if not identical, training for the principal is most likely going to be a waste of time and money.* Untold amounts of district, federal, and other funds are spent each year on the professional development of teachers. Much of this, frankly, is spent in vain. That is not necessarily an indictment of the professional development offered. It is simply that the teachers receive training for which there is no context back in their schools in which to implement that training fully. They may do their best to enact new strategies in their classrooms or even to share their new knowledge with their peers, but until and unless these strategies become part of the expectations, are incorporated by building principals in their supervision, and are provided for either by follow-up training, support, and continued professional discussions, the work falls flat. This was our repeated experience as the Teacher Associates attempted to transform instruction around the state. I have had a front seat in this phenomenon. As a curriculum consultant for a school district, I provided intense support for math teachers to help them use the DCO strategies to get the best results from their standards-based math programs. The superintendent, while agreeing with the proposed plan in theory, resisted requiring the principals to be simultaneously trained, citing time constraints and other priorities as reasons to continually postpone the work sessions set aside for this purpose. When it was clear that the results of the consultancy were spotty because some teachers were viewing the work we were doing as optional, the realization that the supervision piece was missing began to sink in. How could we have expected the principals to support through supervision something in which they were not well versed? The answer was that we couldn't.

I became determined to provide the materials and training for principals that would equip them to be active partners in the transformation of instruction in their buildings. I knew that if principals were to play such a role in the improvement of instruction, they needed to have tools designed for them. Principals have not specialized in every content area and therefore cannot be expected to be content experts, yet they are responsible for supervising instruction and ultimately for student results. DCO and its training protocols were my answer to this challenge. I again acknowledge that principals have many pressing and ballooning responsibilities that pose challenges to the time and effort needed to learn new supervision skills. Daily management, finances, and student issues demand immediate attention. But with the specter of test results that fall below acceptable levels and ones that remain flat or demonstrate unacceptable achievement gaps, the principal can no longer afford to allow these other concerns to exert absolute rule over the allocation of priorities and time. The guarantee of quality instruction is a principal's most critical job, and DCO can help. First, it emphasizes the importance of understanding what good math and science instruction, effective integration of technology, and high-quality literacy instruction actually look like. It then provides some guidelines for the principal in his or her role in improving teaching practice. These guidelines and the tools to facilitate their implementation appear next.

TOOLS FOR THE PRINCIPAL

Guidelines for the Preconference: Planning and Organization

The first section of DCO is the Planning and Organization section. This helps set the scene for a productive preconference, which can actually improve the instructional event before it even occurs. It aligns with important parts of the Implementation, Content, and Classroom Culture sections and attempts to determine the extent to which the teacher has considered those aspects in his or her planning.

Teachers, it should go without saying, must be fully familiar with the criteria of DCO before any observations take place, and the school's instructional goals must be in alignment. This should not be a barrier; the research that underlies DCO is at the core of all best practice approaches.

The Planning and Organization section provides the principal with some key questions to ask prior to the observation that go deeper than the garden variety "What do you plan to be doing tomorrow, and how does it fit into your unit?" In addition to the questions, it provides bulleted guidelines for how to listen to the responses. This assists both the principal and the teacher, in that the teacher is aware of precisely what the principal will be looking for, and the principal is guided as to where to focus attention during the observation. But more important, this can open up discussions about instruction that can cause the teacher to think in some different ways and perhaps alter and improve the plan. The Math/Science and Literacy Versions of Planning and Organization appear in Appendixes A and B respectively.

Box 7.6 gives some examples of how you can structure a preconference using the Planning and Organization indicators to positively impact a lesson before it takes place. This is not unlike a teacher reviewing material with students before a test in the hopes that they will perform better. Any lesson that gets reconsidered as a result of probing questions can only benefit the students. (These conversations are not drawn from live preconferences; they are theoretical and based on the scored examples in Section 1, which were either taped lessons or observed as part of research.)

Box 7.6

How the Planning and Organization Section Can Improve a Lesson Before It Begins

EXAMPLE 1 (FROM 7.2B)

This lesson received a score of 2 on L-IM#2: Teacher's instructional choices are effective in engaging students in literacy activities.

L-PO#1

Principal:	Tell me what you will be teaching on Tuesday and how it fits in with your overall unit.
Teacher:	We are doing a unit on medieval Europe, and I have chosen a story that evokes that period. I will be reading aloud to the students a story set in the Black Forest. *(Teacher describes the story.)*
Principal (sensing that it sounds like a fairy tale, wondering about age appropriateness of the story):	What is the source of that?
Teacher (shows the principal the book):	I got this from the library.
Principal:	Have you ever read this story to fifth graders before? I'm wondering about the sophistication level, seeing that you will be reading it to them so reading difficulty will not be an issue. What do you think?

(Teacher now has an opportunity to rethink her choice of books.)

L-PO#2 and L-PO#3

Principal:	Tell me about how you think the different students in your class will respond to the read-aloud. What are your plans for getting them to interact with the story?
Teacher:	I was planning to read it to them first and ask some questions about what happened.
Principal (hearing little effort to actively engage students or differentiate):	I wonder what it would be like if you started with some initial questions to guide their listening that would relate to some of the elements in the Middle Ages that you wanted to focus on later.
Teacher:	I suppose I could ask them to think about what this story tells us about the social class structure.
Principal:	That would be a great question to start with. How would you get them to actively engage in thinking about that?
Teacher:	Well, I guess I could have them write down what they think.
Principal:	Yes, in their reading journals. And maybe you could have them each share their thoughts with a partner before sharing them with the larger group.
Teacher:	That would be interesting to see what they come up with.

The conversation can then go on to conducting a K-W-L about the Middle Ages and ways to capture the important observations that the students make from the reading that can be applied later on as the study of the Middle Ages progresses. This may bring up the fact that the book does not contain enough "meat" to get to this level, giving another opportunity for the teacher to rethink her choice of books.

EXAMPLE 2 (FROM 7.1B)

This lesson received a score of 1 for CU#1—Classroom management maximizes learning opportunities.

L-PO#6 and MS-PO#6

Principal:	Tell me about how you manage the behavior in your class.
Teacher:	Well, I've been trying to develop a signal with the students that will quiet them down or get them to refocus when they get too noisy. I have a native drum that the students seem to like that I use.
Principal:	That sounds interesting. How do they respond when you beat the drum?
Teacher:	They usually quiet down, but sometimes it takes me a few times to get them to listen.
Principal:	Why do you suppose that happens?
Teacher:	I'm not really sure. I have some pretty active kids in the class.
Principal:	I'm wondering what the consequence is for the class when they don't respond to the drum.

This opens the door for a conversation about how to create a group sense of responsibility for classroom climate and to set expectations for a particular response to the signal for quiet. They can also discuss strategies for introducing consistent consequences in a fair and nonpunitive way that will build respect for everyone in the class, particularly in light of the fact that the signal has been in effect for a while and has not been working.

Guidelines for the Observation: The "Cheat Sheets"

DCO contains some indicators that describe teacher actions, some dealing with student learning and activity, and some that analyze the interaction between the teacher and students. For this reason, a DCO observation is not effectively done sitting inconspicuously in the back of the room. Unlike the concerns of experimenter effect in a research study, where the mere presence of a researcher changes the outcomes of the event, an observation done for the purposes of supervision requires that the principal get closer to the action to understand not only what is occurring at the moment, but to ensure that what he or she is seeing is indicative of usual practice in that class.

Developed to assist you while in the classroom are what I have dubbed the "cheat sheets," which consist of a single page with some key phrases to remind you of what you are looking for and some blank space to make notes. Memorizing the entire DCO is unreasonable, and going into a classroom observation with the entire copy of the document is ungainly and distracting. The cheat sheets, which appear in Appendix G, allow you to go in unencumbered, carrying only what you would for any formal observation: a clipboard, notebook, or pad and a pen. Take care to observe both teacher and students.

Begin the observation by looking around the room, which is the first data point in the Classroom Culture section. What is the quantity and quality of student work displayed? Is it current? Can you tell what the learning goals of the work were? To what extent is individual student thinking in the assignment evident? Does this feel like a room owned by the teacher or a community of learners?

1. **Watch the setup of the lesson.** How much does the teacher need to prep the students before the activity begins? Are there easy connections made to the work preceding this lesson? Are the students engaged and ready to work? Do they seem to know the routine and what is expected of them, moving easily into the activity?

2. **Watch the students in their groups.** How comfortably do the students move into their groups and take control of their learning? Does this seem to be something they do frequently? Do they sit quietly waiting for the teacher to get to them? Do they sit in groups but work individually? (I have likened this to the "parallel play" we see with toddlers.) Is there confusion or order, purposeful chatter or socializing and chaos?

3. **Listen to the students in their groups.** It is now that you will need to get up and circulate. This is the part of the lesson that cannot be scripted or specially crafted for your visit. Do the students converse easily about the concepts? Can they explain to you what they are doing and why? If you ask them to explain the concepts, can they do so as if they have been asked to do this before? Do they seem to own the work, or are they merely performing a task? To what extent are they doing it with understanding? Most important, if they don't understand, how do they react? Do they collaboratively try to figure it out, or do they shut down? Is there an orderly process by which they can seek the assistance of the teacher? Ultimately, you will be looking for how productive this group work is.

4. **Check your "equity box."** Is there a sense of respect and inclusion? Are all students equally engaged? If not, is there a pattern to inclusion versus exclusion? Do the groups seem comfortable with each other? Is the size of the group

such that every student is an equal contributor? Is the teacher monitoring the groups to ensure that everyone is getting the benefit of the learning?

5. **Watch the teacher as he or she moves among the groups.** Is the teacher checking for more than on-task behavior? Is he or she just checking to see if students are on the right track and then moving on? Does the teacher actively engage with the students to probe their thinking and check for understanding? Is he or she keeping track of student responses, misconceptions, or particularly interesting approaches? In other words, is there teaching going on, or is the circulating just pro forma?

6. **If the class is not working in groups, watch how the teacher leads the discussion or activity.** How varied and deep are his or her questions? How does the teacher engage the entire class in the discussion? Does the conversation move on with just a handful of students actively participating? How does the teacher infuse "think time" into the conversation? Does he or she have students jot down some thoughts, write on a whiteboard, or share with a partner, or does the teacher have some other method to ensure that everyone is thinking of the question?

7. **Look for the ending of the lesson.** Is there a defined end to the lesson, or just a bell signaling that time has run out? Is there a reflective piece in which the students either write or share in some way what they have learned and what their questions still are? Is the homework going to further that thinking? Do they know where they are heading tomorrow?

Guidelines for the Postconference

The postconference can sound the death knell for instructional improvement if one is not careful. I remember back to my teaching days when I always anticipated leaving a postconference either with a sense of relief or in tears. Even now, with far better methods of supervision in wide use, postconferences can still have that chilling effect on teachers. They are more likely be seen as something to survive or endure as opposed to a time for engaging and informative professional discussions. Most principals whom I have worked with, like myself in my earliest days of supervision, begin their conference with questions like, "How do you think the lesson went?" "Do you think you reached your goals?" "How would you have improved it?" These questions are designed to allow the teacher to reflect on the lesson rather than be launched into the thoughts of the observer. But, as well meaning as this approach is, it has a few problems:

1. If the teacher is pleased with the outcome of the lesson and thought it went well and the observer did not, that leaves the observer in an extremely awkward position. The ensuing conversation is not likely to leave the teacher thinking about how to improve his or her practice.

2. If there is a lack of trust in the observer, the teacher may not feel comfortable discussing anything that he or she was truly concerned about. The conversation will be forced and tense.

3. The teacher may attempt to trump any criticisms of the observer by focusing on something that indeed could have gone better, but is not at the core of what might need to be improved. The discussion may now be diverted to some more trivial issues, making it more difficult for the observer to address more pressing concerns.

4. Alternatively, the principal might approach the conversation by enumerating the positive actions that he or she noted, moving on later in the discussion to the things that could have been improved on. The teacher will sit through the first half of this conversation waiting for the big "but." If the "but" is significant, the danger is that the teacher will leave the room with little or no memory of the positive feedback and focus only on the suggestions for improvement. The emotions accompanying those thoughts may range anywhere from anger and defensiveness to hurt. It takes a particularly warm, trusting relationship with the principal to leave the postconference actively thinking about how to improve the lesson for the next time. No matter how nicely worded, it still contains the message, "You need to change." The art of the postconference is in reframing the concept of "change" as "evolution." No one wants to change, but everyone hopes to grow and evolve.

In the postconference, DCO guides the discussion centering on pedagogy and student learning. This transforms the experience from an evaluation into a reflective and collaborative inquiry (Love, 2002). It's all about culture and relationships. Because DCO contains indicators of student activity and learning, this is where the conversation begins. The principal, having interacted with students, watching and listening to them, can now use those data to ask questions about student receptiveness to the new learning. By conducting a co-inquiry into student work, it gives the teacher permission to not be perfect. You can generate "advice" together, plan together, and wonder together ("I wonder what would have happened if the students had tried x or y first"). It is helpful to have some "points to ponder" before you begin the conference. This approach adds the metacognitive aspect to the teacher's practice just as the lesson planning does to the students' work.

I recommend requesting the student work resulting from the lesson observed be brought to the postconference. Having student work gives you something clear to focus on and provides something measurable and doable instead of offering vague suggestions. The evidence of learning is now spread out on the desk in front of the two of you—teacher and principal—for consideration. Teachers are hard pressed to defend a weak lesson when the student work is disappointing. The conversation can now focus on where the students are in their understanding. You can note some examples of rich or interesting student thinking, student thinking that you didn't understand, or a student's thinking that indicated that he or she didn't get it. Together, try to unravel what was going on and how to improve the understanding or capitalize on interesting ideas. If there were widespread misconceptions or a general poor showing in the student work, the conversation can now naturally progress to what might be the best strategies to correct those. Operating under the assumption that teachers and principals are equally committed to positive student results, the postconference becomes two colleagues puzzling over how best to reach the learning goals of the lesson.

So, how do we do this? How can we become adept at asking loaded questions without creating barriers? How can we work for improvement without fixing or giving advice, at the same time not manipulating or dancing around the important issues? How can we phrase the questions so that the conference actually becomes a collaborative effort? To make the postconference safe but effective, here are some useful things to consider (Note that there is an attempt to avoid the word *you*. There is a similar attempt to avoid giving advice and using the word *I*.):

- Always first acknowledge the expertise and experience of the teacher.
- Engage in discussions about the *content* and the *students* (discourse, written work, problem solving):

  Instead of asking, "What are *your* goals (or objectives) for the lesson, and do *you* think *you* achieved them?"

  Try asking: "What *concepts* were the *students* learning?" (To help gauge whether the content identified is appropriate, use your state or the national standards as guidelines.)

  Instead of asking: "How do *you* think the lesson went?"

  Try asking: "Do you think *they* have learned it? What should *they* know or be able to do? What will it look like when *they* have learned it?"

  Instead of asking: "What will *you* be doing tomorrow?"

  Try asking: "How does *this concept* lead into what *they* need to learn next?" (This gets at a discussion about the long-term agenda and the development of conceptual understanding. Again, you don't need to be a content expert. You can reference state and national standards.)

This last question may uncover a weakness in teacher content knowledge. You will hear a lack of ability to be fully articulate in separating out the difference between the "topic" and the "concept." Your naïveté can even be a strength here as you struggle to understand from the teacher's explanations what enduring knowledge was at the core of the day's activities. You can be supportive, perhaps acknowledging the difficulty of new programs or the challenges in the class, but this gives you an opportunity to arrange for professional development. When conversations like this become routine and involve the whole staff, it can be a way to begin a real learning community. You can use local assessments to analyze student work and have teachers work together to develop ways to improve student understanding. You can look at state and national data collaboratively, moving the discussion to schoolwide improvement of student results.

Box 7.7

What Do Administrators Say About Collaborative Inquiry in a Postconference?

A team of administrators trained to use this approach in their programs of supervision and evaluation had the following "ahas":

- The suggested questions offered a good framework for reflective questions to have the teacher consider before the postconference.
- The collaborative approach put the teacher at ease, so a deeper conversation was possible.
- The deeper conversation opened up the possibility of problem solving.
- Using student work allowed the conversation to be around what the students were understanding, what they knew, and what they are learning. It was a real assessment!
- It made me realize that you can't fix everything at once.
- It instilled ownership by the teacher.
- Because a good looking lesson can "seduce" an observer, it helps you get past that to what was really happening.
- The tool helps you focus on what to ask to get at the core of what's being learned.

The postconference can also be a place where a good lesson becomes even better. Just as the most capable students need to be challenged, so do accomplished teachers need more than just a "gold star." They need to be urged to rethink or expand their strategies for continuous growth. Frequently, when faced with a well-constructed and implemented lesson, a relieved principal announces to the teacher, "That was great. I have no suggestions for you." This may make the teacher feel supported, but it also leaves him or her with nowhere to go, the entire supervisory process having come to a sudden dead end. The "I wonder what would happen if" approach can be the beginning of an exciting postconference discussion that engages both the principal and the teacher in speculation about how to push the edges even more or create follow-ups that might not have been planned. It works in the same way that the additional challenge works for the gifted student: It causes the accomplished teacher to go deeper into the teaching process for further discoveries. Frankly, it may be the most fun you'll ever have in a postconference. Box 7.8 illustrates how a postconference can cause two different teachers to examine their practice. (These conversations are not drawn from actual postconferences; they are theoretical and based on the scored examples in Section 1, which were either taped lessons or observed as part of research.)

Box 7.8

How a Postconference Can Improve *Any* Lesson

Example 1 (from 7.3B)

This lesson scored a 3 on MS-IM#2: Periods of teacher-student interaction are probing and substantive.

Principal: Now, you mentioned that this was only the second lesson that the children have had on shapes. How much did they already know about shapes?

Teacher: I don't really know. I was assuming that they knew about squares, triangles, and circles, but that they were not familiar with hexagons, rhombuses, and trapezoids, which is what I was trying to teach them about.

Principal: I thought it was really interesting how they all came to the same conclusion about the nine different ways of covering the hexagon. What do you think that indicated about their understanding?

Teacher: I think they really got the concept about the relationships between the shapes, especially that a trapezoid was half a hexagon and there were three triangles in a trapezoid and six in a hexagon.

Principal: Yes, I agree. There wasn't one group that didn't come up with those observations. The open-ended activity really seemed to get them to think. I noticed that there were some children who used the vocabulary and others who still used words like "the blue one." Do you think that some of them already knew those terms?

Teacher: Maybe. I was disappointed that more of them didn't use the words. I had asked them to call it a rhombus.

Principal: What do you think might have gotten them all to use the math terms? Where else might they encounter those words?

Teacher: I have a poem that has the names of the shapes. Maybe I could have started with that.

Principal: That would be great. If you try that tomorrow, let me know if that increases their use of the vocabulary.

The principal has started, as is customary, with something that went well with the lesson, but framed it not in terms of approving of the teacher but rather in being impressed by the performance of the students. That was parallel to the discussion about the uneven result from the shape-describing part of the lesson; it was focused on how what else might be found that would give them another strategy for improving student learning. This makes the teacher think about what else she has available that relates to the skill and gives her something new to try without feeling as though she did something wrong. There is a higher likelihood that she will actually try this to see if it works. If it does, she'll be sure to tell the principal, opening the possibility of another conversation about instruction completely outside the supervisory process.

Example 2 (from 7.5B)

This lesson scored a 5 on L-CO#5: Connections are made between reading and writing.

Principal: What a range of characters you had in that group today! What process did they go through to pick a subject?

Teacher: We did a brainstorm first that gave kids a picture of the variety of personalities that could be chosen. I was really amazed that many of them ended up picking one that wasn't even on the list, even though we had a pretty long list.

Principal: What kind of support did Joey need to produce his story about the Smothers Brothers? That was pretty original thinking to take on two characters.

Teacher: He just thought of it himself, but his special-education teacher worked with him on retelling the story and editing and revising. She originally wanted him to be excused from the assignment, but he loved the *Prince and the Pauper* so much and I think he really got a kick out of trying to be someone else.

Principal: Who surprised you the most?

Teacher: Not sure...they were all special in their own way. I think I was actually most surprised by Lindy, who literally couldn't think of any person in the world who she might be interested in enough to try out their life for a day. She was stuck for several days, and I tried several methods—free association, suggesting popular celebrities and fictional characters—nothing. I was almost afraid she wasn't going to produce a story. Then she decided to be a chipmunk. I'll be watching her carefully for the next project, which is going to start next week.

Principal: What will you be doing?

Teacher: We are going to be tackling some Shakespeare. I have copies of *Romeo and Juliet* that have been abridged but not rewritten. I think we're going to try to put it on before the end of the year. I'll see if I can get Lindy to take on one of the bigger roles. After this last experience, doing a play will offer another way of talking about our own identity and what it feels like to pretend to be someone else.

This conversation, instead of cutting off discussion with a "that was great" kind of comment, opened the door for thinking about what made it successful and how specific children reacted to the assignment. It also led the teacher to consider the connection between this project and the next one: that of being in the skin of someone else. She is going to be focusing on at least two children to see how they do in relation to their performance this time.

INTRODUCING DCO TO YOUR TEACHERS

While the supervision of instruction by building administrators was the raison d'etre of the DCO system from the beginning, it can be used to improve instruction in a number of different ways. Because some policies governing how teachers are evaluated and systems have been put in place, it may not be feasible or advisable to supplant those with DCO without significant groundwork. Foisting this as an evaluative tool on teachers without the proper context can be a disaster. Its comprehensive nature can be intimidating. Using it as a measure of teacher competence in the absence of a collaborative investigation of what it is and how, with appropriate teacher input, it should be used for the improvement of your overall instructional program can land you in trouble that is easily diverted. Two stories tell how different districts created vastly different results through divergent leadership approaches (see Box 7.9 and Example 7.10). These stories aside, the instrument can be useful immediately to schools in a number of settings.

Box 7.9

When Good Ideas Go Bad

INTRODUCE DCO INTO YOUR SYSTEM OF SUPERVISION AND EVALUATION

- The guidelines in DCO can lay the groundwork for improved instructional practice.
- A common language for professional competence enhances communication between principals and teachers.
- This common language can raise the professional discourse among peers and contribute to a professional learning community that is truly focused on improvements in instruction and achievement.

How It Went Bad

A superintendent had just completed training in DCO. He felt that it would benefit his faculty in general and wanted to use it as an evaluation for a professional development initiative that he had spent considerable time and resources providing for his teachers. He requested a mass training of his teachers. Being very new at this, my associates and I agreed to do the training. We created small discussion groups and conducted the training on one of the district's big inservice days. The reaction of the teachers that day was mixed; some were intrigued and excited by the ideas, while others were skeptical about a standards-based approach and resistant to looking at their instruction differently. In several of the discussion groups, the conversation turned testy.

The next week, the superintendent was served with a grievance from his teacher's union alleging a change in evaluation procedures without properly negotiating such a change. The superintendent dropped his plans, thereby ending the grievance. His teachers continued on without the benefit that could have been derived from a more collaborative approach.

Example 7.10

INTRODUCING DCO INTO THE FABRIC OF YOUR SCHOOL

Two coprincipals were concerned about their school's low performance on state test results in mathematics, despite their general population, which had all the demographic characteristics that successful schools typically have. There was discontent in the community, and there were demands for action. These principals gathered the other principals in their district, along with four math teacher leaders, and took a credit-bearing course on the concepts and use of the DCO approach. This included the analysis of classroom events on videotape, the debriefing of live classroom observations, and an emphasis on handling the postconference for maximum impact on instructional practice.

After the course, all the administrators and teacher leaders agreed that the general approach to mathematics would be beneficial to their school. Their next step was to arrange for a similar course aimed directly at teachers to explore the standards-based approach to mathematics instruction. All the administrators and teacher leaders who took the first course *retook the adapted course along with all the teachers* in the school. Together they all grappled with the new approaches, the changes that would need to occur (including new math materials), the support that would need to be ongoing for both teachers and the system in general, and how best to use the resource of the math teacher leaders in this whole process.

A year later, many changes were in place, and the school began to see its math scores rise. The school then adopted a consultancy model to raise its reading and writing scores that included several elements of the model used in math. Overall, the climate of the school improved, and the principals were grateful for the assistance received and proud of all their accomplishments.

Teacher Self-Assessment and Professional Growth Plans

Most schools have a system in place for teachers to set annual goals, which may guide the sort of professional development that they pursue that year. Introducing DCO as a self-assessment tool, you can have teachers reflect on the various components and together choose with them an area or two to focus on. This could be done as individuals, or your entire faculty could decide together where they want to place their efforts. They might even be guided by student data to help make decisions about where the greatest needs of improvement lie.

Peer Coaching and Mentoring

Mentoring and peer coaching have become much more prevalent in schools in recent years. Research demonstrates that with many more employment opportunities available to them, young teachers expect support to help them succeed. If they don't get that support, they leave (Johnson, Berg, & Donaldson, 2005). This research has prompted schools to look for solutions. There are some mentoring programs (Educational Testing Service, 2007; New Teacher Center, 2007) that are in use across the country, while some schools have tried a home-grown approach. DCO can provide assistance to peer coaches and local mentors to help focus their classroom observation skills and to guide them in their work to support their mentored teacher in his or her growth in confidence and professional expertise.

Group Lesson Study and Study Groups

As more evidence has surfaced about the concept of making teaching practice public, schools have moved to incorporate the concepts of professional learning communities (DuFour & Eaker, 1998) into their school cultures. DCO makes an excellent topic for a study group or as a framework for lesson study, similar to the method that Japanese teachers use to hone their practice (TIMSS, 2004). The most powerful use of DCO has been in groups where the trust and relationships had developed to create enough safety to fully expose one's work for feedback from colleagues. I have worked with teams of principals, some of whom were willing volunteers, to videotape a sequence of preconferences, observations, and postconferences with a cooperative teacher. Using DCO as a lens through which to view the entire process, and a "Critical Friends" protocol (NSRF, 2000) for the presentation and discussion, we were able to view and accurately analyze the dynamics of this very complex set of events. Everyone was able to grow from the experience.

An alternative method for getting a form of lesson study going in your school is to avail your teachers of the DCO instrument and use it to focus a discussion about a series of videotaped classrooms. There are ample choices of commercially available tapes in many different content areas that can be used for this purpose. Some of those made in the earlier days of the standards-based movement can be used to demonstrate the attempt of new, good ideas that have not been fully formed yet. One principal showed two tapes of fourth-grade science classes at an extended faculty meeting. These tapes varied significantly in the level of inquiry and concept development, although both teachers were working toward increased depth of thinking and student engagement. The principal reported that the ensuing conversation among the teachers was the best professional discussion they had ever had at such a meeting. Once the conversation has begun, you can begin to ask the questions about how to best benefit from DCO in your setting and make plans for implementing a plan of action.

CONCLUDING THOUGHTS

There is nothing said in this book that hasn't come up in some other venue. I acknowledge and express my appreciation for the body of research and literature that has laid the basis for DCO. I don't know what it will take or what successes have to be documented, whether it be the 90-90-90 Schools (Reeves, 2006), the schools that present annually at the Model Schools Conference hosted by the International Center for Education Leadership, or the successes experienced by individual school districts such as the El Centro District in California (Amaral, Garrison, & Klentschy, 2002), to make us sit up and take notice. The fact is that these examples and the body of research tell us what works and what doesn't. Michael Schmoker expresses the same perplexed sense of urgency:

> But don't we want more? Agreement among educators, researchers, and consultants on the effectiveness of these practices is no less than astonishing.

Shouldn't we wish to see these practices adopted . . . Clearly, they haven't been, not even by low-performing schools that are right next door to dramatically improved schools and districts. Despites some small progress, a coherent curriculum and productive collaboration are still all too rare, even among those who have attended the right conferences, read the right books, and are well acquainted with the fundamental concepts of collaborative learning communities. (Schmoker, 2006, p. 150)

DCO is one system that takes this research on a very practical level and attempts to bring into practice that which has proven its effectiveness before. I know through my professional work in and with schools and from my opportunity to be involved in national studies that this research has not yet penetrated our classrooms deeply or widely enough. I have observed whole schools and individual teachers attempt to implement pieces of what has been identified as best practice. But too often, what they have achieved with their efforts has been merely the veneer of best practice. It has been the watching of these "near misses" that inspired the "good ideas gone bad" vignettes in this book. Even as I write these words, I know that I say nothing revolutionary, but I also know that the benefits of what we know have reached far too few of our students.

While I hope that this approach and these tools can be of use to any professional educator, I write this for the principals out there who are under such pressure to make a difference. I have heard Michael Fullan say something to the effect of, "Take a changed individual and return him/her to the same culture, and the culture wins every time." This approach should be school based and not appear to be coming from some outside training whose results fade as teachers return to their particular reality. It requires your full attention and support. It is my hope that this system, with its perspective firmly based in school practice, will offer a tangible method of grappling with the intensely complex task of improving instruction and actually affecting student achievement. Use these tools as you see fit. They are laden with multiple layers that portray an ideal of practice we may never completely reach. They lay out the picture of optimal teaching and learning, coupled with systems in place for you to help teachers reach those levels of accomplished practice. There is something in here for everyone, and we know that we can all stand a bit of professional growth, regardless of our years and accumulated expertise. Our laws now ask that we strive not only for more successful and equitable student outcomes, but for every teacher to meet the highest standard of professional excellence. This cannot happen without you. I make this point in a chapter of *Teaching Science in the 21st Century*:

While training teachers is an essential component of programs to improve student results . . . , it is at the level of the school at which efforts must be aimed. A knowledgeable and passionate principal who can insure that *all* teachers are held to a high standard (as high a standard as that to which we now hold our students) is as essential as any professional development strategy. Until we have the active and informed participation of *every* principal combined with the expectation for a level of quality professional practice from *every* teacher, our results will continue to disappoint us. (Saginor, 2006b, p. 175)

Appendix A

Questions for the Preconference: Math/Science Version

SECTION I: PLANNING AND ORGANIZATION CRITERIA

Indicator	Examples of Evidence
MS-PO#1. What will you be teaching, and how does it fit into the total unit? How will you know if the students are learning? *(Is the curriculum aligned with standards and assessments and central to the lesson, or is it simply topic based?)* *(Is the teacher prepared to teach and assess the content of the lesson?)*	**Have teacher:** • note the source of the lesson (text, national, state, or local standard) • identify the specific concepts and skills to be taught and how they connect with what came before and what will follow • describe the planned activities and how they will lead directly to the content, concepts, and skills • identify what assessments are planned and how they will reflect understanding of the concepts **Listen for the extent to which the teacher:** • can speak easily about the mathematics • clearly connects the learning activities with the concepts contained in them • can clearly describe what a student will understand and be able to do as a result of learning this concept, and how the teacher will use formative assessment to adapt instruction as necessary
MS-PO#2. What kinds of materials will you be using and how are they organized? *(Are supplies and equipment available to adequately conduct the lesson?)*	**Listen to the extent to which:** • books and other written and manipulative materials are available and related to the concepts involved • materials are sufficient for all students to have access to them • materials are organized and ready to be distributed with minimum disruption to the lesson • there is sufficient amount of appropriate, working technology equipment
MS-PO#3. How is the lesson organized for teacher and students to interact? *(How substantive and respectful will teacher-student and student-student interactions be?)* *(How student-centered is the lesson?)*	**Listen for the extent to which:** • teacher will interact respectfully with students as individuals, pairs, and small groups • teacher will lead but not dominate discussions • students will actively work together in small groups • students will converse about what they are learning • teacher will encourage student interaction • teacher will allow adequate time for student reflection

Indicator	Examples of Evidence
MS-PO#4. Are investigative tasks essential elements of the lesson plan?	**Listen for the extent to which:** • students have opportunities to ask their own questions or design investigation questions • students manipulate equipment and materials • students gather, record, or analyze data • students make notes, drawings, or summaries in journal or lab book • students apply what they learn to real-world situations
MS-PO#5. Describe the students in your class and how you approach their differences. *(Is the lesson organized to address students' developmental levels, learning styles, and equity of access and opportunity?)*	**Listen for the extent to which:** • diverse learning styles will be addressed with multiple opportunities to interact with the content (i.e., group work, individual work, varied activities) • assignments or tasks will be accessible to all students • students from underrepresented groups are fully engaged in activities and conversations • exceptional students will be challenged
MS-PO#6. Describe the behavior management system in your classroom. *(Do the classroom management procedures maximize learning opportunities?)*	**Listen for the extent to which:** • teacher is confident and comfortable anticipating the class • there are clearly stated classroom norms that emphasize responsibility and respect • teacher will manage the classroom control with respect
MS-PO#7. How will you end the lesson? *(Is the lesson organized for adequate wrap-up and closure?)*	**Listen for the extent to which:** • time is available for students to articulate what was learned • teacher reviews what students have said • students complete data sheets or present conclusions about their work • clear assessments, both formative and summative, of reaching the identified standard will be observed or are planned
MS-PO#8. Does the lesson plan incorporate student or teacher use of technology?	**Have teacher describe the extent to which:** • students use computers in small groups or individually • students use graphing calculators, SMART Boards, microscopes, or other technological tools • teacher and staff are trained in use of technology
MS-PO#9. Does the teacher employ appropriate instructional strategies in planning the use of technology?	**Have teacher describe the extent to which:** • teacher plans appropriate strategies in use of the Internet • learning concepts drive the use of technology • activities are age appropriate • activities demonstrate understanding of current research
MS-PO#10. Is technology used in managing, planning, and communication?	**Have teacher describe the extent to which:** • teacher uses e-mail to peers, parents, and students • teacher uses technology for administrative tasks (grades, record keeping, making notes, and acquiring pictures, text, and sound) • teacher uses technology to manage teaching and learning effectively (lesson planning, presentations, handouts)
MS-PO#11. Do policies exist for the use of technology?	**Have teacher describe the extent to which:** • there is an Internet use policy or code that all students are aware of • evenly balanced fund resources ensure that technology reaches all students • educational goals drive technology use • administrators' vision and support for the effective use of technology are evident

Appendix B

Questions for the Preconference: Literacy Version

SECTION I: PLANNING AND ORGANIZATION CRITERIA

Question/Indicator	Examples of Evidence
L-PO#1. What will you be teaching and how does it fit into the total unit? How will you know if the students are learning? *(Is the curriculum aligned with standards and assessments and central to the lesson, or is it simply topic based?)* *(Is the teacher prepared to teach and assess the content of the lesson?)*	**Have teacher:** • note the source of the lesson (standards, text, reading selection) • identify the specific concepts and skills to be taught and how they connect with what came before and what will follow • describe the planned activities that will directly focus on lesson content, concepts, and skills • identify what assessments are planned and how they will reflect understanding of the concepts **Listen for the extent to which the teacher:** • can speak easily about the development of literacy • can clearly connect the learning activities with the skills contained in them • can clearly describe what a student will understand and be able to do as a result of the lesson • holds the students accountable for group or center work
L-PO#2. How is the lesson organized for teacher and students to interact? *(How substantive and respectful will teacher-student and student-student interactions be?)* *(How student-centered is the lesson?)*	**Listen for the extent to which:** • teacher will organize and manage student learning for whole groups, individuals, and small groups • groups or centers will be set up for substantive learning • teacher will lead but not dominate discussions • teacher will interact respectfully with students • students will converse about what they are learning • students have opportunities to ask their own questions
L-PO#3. Describe the students in your class and how you approach their differences. *(Is the lesson organized to address students' developmental levels, learning styles, and equity of access and opportunity?)*	**Listen for the extent to which:** • diverse learning styles will be addressed with multiple opportunities to interact with the content (i.e., group work, individual work, varied activities) • assignments or tasks will be accessible to all students • students from underrepresented groups are fully engaged in activities and conversations • exceptional students will be challenged

Question/Indicator	Examples of Evidence
L-PO#4. How is the time organized for the lesson? *(Is the lesson organized for time to reflect on the lesson and its content?)*	**Listen for the extent to which:** • time is apportioned for teaching skills and practice or application • transitions are planned for and organized • time is apportioned for large-group, small-group, and individual think time
L-PO#5. How will you end the lesson? *(Is the lesson organized for adequate wrap-up and closure?)*	**Listen for the extent to which:** • time is available for students to articulate what was learned • teacher reviews what students have said • students have time for reflection • students compare and share work • clear assessments of reaching the identified skills are observed or are planned
L-PO#6. Describe the behavior management system in your classroom. *(Do the classroom management procedures maximize learning opportunities?)*	**Listen for the extent to which:** • the teacher seems confident and comfortable anticipating the class • there are clearly stated classroom norms that emphasize responsibility and respect • students are made familiar with the classroom norms • there are clearly stated consequences for specific behaviors • teacher manages classroom control with respect • students are provided with strategies for self-correction

Appendix C

The Math/Science Version

Indicators	Examples of Evidence
MS-IM#1. Teacher demonstrates confidence as a facilitator of mathematical and scientific learning and growth	• Teacher speaks fluently and in depth about concepts • Teacher allows student questions and can expand on topic as necessary • Lesson is not overly scripted; teacher demonstrates ability to adapt the task as necessary to guide and deepen student learning • Teacher encourages students to actively grapple with concepts • Teacher presents himself or herself as a learner along with students, indicating what he or she doesn't know and voicing satisfaction about learned information
MS-IM#2. Periods of teacher-student interaction are probing and substantive	• Questions expose and draw on students' prior knowledge • Questions and dialogue emphasize higher order thinking (students compare, contrast, classify, use analogies and metaphors; Marzano, 1999) • Teacher probes with challenging activities in addition to questions • Students are encouraged to develop a metacognitive sense of their learning
MS-IM#3. Teacher's instructional choices are effective in engaging students in active and thoughtful learning	• Students are engaged and excited about finding answers to questions posed by the activity • Objectives are clearly stated (sometimes in an inquiry; this comes out later in the lesson and might not be observed at first) • Activities are likely to lead to student learning in the stated objectives • Teacher does not dominate discussions • Tasks are challenging; teacher sets high expectations • Both teacher-directed instruction and constructivist methods are used as appropriate for task and diverse learning needs

Indicators	Examples of Evidence
MS-IM#4. Students have opportunities to construct their own knowledge (Note: If this is not directly observed in the lesson, teacher can identify when and how in the unit this will occur.)	• Investigative tasks are essential elements of the lesson • Curiosity and perseverance are encouraged • Students apply existing knowledge and skills to new situations and integrate new and prior knowledge • Students make notes, drawings, or summaries in a journal or lab book that becomes part of their ongoing resources • Students have opportunities to do more than follow procedures; they ask their own questions, choose their own strategies, or design investigations • Students manipulate materials and equipment • Teachers and students discuss which technologies to use for various products and processes and why to use them
MS-IM#5. The pace of the lesson is appropriate for the developmental level of the students, and there is adequate time for wrap-up and closure of the lesson	• Students have time to engage in the tasks, and there is adequate time to practice new skills • Teacher "wait time" is sufficient to allow all students to have a chance to think of answers • Teacher adjusts time periods to accommodate students if necessary • Time is available for students to review, reflect on, and articulate what was learned, either through class discussions, journal writing, completion of data sheets, or presentations
MS-IM#6. Periods of student-student interaction are productive and enhance individual understanding of the lesson	• Students have opportunities to collaborate in pairs or small groups • Student group work is structured to lead students to greater understanding; outcomes are clearly stated • Student discussions demonstrate thinking and learning about the concepts contained in the activities
T-IM#7. Teacher models technology integration	• Teacher uses the equipment in class and suggests technology tools to expand student learning • Teacher has backup plans in case of a problem with the technology
T-IM#8. Students use electronic resources efficiently and productively	• Students use planned strategies to contact resources and collect information • Within a lesson or unit, students use many available resources, including the Internet • Students process and evaluate the information collected • Students communicate appropriate school-related information through the use of electronic tools (e.g., newsletters, Web pages)

SECTION III. CONTENT OF THE LESSON

Indicators	Examples of Evidence
MS-CO#1. Academic standards are central to the instructional program	• Content is aligned with the appropriate national or state standards • The standard and content is clearly identified and understood by students OR • The standard and content will intentionally emerge from the activities
MS-CO#2. Teacher shows an understanding of the concepts and content of the lesson	• Teacher can articulate clearly what concepts are intentionally contained within the activities • The activities and instructional strategies are crafted to lead to the understanding of those concepts • Teacher provides accurate information • Teacher asks questions that reflect substantive understanding of the topic • Teacher elicits more than just facts or introduces confounding factors to deepen thinking • Teacher encourages students to question, probe, explain answers, and extend knowledge
MS-CO#3. Teacher collects and assesses evidence of student progress to enhance teaching and learning	• Assessment is systematic and ongoing so that teacher can track student progress and adjust instruction • Student misconceptions are identified so that they can adjust their thinking • Agreed-on standards are used to judge the quality of student products and performances • Assessments are varied (journals, performance tasks, presentations, tests) and target concepts and skills • Students self-assess by using rubrics or reviewing past work to see their progress • Assessments clearly indicate conceptual closure
MS-CO#4. Students are intellectually engaged with concepts contained in the activities of the lesson	• Students are engaged in substantive discourse about the concepts with teacher and other students • Students do more than just guess; they check their hypotheses to discover important concepts that lead them to learn the concepts • Student responses reflect real thinking, not just "canned answers" or simple procedural steps • Students come to conceptual closure about what they have learned by the end of a unit
MS-CO#5. Connections are made between concepts in this lesson and previous and future lessons in the unit, other subjects, or applications in the real world	• Teacher identifies the connections • Student activities and discussions lead to having them make connections • The connections made are more than just mentioning them; they are used to further understanding of the current concepts • Teacher provides examples and students discuss real-world applications • Students are provided with opportunities to actually apply new learning in the real world

Indicators	Examples of Evidence
MS-CO#6. The lesson incorporates abstractions, theories, and models as appropriate	• Teacher explains and students discuss how concept fits in an existing theory or relates to other theories • Students create models and other nonlinguistic representations that depict the concepts • Models portray concepts accurately • Models help students make the connections to the abstract concepts
T-CO#7. Students use electronic resources to support the learning of the content of the lesson	• Students collect resources and conduct collaborative research (e.g., World Wide Web, CD-ROM) in a focused, productive way for specific educational purposes • Students are taught skills needed for critical analysis of information obtained through the use of electronic resources • Students demonstrate the ability to distinguish fact from opinion or bias, and they consider the reliability and validity of their sources
T-CO#8. Students understand appropriate use of technology tools	• Students and teachers select technology tools appropriate to the learning task (simulations, word processing, spreadsheets, databases, modeling) • Technology (computers, calculators, microscopes, probes, video, etc.) is used to enhance and extend capability for data collection, recording, analysis, and presentation • More time is spent on content than on decorative and extrinsic elements

SECTION IV. CLASSROOM CULTURE

Indicators	Examples of Evidence
MS-CU#1. Classroom management maximizes learning opportunities	• Teacher maintains a level of order conducive to learning (students are attending to the teacher and the activity) • There is an atmosphere of freedom and flexibility within that order • Classroom norms emphasize personal and collective responsibility to create a learning community • Directions to students are clear to avoid confusion and constant questions, which interrupt the flow of the activity • During group times, students not working with teacher are engaged in relevant and important work

(Continued)

(Continued)

Indicators	Examples of Evidence
MS-CU#2. Classroom routines are clear and consistent	• There are clearly stated classroom norms • There is a minimum of disruption and inappropriate interruptions; transition times are seamless • Routines for noninstructional duties are clearly established, and students follow them consistently
MS-CU#3. Behavior is respectful and appropriate	• Teacher manages classroom control preventively and with respect • If correction is needed, teacher handles the situation with respectful control and minimum disruption • There are clearly stated consequences for specific behaviors, and they are applied consistently • The atmosphere of the classroom feels safe, and there is an absence of bullying, harassment, and inappropriate language • Students are provided with strategies for self-monitoring and correction
MS-CU#4. The classroom culture generates enthusiasm for the exploration of mathematical and scientific ideas	• Many mathematical and scientific tools and resources are prominent and frequently used • Students generate ideas, questions, propositions, and solutions • Students are encouraged to use multiple approaches to solve problems (numeric, algebraic, and graphic in math; open-ended inquiry in science) • Students are engaged and motivated to participate • There is student math and science work displayed
MS-CU#5. Teacher shows respect for students' ideas, questions, and contributions to the lesson and works collaboratively with students	• Teacher has routines that encourage all students to participate • Adequate time is provided for discussion • Teacher listens carefully to student responses, not always looking for a predetermined answer • Teacher accepts ideas without judging and respectfully helps students untangle their misconceptions • Teacher supports and facilitates work of students as individuals and in small and large groups
MS-CU#6. Students show respect for and value each others' ideas, questions, and contributions to the lesson; students work collaboratively	• Students readily share ideas and listen to each other in large and small groups • No student dominates • Students discuss alternative ideas • Students challenge and question each other respectfully • Students coordinate efforts and share responsibility for group results
MS-CU#7. All students have equal access to the total educational resources of the classroom	• Students have equal access to teacher attention, materials, technology, and assigned roles • The pattern of inclusion of all students shows attention to issues of gender, race, ethnicity, special needs, and socioeconomic status

Indicators	Examples of Evidence
	• Teacher discourages dominance of individual students and encourages reticent students • Groupings maximize each student's ability to participate; group dynamics are monitored by the teacher • Teacher addresses diverse needs and abilities • Teacher recognizes exceptional participation and creates opportunities for students to exceed standards
T-CU#8. Students exhibit positive attitudes or leadership in using technology to support learning	• Students mentor each other and troubleshoot with technology • Students take charge of their own learning and are able to make choices about when and how to use technology to support that learning • Students have backup plans in case of a problem with the technology
T-CU#9. All students are guaranteed equity of access and opportunities for learning through a wide variety of technologies regardless of gender, economics, race, first language, special education, ability, or learning style	• Gender inequities are recognized and addressed • Technologies support learning that is socially and culturally diverse • Special provisions are made to increase access for students who do not have access to technology at home • Assistive technology is used to enable all students to achieve the learning goals • Each computer has Internet access • Network access allows use of file and print services • Phone is available for outside communication • Internet response is rapid enough for viable use
T-CU#10. Appropriate technologies are present and available in the classroom in sufficient quantity	• Students and teachers have as-needed access to technology adequate in quantity and variety (computers, calculators, microscopes, probes, video, etc.), such as: equipment and software (simulations, word processing, spreadsheets, databases, modeling), tutorials and other support materials, assistive technologies for diverse learning needs, technology for administrative tasks, and communication tools (i.e., telephone, fax)
T-CU#11. Physical layout of technology makes the resources accessible and supports learning for all students	• Equipment is easy and safe to use and in good repair • Equipment and resources are arranged so that teacher can easily monitor and guide the use of technology • Students move freely in the classroom to access technology as needed • The layout and location of technology tools contribute to their regular use
T-CU#12. Students understand ethical and appropriate uses of technology	• Teachers model ethical use of technology • Students demonstrate ethical use of technology • Ongoing discussion of ethical use is evident • Students dialogue about uses of technology in daily life and the advantages, disadvantages, and responsibilities of those uses (from the International Society for Technology in Education)

Appendix D

The Literacy Version

Indicators	Examples of Evidence
L-IM#1. Teacher shows an understanding of how to use text to build reading fluency, comprehension, and writing skills in the students	• There is evidence of a balanced program including decoding skills, comprehension, and writing • The teacher models the skills of good readers and writers • Spelling and vocabulary are taught in context • Multiple decoding strategies (sounding out, beginning and ending sounds, blending sounds, using context or pictures, sight words, "word wall," etc.) are used in reading instruction • When teacher introduces a new phonogram, students have opportunity to practice it (K–2) • Teacher reviews old phonograms, and students demonstrate recognition and mastery (K–2) • Teacher employs a variety of techniques and materials, including choral chanting, skywriting, use of chalkboard or chart (K–2) • Multiple reading strategies (pre-reading, making predictions, asking questions, identifying important themes, analyzing text structure, making connections and inferences, evaluating, summarizing, re-reading) are evident • Teacher builds students' independent use of all these strategies and provides opportunities to use them in appropriate contexts • Both meaning making and fluency building are the focus of these activities • There is evidence that writing is taught through a multiphase process, including prewriting, drafting, conferencing, revising, editing, and publishing • Teacher conducts direct instruction in writing skills (topic development, organization, sentence/paragraph creation and structure, developing tone, voice, purpose, etc.) • Instruction is given in the different writing genres (response to text, report, narrative, procedure, persuasive, reflective essay)

Indicators	Examples of Evidence
L-IM#2. Teacher's instructional choices are effective in engaging students in literacy activities	• Assignments are varied in nature and difficulty so that all students are engaged in the activity • Lesson construction has been purposefully planned for active engagement of all students • During read-alouds, teacher reads with animation and stops to ask questions, involve students, and describe new or relevant vocabulary without interrupting the flow of the story • Students have text or reading response journals to follow along with during read-alouds • Books used are appropriate, and the students are engaged in reading or listening Prewriting Phase • Teacher clearly defines the purpose of the writing • Teacher activates background knowledge about the topic • Students are encouraged to use a graphic organizer • Teacher helps students generate possible language for their writing • Teacher gives feedback on students' prewriting
L-IM#3. Students have opportunities to construct their own meaning	• Students write or tell their reactions and connections to the reading selection • Students can discuss strategies they use for understanding text • Activities are used to help students "own" their new learning; elements of choice are part of the lesson strategies • Students write frequently and can discuss the writing process Drafting phase • Teacher encourages students to get ideas down without focusing too intently on spelling, grammar, or editing (Note: If this is not directly observed in the lesson, teacher can identify when and how in the unit this will occur) • Students write their ideas easily and freely, knowing they can edit, correct, or change things later (Note: If this is not directly observed in the lesson, teacher can identify when and how in the unit this will occur)
L-IM#4. The pace of the lesson is appropriate for the developmental level of the students, and there is adequate time for wrap-up and closure of the lesson	• Students have time to complete work • Some activities allow for students to work at their own pace • Adequate time is provided for discussion and processing of learning • When appropriate, teacher holds whole-class discussions to clarify expectations or provide direction • All students have opportunities to participate • Pace is adjusted as necessary • There is closure at the end of the lesson

(Continued)

(Continued)

Indicators	Examples of Evidence
L-IM#5. Periods of student-student interaction are productive and enhance individual understanding of the lesson	• Tasks for each reading group or "center" are clear for students to engage in productive learning at all times • Students use reading group or center time when teacher is not with group to support each other and continue to build their reading skills • Students working with the teacher engage in cross-talk with and respond to each other and not just the teacher • Students are encouraged to have peer conferences during drafting and editing stages • Student peer conferences add to the quality of student writing products • Teacher provides opportunities for students to share their writing with each other

SECTION III. CONTENT OF THE LITERACY LESSON

Indicator	Examples of Evidence
L-CO#1. Academic standards and assessments are central to the literacy program	• The content is aligned with state or national standards • Rubrics and processes used in reading and writing are clearly established and are understood by all students • Agreed-on processes of reading, writing, and other literacy skills are used to judge the quality of student products and performances
L-CO#2. Teacher has depth of knowledge of the content and concepts, and he or she is skilled in using text to build meaning	• Teacher clearly connects the learning activities with the skills they are intentionally designed to elicit • Teacher models appropriate reading and writing strategies • Information provided is clear and accurate • Teacher takes advantage of reading material to discuss background knowledge or vocabulary • Teacher refers directly to the text to build understanding • Teacher asks a variety of types of questions (probing for meaning, clarification, inference, evaluation) • Teacher has students justify answers by referring to text • Teacher addresses misconceptions and misunderstandings • Teacher connects content in reading selection to previously learned material in this unit or others • Teacher reads difficult passages and helps students understand the material (students follow with finger if necessary; K–2) (Note: if this is not directly observed in the lesson, teacher can identify when and how in the unit this will occur)

Indicators	Examples of Evidence
L-CO#3. Teacher collects and assesses evidence of student progress to enhance teaching and learning	• Assessment is systematic and ongoing so that teacher can track student progress and adapt instruction • Clear criteria are used to judge student work • Student misconceptions are identified through formative assessment so that students can adjust their thinking • Assessments clearly target concepts *and* skills • Assessments are varied in the kind of tasks required • Teacher gives oral and written feedback • Assessments test spelling and vocabulary with an emphasis on context • Teacher guides students to focus on criteria or rubrics to edit writing for final copy • There is evidence that teacher conducts both informal and scheduled reading and writing conferences that are focused and positive • Assessments clearly indicate conceptual closure
L-CO#4. Students demonstrate the building of their literacy skills	• Students demonstrate building fluency by reading aloud with expression, accuracy, and appropriate pace, and by following text (with their fingers if needed at the K–2 level) • Sound symbol patterns previously taught are recognized and used correctly in new reading and writing situations • Students demonstrate building vocabulary by using new words in their speech and writing • Students engage in literature discussions to reflect on and react to reading selections, and they directly refer to the text to demonstrate and improve comprehension • Students are developing a metacognitive understanding of the skills and strategies they are using so that they fully understand the processes of reading and writing • Students are building their writing ability—using invented spelling that demonstrates grade-appropriate sound-symbol correspondence at the K–2 level—using writing resources as necessary (dictionary, thesaurus, etc.) • Students have many opportunities to practice writing
L-CO#5. Connections are made between reading and writing and other subjects and have applications to the real world	• Teacher makes connections between writing assignments and reading selections • Students have opportunities to write about what they are reading • Teacher connects reading and writing to other texts and other content areas • Teacher asks students to make these connections • Student activities and discussions further lead to having them make connections • Teacher uses reading and writing assignments to point out vocabulary, syntax, and usage • Reading and writing skills are taught in a context and have relevance to students • Students discuss real-world applications • Students are provided with opportunities to actually apply new learning in the real world

SECTION IV. CLASSROOM CULTURE OF THE LITERACY LESSON

Indicators	Examples of Evidence
L-CU#1. Classroom management maximizes learning opportunities	• Teacher maintains a level of order conducive to learning (students are attending to the teacher and the activity) • There is an atmosphere of freedom and flexibility within that order • Classroom norms emphasize personal and collective responsibility to create a learning community • Directions to students are clear to avoid confusion and constant questions, which interrupt the flow of the activity • During group times, students not working with teacher are engaged in relevant and important work
L-CU#2. Classroom routines are clear and consistent	• There are clearly stated classroom norms • There is a minimum of disruption and inappropriate interruptions; transition times are seamless • Routines for noninstructional duties are clearly established, and students follow them consistently
L-CU#3. Behavior is respectful and appropriate	• Teacher manages classroom control preventively and with respect • If correction is needed, teacher handles the situation with respectful control and minimum disruption • There are clearly stated consequences for specific behaviors, and they are applied consistently • The atmosphere of the classroom feels safe, and there is an absence of bullying, harassment, and inappropriate language • Students are provided with strategies for self-monitoring and correction
L-CU#4. Literacy is valued, and reading and writing are enthusiastically promoted	• Literacy is approached with enthusiasm by teacher and students • Student work displayed is connected to curriculum or in some way used by children or teacher • Writing is valued and enthusiastically promoted • Many types of authentic reading materials are displayed and are available to students for reference during class • Dictionaries, thesaurus, style manuals, and literacy resources are available for students to use at all times; teacher encourages students to use these when reading and writing
L-CU#5. Teacher shows respect for student ideas, questions, and contributions and works collaboratively with students	• Teacher has routines that encourage all students to participate • Adequate time is provided for discussion • Teacher listens carefully to student responses, not always looking for a predetermined answer • Teacher accepts ideas without judging and respectfully helps students untangle their misconceptions • Teacher supports and facilitates work of students as individuals and in small and large groups

Indicators	Examples of Evidence
L-CU#6. Students show respect for and value each others' ideas, questions, and contributions to the lesson; students work collaboratively	<ul><li>Students readily share ideas and listen to each other in large and small groups</li><li>No student dominates</li><li>Students discuss alternative ideas</li><li>Students challenge and question each other respectfully</li><li>Students coordinate efforts and share responsibility for group results</li></ul>
L-CU#7. All students have equal access to the total educational resources of the classroom	<ul><li>Students have equal access to teacher attention, materials, technology, and assigned roles</li><li>The pattern of inclusion of all students shows attention to issues of gender, race, ethnicity, special needs, and socioeconomic status</li><li>Teacher discourages dominance of individual students and encourages reticent students</li><li>Groupings maximize each student's ability to participate; group dynamics are monitored by the teacher</li><li>Teacher addresses diverse needs and abilities</li><li>Teacher recognizes exceptional participation and creates opportunities for students to exceed standards</li></ul>

Appendix E

The "Cross-Walks"

THE CRITERIA OF DIAGNOSTIC CLASSROOM OBSERVATION (DCO) AND THE DOMAINS OF DANIELSON'S (1986) FRAMEWORK FOR TEACHING

DCO Section I: Planning/Organization
This section is designed to guide a preconference with the teacher to be observed to assess the quality of planning of the lesson.

Danielson Domain I: Danielson Planning and Preparation
This section is part of the observation process and measures goals, teacher knowledge, design of instruction, and assessment.

DCO Section II: Implementation of the Lesson
This section focuses on the effectiveness of instruction and learning that occur during the lesson. Observations of both teacher and student activity are noted.

Danielson Domain II: Instruction
This section measures teacher instructional practices.

DCO Section III: Content of the Lesson
This section notes the accuracy, importance, alignment with state and national standards, level of abstraction, and connections to other concepts of the content. Training also includes how to recognize conceptual closure, correction of student misconceptions, and the effectiveness of student assessment.

No Corresponding Danielson Domain

DCO Section IV: Classroom Culture
This section assesses the learning environment, classroom management, the level of student engagement, the nature of the working relationships, and issues of equity.

Danielson Domain III: Classroom Environment
This section measures the level of respect and rapport, classroom management, the culture of learning, and organization of physical space.

Danielson Domain IV: Professional Practice
This section deals with the relationship of the teacher to colleagues, the school district, families, and professional responsibilities and conduct.

No Corresponding DCO Domain

In DCO, the integration of technology is woven throughout the entire tool.

There is no technology component in the Danielson Framework.

THE CRITERIA OF DIAGNOSTIC CLASSROOM OBSERVATION AND THE SKILLFUL TEACHER

DCO Section I : Planning and Organization
This section guides the preconference: probing teacher thinking and forethought for implementation, content, and classroom culture.

Skillful Teacher **Parameters**
The parameters are space, time, routines, and objectives.

DCO Section II: Implementation of the Lesson
This section involves engagement of learners, confidence and preparation of teacher, teacher-student interaction, student-student interaction, constructing one's own knowledge, pacing, and use of technology.

Skillful Teacher **Parameters**
The parameters are attention, principles of learning (active participation, degree of momentum, guidance, saying and doing), clarity (purpose), models of teaching (learning opportunities), and learning experiences (learning opportunities).

DCO Section III: Content of the Lesson
This section rates teacher knowledge, alignment with standards, assessment (multiple forms), metacognition, connections, conceptual closure, abstractions and models, use of literacy as a learning tool, and use of technology to build content learning.

Skillful Teacher **Parameters**
The parameters are principles of learning (meaning, contiguity, critical attributes, application in setting, active participation, feedback, reinforcement, keeping students open and thinking, end without closure), organization of curriculum, clarity (cognitive empathy), and assessment (multiple forms).

DCO Section IV: Classroom Culture
This section rates behavior management, enthusiasm, mutual respect, development of a learning community, listening to and considering alternative ideas, and equity of access to all learning resources of the classroom (teacher attention, materials, participation, and technology).

Skillful Teacher **Parameters**
The parameters are discipline, classroom climate (negotiating the rules of the classroom game), and risk taking and confidence.

**THE CRITERIA OF DIAGNOSTIC CLASSROOM OBSERVATION (DCO)
AND THE HORIZON, INC. OBSERVATION PROTOCOL**

DCO Section I: Planning/Organization
This section is designed to guide a preconference with the teacher to be observed to assess the quality of planning of the lesson, as anticipated by the criteria, indicators, and evidence of the three subsequent sections.

Horizon Section I: Purpose of the Lesson and Design
In Section I, Section B compares the teacher's stated purpose and the extent to which the activities are focused on algorithms versus conceptual understanding as observed. Section C evaluates the extent to which the lesson has been planned to address the key indicators of the following sections.

DCO Section II: Implementation of the Lesson
This section focuses on the effectiveness of instruction and learning that occur during the lesson. Observations of both teacher and student activity are noted. Examples of evidence are outlined.

Horizon Section II: Implementation
This section measures teacher instructional practices with a high degree of correlation with the indicators in DCO. No examples of evidence are presented.

DCO Section III: Content of the Lesson
This section notes the accuracy, importance, alignment with state and national standards, level of abstraction, and connections to other concepts of the content. Training also includes how to recognize conceptual closure, correction of student misconceptions, and the effectiveness of student assessment.

Horizon Section III: Content
This section measures the quality of the content with a high degree of correlation with the indicators in DCO. No examples of evidence are presented.

DCO Section IV: Classroom Culture
This section assesses the learning environment, classroom management, the level of student engagement, the nature of the working relationships, and issues of equity.

Horizon Section IV: Classroom Culture
This section measures the level of respect, rapport, and equity with a high degree of correlation with the indicators of DCO. No examples of evidence are presented.

In DCO, the integration of technology is woven throughout the entire tool.

There is no technology component in the Horizon Observation Protocol.

DCO has a Literacy Version and a Composite Version for all content areas.

The Horizon Observation Protocol is directed toward mathematics and science only.

Appendix F

The Score Sheets

**IMPLEMENTATION OF THE LESSON: MATH/SCIENCE
AND COMPOSITE VERSIONS**

MS-IM#1. Teacher demonstrates confidence as a facilitator of mathematical and scientific learning and growth

1	2	3	4	5
no evidence	limited evidence	moderate evidence	consistent evidence	extensive evidence

Supporting evidence for rating/comments:

MS-IM#2. Periods of teacher-student interaction are probing and substantive

1	2	3	4	5
no evidence	limited evidence	moderate evidence	consistent evidence	extensive evidence

Supporting evidence for rating/comments:

MS-IM#3. Teacher's instructional choices are effective in engaging students in active and thoughtful learning

1	2	3	4	5
no evidence	limited evidence	moderate evidence	consistent evidence	extensive evidence

Supporting evidence for rating/comments:

(Continued)

(Continued)

MS-IM#4. Students have opportunities to construct their own knowledge (Note: If this is not directly observed in the lesson, teacher can identify when and how in the unit this will occur.)

1	2	3	4	5
no evidence	limited evidence	moderate evidence	consistent evidence	extensive evidence

Supporting evidence for rating/comments:

MS-IM#5. The pace of the lesson is appropriate for the developmental level of the students, and there is adequate time for wrap-up and closure of the lesson

1	2	3	4	5
no evidence	limited evidence	moderate evidence	consistent evidence	extensive evidence

Supporting evidence for rating/comments:

MS-IM#6. Periods of student-student interaction are productive and enhance individual understanding of the lesson

1	2	3	4	5
no evidence	limited evidence	moderate evidence	consistent evidence	extensive evidence

Supporting evidence for rating/comments:

Composite-IM#7. Best practices in reading as a learning tool are evident

1	2	3	4	5
no evidence	limited evidence	moderate evidence	consistent evidence	extensive evidence

Supporting evidence for rating/comments:

Composite-IM#8. Best practices in the use of writing as a learning tool are evident

1	2	3	4	5
no evidence	limited evidence	moderate evidence	consistent evidence	extensive evidence

Supporting evidence for rating/comments:

Composite-IM#9.Connections are made between reading and writing

1	2	3	4	5
no evidence	limited evidence	moderate evidence	consistent evidence	extensive evidence

Supporting evidence for rating/comments:

T-IM#7. Teacher models technology integration

1	2	3	4	5
no evidence	limited evidence	moderate evidence	consistent evidence	extensive evidence

Supporting evidence for rating/comments:

T-IM#8. Students use electronic resources efficiently and productively

1	2	3	4	5
no evidence	limited evidence	moderate evidence	consistent evidence	extensive evidence

Supporting evidence for rating/comments:

IMPLEMENTATION OF THE LESSON: LITERACY VERSION

L-IM#1. Teacher shows an understanding of how to use text to build reading fluency, comprehension, and writing skills in the students

1	2	3	4	5
no evidence	limited evidence	moderate evidence	consistent evidence	extensive evidence

Supporting evidence for rating/comments:

L-IM#2. Teacher's instructional choices are effective in engaging students in literacy activities

1	2	3	4	5
no evidence	limited evidence	moderate evidence	consistent evidence	extensive evidence

Supporting evidence for rating/comments:

(Continued)

(Continued)

L-IM#3. Students have opportunities to construct their own meaning

1	2	3	4	5
no evidence	limited evidence	moderate evidence	consistent evidence	extensive evidence

Supporting evidence for rating/comments:

L-IM#4. The pace of the lesson is appropriate for the developmental level of the students, and there is adequate time for wrap-up and closure of the lesson

1	2	3	4	5
no evidence	limited evidence	moderate evidence	consistent evidence	extensive evidence

Supporting evidence for rating/comments:

L-IM#5. Periods of student-student interaction are productive and enhance individual understanding of the lesson

1	2	3	4	5
no evidence	limited evidence	moderate evidence	consistent evidence	extensive evidence

Supporting evidence for rating/comments:

CONTENT OF THE LESSON: MATH/SCIENCE AND COMPOSITE VERSIONS

MS-CO#1. Academic standards are central to the instructional program

1	2	3	4	5
no evidence	limited evidence	moderate evidence	consistent evidence	extensive evidence

Supporting evidence for rating/comments:

MS-CO#2. Teacher shows an understanding of the concepts and content of the lesson

1	2	3	4	5
no evidence	limited evidence	moderate evidence	consistent evidence	extensive evidence

Supporting evidence for rating/comments:

MS-CO#3. Teacher collects and assesses evidence of student progress to enhance teaching and learning

1	2	3	4	5
no evidence	limited evidence	moderate evidence	consistent evidence	extensive evidence

Supporting evidence for rating/comments:

MS-CO#4. Students are intellectually engaged with concepts contained in the activities of the lesson

1	2	3	4	5
no evidence	limited evidence	moderate evidence	consistent evidence	extensive evidence

Supporting evidence for rating/comments:

MS-CO#5. Connections are made between concepts in this lesson and previous and future lessons in the unit, other subjects, or applications in the real world

1	2	3	4	5
no evidence	limited evidence	moderate evidence	consistent evidence	extensive evidence

Supporting evidence for rating/comments:

MS-CO#6. The lesson incorporates abstractions, theories, and models as appropriate

1	2	3	4	5
no evidence	limited evidence	moderate evidence	consistent evidence	extensive evidence

Supporting evidence for rating/comments:

Composite-CO#7. Teacher shows an understanding of how to use text to build comprehension of the content

1	2	3	4	5
no evidence	limited evidence	moderate evidence	consistent evidence	extensive evidence

Supporting evidence for rating/comments:

(Continued)

(Continued)

T-CO#7. Students use electronic resources to support the learning of the content of the lesson

1	2	3	4	5
no evidence	limited evidence	moderate evidence	consistent evidence	extensive evidence

Supporting evidence for rating/comments:

T-CO#8. Students understand appropriate use of technology tools

1	2	3	4	5
no evidence	limited evidence	moderate evidence	consistent evidence	extensive evidence

Supporting evidence for rating/comments:

CONTENT OF THE LESSON: LITERACY VERSION

L-CO#1. Academic standards and assessments are central to the literacy program

1	2	3	4	5
no evidence	limited evidence	moderate evidence	consistent evidence	extensive evidence

Supporting evidence for rating/comments:

L-CO#2. Teacher has depth of knowledge of the content and concepts, and he or she is skilled in using text to build meaning

1	2	3	4	5
no evidence	limited evidence	moderate evidence	consistent evidence	extensive evidence

Supporting evidence for rating/comments:

L-CO#3. Teacher collects and assesses evidence of student progress to enhance teaching and learning

1	2	3	4	5
no evidence	limited evidence	moderate evidence	consistent evidence	extensive evidence

Supporting evidence for rating/comments:

L-CO#4. Students demonstrate the building of their literacy skills

1	2	3	4	5
no evidence	limited evidence	moderate evidence	consistent evidence	extensive evidence

Supporting evidence for rating/comments:

L-CO#5. Connections are made between reading and writing and other subjects and have applications to the real world

1	2	3	4	5
no evidence	limited evidence	moderate evidence	consistent evidence	extensive evidence

Supporting evidence for rating/comments:

CLASSROOM CULTURE: ALL VERSIONS

CU#1. Classroom management maximizes learning opportunities

1	2	3	4	5
no evidence	limited evidence	moderate evidence	consistent evidence	extensive evidence

Supporting evidence for rating/comments:

(Continued)

(Continued)

CU#2. Classroom routines are clear and consistent

1	2	3	4	5
no evidence	limited evidence	moderate evidence	consistent evidence	extensive evidence

Supporting evidence for rating/comments:

CU#3. Behavior is respectful and appropriate

1	2	3	4	5
no evidence	limited evidence	moderate evidence	consistent evidence	extensive evidence

Supporting evidence for rating/comments:

L-CU#4. Literacy is highly valued, and reading and writing are enthusiastically promoted

1	2	3	4	5
no evidence	limited evidence	moderate evidence	consistent evidence	extensive evidence

Supporting evidence for rating/comments:

MS-CU#4. The classroom culture generates enthusiasm for the exploration of mathematical and scientific ideas

1	2	3	4	5
no evidence	limited evidence	moderate evidence	consistent evidence	extensive evidence

Supporting evidence for rating/comments:

CU#5. Teacher shows respect for student ideas, questions, and contributions and works collaboratively with students

1	2	3	4	5
no evidence	limited evidence	moderate evidence	consistent evidence	extensive evidence

Supporting evidence for rating/comments:

MS-CU#6. Students show respect for and value each others' ideas, questions, and contributions to the lesson; students work collaboratively

1	2	3	4	5
no evidence	limited evidence	moderate evidence	consistent evidence	extensive evidence

Supporting evidence for rating/comments:

CU#7. All students have equal access to the total educational resources of the classroom

1	2	3	4	5
no evidence	limited evidence	moderate evidence	consistent evidence	extensive evidence

Supporting evidence for rating/comments:

T-CU#8. Students exhibit positive attitudes or leadership in using technology to support learning

1	2	3	4	5
no evidence	limited evidence	moderate evidence	consistent evidence	extensive evidence

Supporting evidence for rating/comments:

T-CU#9. All students are guaranteed equity of access and opportunities for learning through a wide variety of technologies regardless of gender, economics, race, first language, special education, ability, or learning style

1	2	3	4	5
no evidence	limited evidence	moderate evidence	consistent evidence	extensive evidence

Supporting evidence for rating/comments:

T-CU#10. Appropriate technologies are present and available in the classroom in sufficient quantity

1	2	3	4	5
no evidence	limited evidence	moderate evidence	consistent evidence	extensive evidence

Supporting evidence for rating/comments:

(Continued)

(Continued)

T-CU#11. Physical layout of technology makes the resources accessible and supports learning for all students

1	2	3	4	5
no evidence	limited evidence	moderate evidence	consistent evidence	extensive evidence

Supporting evidence for rating/comments:

T-CU#12. Students understand ethical and appropriate uses of technology

1	2	3	4	5
no evidence	limited evidence	moderate evidence	consistent evidence	extensive evidence

Supporting evidence for rating/comments:

Appendix G

The "Cheat Sheets"

THE MATH/SCIENCE VERSION

Name of teacher: _____ Date of observation: _____

Math/Science Implementation	Notes, Examples
Teacher facilitation—Teacher speaks in depth about concepts, encourages students to grapple	
Student engagement—Are students engaged in active, thoughtful learning, constructing their own knowledge? Diverse instructional strategies? Developing a metacognitive sense?	
Pace—Appropriate to the lesson? To student learning? "Wait time?" Reflection time built in?	
Student-student interaction—Is it helping students reach a better understanding?	
Math/Science Content	Notes, Examples
Standards—Lesson/tasks/assessments aligned with standards?	
Conceptual understanding—Does teacher demonstrate depth of knowledge? Are students grappling with concepts? How is teacher assessing/planning to assess?	
Content—Are concepts to be learned clear? Skills? Are expectations evident? Does teacher address student misconceptions? How?	
Connections—Is the lesson related to real-world situations? Other disciplines? Previous/future lessons?	
Abstractions—Does the teacher incorporate new concepts into existing theories and use models as appropriate? Are models accurate?	

(Continued)

(Continued)

Math/Science Classroom Culture	Notes, Examples
Classroom behavior—Climate is structured but flexible; expectations are clear and consistent; routines are smooth; interruptions minimal; safe, respectful environment?	
Enthusiasm—Do teacher, students, and classroom exude enthusiasm for learning math and science? Are curiosity and perseverance in inquiry and concept exploration evident?	
Collaboration and respect—Do the teacher and students respect each other? Are students and teacher collaborating?	
Student participation—Is student participation encouraged and valued? Are students participating in relevant and important work at all times?	
Equity of access—Are all students actively included? Are there patterns of inclusion or exclusion? Does teacher monitor groups for equity?	

The Literacy Version

Name of teacher: _____   Date of observation: _____

Literacy Implementation	Notes, Examples
Teacher as builder of literacy skills—Are both fluency and meaning making evident; multiple strategies; skills taught in context? Do guided reading groups enhance student skills and comprehension? Is the writing process taught?	
Student engagement—Is lesson designed so students are engaged in active, thoughtful learning, constructing their own knowledge? Is there appropriate use of guided reading groups, read-alouds, journals?	
Pace—Appropriate to the lesson? To student learning? "Wait time?" Reflection time built in?	
Student-student interaction—Is it helping students reach a better understanding? Reading centers used to best advantage?	
Literacy Content	Notes, Examples
Standards—Lesson/tasks/assessments aligned with standards?	

Conceptual understanding—Does teacher demonstrate depth of knowledge; provide accurate information? Do teacher and students use text to make meaning?	
Assessments—Are they systematic and ongoing? Are expectations evident? Does teacher address student misconceptions? How does teacher give feedback?	
Students building literacy skills—Fluency, vocabulary usage, ability to discuss text? Developing a metacognitive sense of learning?	
Connections—Is there a connection between reading and writing? Is the lesson related to real-world situations? Other disciplines? Previous/future lessons?	
Literacy Classroom Culture	*Notes, Examples*
Classroom behavior—Climate is structured but flexible; expectations are clear and consistent; routines are smooth; interruptions minimal; safe, respectful environment?	
Enthusiasm—Teacher, students, and classroom exude enthusiasm for reading and writing? Both reading and writing valued?	
Collaboration and respect—Do the teacher and students respect each other? Are students and teacher collaborating? Helping each other? Polite?	
Student participation—Is student participation encouraged and valued? Students participating in relevant and important work at all times?	
Equity of access—Are all students actively included? Are there patterns of inclusion or exclusion? Does teacher monitor groups for equity?	

The Composite Version

Name of teacher: _____   Date of observation: _____

Implementation	*Notes, Examples*
Teacher facilitation—Teacher speaks in depth of concepts, encourages students to grapple?	
Student engagement—Are students engaged in active, thoughtful learning? Are they constructing their own knowledge? Diverse instructional strategies? Learning needs?	

(Continued)

(Continued)

Pace—Is the pace appropriate to the lesson? To student learning? Is there time for wrap-up and reflection?	
Student-student interaction—Is it helping students reach a better understanding?	
Students building literacy skills—Is the teacher incorporating reading and writing strategies to assist students in gaining a metacognitive understanding of their learning processes?	
Content	*Notes, Examples*
Content understanding—Are teacher and students using text to further understanding of the content?	
Conceptual understanding—Does teacher demonstrate depth of knowledge? Are students grappling with concepts? How is teacher assessing/planning to assess?	
Content—Are concepts to be learned clear? Skills? Are expectations evident? Does teacher address student misconceptions? How?	
Connections—Is the lesson related to real-world situations? Other disciplines? Previous/future lessons?	
Abstractions—Does the teacher incorporate new concepts into existing theories and use models as appropriate? Are models accurate?	
Literacy as a learning tool—Is teacher using text to build comprehension of the content?	
Classroom Culture	*Notes, Examples*
Classroom behavior—Climate is structured but flexible; expectations are clear and consistent; routines are smooth; interruptions minimal; safe, respectful environment?	
Enthusiasm—Teacher, students, and classroom exude enthusiasm for learning? Both reading and writing are valued as part of learning process?	
Collaboration and respect—Do the teacher and students respect each other? Are students and teacher collaborating? Helping each other? Polite?	
Student participation—Is student participation encouraged and valued? Students participating in relevant and important work at all times?	
Equity of access—Are all students actively included? Are there patterns of inclusion or exclusion? Does teacher monitor groups for equity?	

References

Ainsworth, L., & Viegut, D. (Eds.). (2006). *Common formative assessments: How to connect standards-based instruction and assessment.* Thousand Oaks, CA: Corwin Press.

Amaral, O., Garrison, L., & Klentschy, M. (2002, Summer). Helping English learners increase achievement through inquiry-based science instruction. *Bi-Lingual Research Journal, 26*(2), 213–239.

American Association for the Advancement of Science. (1989). *Science for all Americans.* New York: Oxford University Press.

American Association for the Advancement of Science. (1993). *Benchmarks for science literacy.* New York: Oxford University Press.

American Association for the Advancement of Science. (1998). *Blueprints for reform: Science, mathematics, and technology education.* New York: Oxford University Press.

American Association for the Advancement of Science. (2001). *Atlas of science literacy.* Arlington, VA: National Science Teachers Association.

Annenberg Foundation/CPB. (1987). *A private universe* [Videotape]. Burlington, VT: Author.

Annenberg/CPB Math and Science Collection. (1995). *Science images* [Videotape]. Burlington, VT: Author.

Annenberg/CPB Math and Science Collection. (1996). *Teaching math: A video library* [Videotape]. Burlington, VT: Author.

Annenberg/CPB Math and Science Collection. (2000). *Teaching high school science* [Videotape]. Burlington, VT: Author.

Annenberg/CPB Math and Science Collection. (2002). *Teaching reading: A library of practices* [Videotape]. Burlington, VT: Author.

Ball, D. L. (1992, Summer). Magical hopes: Manipulatives and the reform of math education. *American Educator, 16*(2), 14–18, 46–47.

Ball, D. L., & Friel, S. N. (1991). What's all this talk about discourse? *Arithmetic Teacher, 39*(3), 44–48.

Ball, D., Lubienski, S. T., & Mewborn, D. S. (2001). Research on teaching mathematics: The unsolved problem of teacher's mathematical knowledge. In V. Richardson (Ed.), *Handbook of research on teaching* (4th ed., 433–456). Washington, DC: American Educational Research Association.

Bamburg, J. D. (1994). *Raising expectations to improve student learning* (Report from the Urban Monograph Series). Oak Brook, IL: North Central Regional Educational Laboratory.

Berlinghoff, W. P., Sloyer, C., & Hayden, R. W. (2000). *Math connections.* Armonk, NY: It's About Time, Inc., Herff Jones Education Division.

Billmeyer, R., & Barton, M. L. (1998). *Teaching reading in the content areas: If not me, then who?* Aurora, CO: Mid-Continent Research for Education and Learning.

Black, P., Harrison, C., Lee, C., Marshall, B., & Wiliam, D. (2003). *Assessment for learning: Putting it into practice.* Berkshire, UK: Open University Press.

Black, P., & Wiliam, D. (1998). Inside the black box: Raising standards through classroom assessment. *Phi Delta Kappan, 80,* 139–148.

Bloom, B. S. (1984). *Taxonomy of educational objectives.* Boston: Allyn and Bacon.

Boke, N., & Hewitt, G. (2004). *Reading to learn: A classroom guide to reading strategy instruction.* Montpelier, VT: Vermont Strategic Reading Initiative.

Budge, D. (2005, February 18). *Tasting the assessment soup.* Retrieved February 7, 2008, from http://www.tes.co.uk/search/story/?story_id=2074776

Byers, G. O. (2001). *Daily oral language.* Great Source Education Group. Retrieved 2006 from http://www.bsu.edu/elementaryeducation/media/pdf/vita-byers.pdf

Cohen, E., & Lotan, R. (Eds.). (1997). *Working for equity in heterogeneous classrooms: Sociological theory in action.* New York: Teachers College Press.

Daggett, W. R. (1995). *Testing and assessment in American schools: Committing to rigor and relevance* (Report of the Third Annual Model Schools conference). New York: International Center for Leadership in Education.

Daggett, W. R. (2000, May). *Managing change in the 21st century.* Address given to school leaders in Burlington, VT.

Daggett, W.R. (2007). *Rigor/Relevance Matrix*. International Center for Leadership in Education: Retrieved December 2, 2007 from http://www.LeaderEd.com.

Danielson, C. (1986). *Enhancing professional practice: A framework for teaching*. Alexandria, VA: ASCD.

Darling-Hammond, L. (2000a, September 13). Doing what matters most: Investing in quality teaching (ID Number 10417). *TCRecord: The Voice for Scholarship in Education*. Retrieved February 13, 2008, from http://www.tcrecord.org

Darling-Hammond, L. (2000b). Teacher quality and student achievement: A review of state policy evidence. *TCRecord: The Voice for Scholarship in Education, 102*(1), 28–56.

DuFour, R., & Eaker, R. (1998). *Professional learning communities at work: Best practices for enhancing student achievement*. Bloomington, IN: National Educational Service.

Duckworth, E. (1987). *The having of wonderful ideas and other essays on teaching and learning*. New York: Teachers College Press.

Education Commission of the States. (2006). *In pursuit of quality teaching: Five key strategies for policymakers*. Retrieved February 7, 2008, from http://www.ecs.org/ecsmain.asp?page=/html/publications/home_publications.asp

Education Trust. (2006). *Teaching inequality: How poor and minority children are shortchanged on teacher quality*. Washington, DC: Author.

Educational Testing Service. (2007). *Pathwise Framework Induction Program*. Retrieved March 2007 from http://www.ets.org/portal/site/ets/menuitem

Evans, R. (1996). *The human side of school change*. New York: Jossey-Bass.

Fullan, M. (2001a). *Leading in a culture of change*. San Francisco: Jossey-Bass.

Fullan, M. (2001b). *The new meaning of educational change*. New York: Teachers College Press.

Gabriel, J. G. (2005). *How to thrive as a teacher leader*. Alexandria, VA: ASCD.

Glickman, C. D. (1990). *Supervision of instruction: A development approach* (2nd ed.). Boston: Allyn and Bacon.

Grant, C. M., Nelson, B. S., Davidson, E., Sassi, A., Weinberg, A. S., & Bleiman, J. (2002). *Lenses on learning: A new focus on mathematics and school leadership*. Lebanon, IN: Dale Seymour.

Gray, W. S., Monroe, M., Artley, A., & Arbuthnot, M. H. (1956). *The new* We Look and See: *Kindergarten to 1st grade* (First pre-primer in series). Saddle River, NJ: Scott-Foresman.

Horizon Research, Inc. (1997). *Local systemic change classroom observation protocol*. Washington, DC: National Science Foundation.

Hunter, M. (n.d.). *Eight steps to lesson design*. Retrieved February 7, 2008, from http://faculty.mdc.edu/jmcnair/Joe14pages/Eight%20Steps%20to%20Lesson%20Design%20-%20Madely%20Hunter.htm

International Society for Technology in Education. (2000). *National educational technology standards for students: Connecting curriculum and technology*. Washington, DC: Author.

Jernstedt, G. C. (2005, August). *Learning and the brain*. Address given to school leaders in Killington, VT.

Johnson, D. W., Johnson, R. T., & Holubec, E. J. (1994). *The new circles of learning: Cooperation in the classroom and school*. Alexandria, VA: ASCD.

Johnson, S. M., Berg, J. H., & Donaldson, M. L. (2005). *Who stays in teaching and why: A review of the literature on teacher retention*. Cambridge, MA: The Project on the Next Generation of Teachers. Retrieved February 7, 2008, from http://assets.aarp.org/www.aarp.org_/articles/NRTA/Harvard_report.pdf

Keeley, P. (2005). *Science curriculum topic study*. Thousand Oaks, CA: Corwin Press.

Keeley, P. (2004). *Uncovering students' ideas in science: 25 formative assessment probes*. Arlington, VA: National Science Teachers Association.

Kohn, A. (1996). *Beyond discipline: From compliance to community*. Alexandria, VA: ASCD.

Lambert, L. (1998). *Building leadership capacity in schools*. Alexandria, VA: ASCD.

Love, N. (2002). *Using data/getting results: A practical guide for school improvement in mathematics and science*. Norwood, MA: Christopher-Gordon.

McIntosh, P. (1988). *White privilege and male privilege: A personal account of coming to see correspondences through work in women's studies* (Working Paper 189). Wellesley, MA: Wellesley College Center for Research on Women.

Marzano, R. J. (1999, December). *Strategies that impact student achievement*. Paper presented at the ASCD Conference, Boston.

Marzano, R. J., Pickering, D. J., & Marzano, J. S. (2003). *Classroom management that works: Research-based strategies for every teacher*. Alexandria, VA: ASCD.

McLaughlin, M. (1995, December). *Creating professional learning communities*. Keynote address presented at the annual conference of the National Staff Development Council, Chicago.

National Council for Teachers of Mathematics. (1989). *Curriculum and evaluation standards for school mathematics*. Reston, VA: NCTM.

National Reading Panel. (2000). *Teaching children to read: An evidence-based assessment of the scientific research literature on reading and its implications for reading instruction*. Washington, DC: National Institute of Child Health and Human Development.

National Research Council. (2000a). *How people learn: Brain, mind, experience, and school*. Washington, DC: National Academy Press.

National Research Council. (2000b). *Inquiry and the national education standards: A guide for teaching and learning.* Washington, DC: National Academy Press.

National Research Council. (2004). *How students learn: Mathematics in the classroom.* Washington, DC: National Academies Press.

National Research Council, (1995). *National Science Education Standards.* Washington, DC: National Academy Press.

National School Reform Faculty. (2000). *Critical friends groups.* Bloomington, IN: Harmony Education Center. Retrieved February 7, 2008, from http://www.nsrfharmony.org/ faq.html#1

National Study of School Evaluation. (2002). *Indicators of quality.* Education Reform Network. Available from http://www.nsse.org/

New Teacher Center. (2007). *The New Teacher Center induction model.* Santa Cruz, CA: University of California, Santa Cruz. Retrieved February 7, 2008, from http://www.newteachercenter.org/ti_induction_model.php

No Child Left Behind Act of 2001. Retrieved February 7, 2008, from http://www.ed.gov/policy/elsec/leg/ esea02/index.html

Ogle, D. (1986). *KWL instruction reading strategy.* Retrieved February 8, 2008, from http://boe.gree .k12.wv.us/ronceverte/kwl2.html

Piaget, J. (1978). *Success and understanding.* Cambridge, MA: Harvard University Press.

Reeves, D. (2006). *Accountability in action: A blueprint for learning organizations* (2nd ed.). Englewood, CO: Advanced Learning Press.

Rose, C. M., Minton, L., & Arline, C. B. (2006). *Uncovering student thinking in mathematics: 25 formative assessment probes.* Thousand Oaks, CA: Corwin Press.

Saginor, N. (1999). *Is "good" good enough? Excellence in teaching redefined.* Unpublished doctoral dissertation, University of Vermont, Burlington.

Saginor, N. (2006a). *Formative assessment: The what and the why.* Presentation to the Riverdell Interstate School District.

Saginor, N. (2006b). The principal as leader in changing the face of science instruction: Implications for building level leadership. In J. Rhotan & P. Shane (Eds.), *Teaching science in the 21st century* (p. 175). Arlington, VA: NSTA Press.

Santa, C. M., Havens, L. T., & Valdes, B. J. (2004). *Project CRISS: Creating independent student-owned strategies.* Dubuque, IA: Kendall/Hunt.

Saphier, J., & Gower, R. (1997). *The skillful teacher: Building your teaching skills.* Acton, MA: RBT, Inc.

Saphier, J., Haley-Speca, M., & Gower, R. (2008). *The skillful teacher: Building your teaching skills* (6th ed.). Action, MA: RBT, Inc.

Schmoker, M. (2006). *Results now: How we can achieve unprecedented improvements in teaching and learning.* Alexandria, VA: ASCD.

Senge, P. M., Kleiner, A., Roberts, C., Ross, R. B., & Smith, B. J. (1994). *The fifth discipline fieldbook: Strategies and tools for building a learning organization.* New York: Doubleday.

Shulman, L. S. (1987). Knowledge and teaching: Foundations of the new reform. *Harvard Educational Review, 57*(1), 1–22.

Southwest Educational Development Laboratory. (2000). *Technology in education series* [Videotape]. Phoenix, AZ: Author.

Tarule, J. M. (1996). Voices in dialogue: Collaborative ways of knowing. In N. R. Goldberger, J. M. Tarule, B. M. Clinchy, & M. F. Belenky (Eds.), *Knowledge, difference, and power: Essays inspired by women's ways of knowing* (pp. 274–304). New York: Basic Books.

Third International Mathematics and Science Survey. (1995). Washington, DC: International Center for Education Statistics.

Tomlinson, C. A. (1999). *The differentiated classroom: Responding to the needs of all learners.* Alexandria, VA: ASCD.

Tomlinson, C. A. (2004). *How to differentiate instruction in mixed ability classrooms* (2nd ed.). Alexandria, VA: ASCD.

Trends in International Mathematics and Science Study. (2004). *Highlights from the TIMSS study, 2003.* Washington, DC: International Center for Education Statistics.

U.S. Department of Education. (2006). *Reading First.* Retrieved February 7, 2008, from http:// www.ed.gov/ programs/readingfirst/index.html

Vella, J. (2002). *Learning to listen, learning to teach: The power of dialogue in educating adults.* San Francisco, CA: Jossey-Bass.

Vygotsky, L. S. (1978). *Mind and society: The development of higher mental processes.* Cambridge, MA: Harvard University Press.

Wiggins, G., & McTighe, J. (1998). *Understanding by design.* Alexandria, VA: ASCD.

Index

CORWIN PRESS

The Corwin Press logo—a raven striding across an open book—represents the union of courage and learning. Corwin Press is committed to improving education for all learners by publishing books and other professional development resources for those serving the field of PreK–12 education. By providing practical, hands-on materials, Corwin Press continues to carry out the promise of its motto: **"Helping Educators Do Their Work Better."**